Wonju

THE GETTYSBURG OF THE KOREAN WAR

J. D. COLEMAN

Also by J. D. Coleman

Pleiku: The Dawn of Helicopter Warfare in Vietnam

Incursion: From America's Chokehold on the NVA
Lifelines to the Sacking of the Cambodian Sanctuaries

Wonju

THE GETTYSBURG OF THE KOREAN WAR

J. D. COLEMAN

Brassey's
Washington, D.C.

Library of Congress Cataloging-in-Publication Data

Coleman, J. D.
    Wonju : the Gettysburg of the Korean War / J.D. Coleman.—1st ed.
      p. cm.
    Includes bibliographical references (p.) and index.
    ISBN 1-57488-212-0 (cloth : alk. paper)
    1. Korean War, 1950–1953—Campaigns—Korea (South)—Waenju-si.
    I. Title.
    DS918.2.W66 C65 2000
    951.904′242—dc21   00-063023

Printed in Canada on acid-free paper that meets the
American National Standards Institute Z39-48 Standard.

Brassey's
22841 Quicksilver Drive
Dulles, Virginia 20166

First Edition

10 9 8 7 6 5 4 3 2 1

Contents

Maps vii

Preface ix

Acknowledgments xi

Abbreviations xiii

Introduction
February 1951—The Month of Destiny *1*

1 | The *Inmun Gun* *5*

2 | Bugles, Whistles, and Shepherd's Horns *16*

3 | Withdrawal from North Korea *30*

4 | Ridgway Takes Command *37*

5 | The Third Phase Offensive *44*

6 | Rekindling the Offensive Spirit *54*

7 | Thunderbolt and Twin Tunnels *63*

8 | Thrusts, Counters, Deceptions, and Plans 75

9 | Operation Roundup Unfolds *85*

10 | Prelude to Disaster *95*

11 | Peng's Plan for the Fourth Phase Offensive   *107*

12 | The Agony of Another Gauntlet   *112*

13 | Failed Rescue   *128*

14 | Into the Valley of Death   *141*

15 | Revelations and Recriminations   *155*

16 | Establishing the Wonju Line   *171*

17 | First Fight at Chip'yong-ni   *183*

18 | First Decision at Wonju   *194*

19 | Climax at Chip'yong-ni   *209*

20 | Final Decision at Wonju   *226*

21 | Transitioning to "Killer"   *242*

22 | In the Final Analysis   *259*

Appendices   *268*

Notes   *272*

Bibliography   *289*

Index   *291*

About the Author   *303*

Maps

East Central Asia   *xi*
Korea   *2*
The Pusan Perimeter   *8*
The Capture of Seoul   *11*
The Battlefront, 23 November 1950   *20*
Organization of UN Forces in Korea   *22*
Battle of the Ch'ongch'on   *26*
The 2d Infantry Division at Kunu-ri   *28*
Eighth Army Withdrawal   *32*
Enemy Third Phase Offensive   *47*
NK II Corps and V Corps Attacks   *56*
Operation Thunderbolt   *66*
Battle at Twin Tunnels   *72*
Operation Thunderbolt II   *76*
Operation Roundup—The X Corps Plan   *81*
Battle for Hoengsong   *113*
Battle of Hoengsong: Massacre Valley   *142*
Defending the Wonju Line   *172*
Chip'yong-ni   *185*
Hill 255   *199*
Hill 342   *228*
Battle at Sillim-ni   *250*
Operation Killer   *257*

Preface

Although only a staff sergeant in an airborne infantry rifle company in February 1951, I always believed that the battles fought in and around Wonju during that period were significant. Yet, for years, I searched histories of the war in vain for some mention of that bloody campaign. Not until the late 1980s did Korean War historians began to pick up on the fact that there was more to the war in February 1951 than Chip'yong-ni. Then, published in rapid succession, three books provided some coverage of those Wonju battles, but substantial gaps remained to be filled.

About that time, I was distributing questionnaires to former members of the 187th Airborne Regimental Combat Team to seek input for a book about the regiment in Korea. The response from Col. William E. "Bill" Weber, who had commanded K Company in February 1951, made it quite clear that the battles at Wonju were significant. Subsequent conversations with Bill provided the genesis of the subtitle for this book. Bill was persuaded that when the Chinese retreated after defeats at Wonju and Chip'yong-ni, the situation was much the same as when Robert E. Lee's army retired from Gettysburg. Colonel Weber believed that the Chinese field commanders knew that they no longer could win the war and, worse, could very well lose it. Lee crossed the Potomac and headed back to Virginia troubled by the same awareness.

The three books published during the late 1980s were the Army's history, *Ebb and Flow*, by Billy C. Mossman; *The Forgotten War* by Clay Blair; and *Ridgway Duels for Korea*, by Lt. Col. Roy E. Appleman. They provided a foundation upon which I could build the story of these battles. The National Archives yielded nearly 1,500 pages of records of the units involved in them. These records were invaluable in cross-checking and verifying information. The National Archives also provided black-and-white copies of the tactical maps used in 1951, so that I could plot locations of units with some degree of precision.

My greatest regret is that I did not start this project several years earlier when more valuable sources were still alive and able to provide insiders' views of the battles. Nevertheless, many veterans, alive and healthy, were willing to share their insights. Their stories make up the flesh of this book.

I have always followed a strict rule in portraying wartime experiences. No matter how fascinating or interesting a story might be, I will not use it unless I obtain independent corroboration of its authenticity. In no case in this book have accounts been fictionalized to improve the story line. What the reader sees on the printed page is what happened, and I have portrayed it with as much historical accuracy and humanity as possible. Historians and old soldiers who wish to query me to examine facts or events in greater detail can contact me at P.O. Box 1592, Kalispell, MT 59903.

Chapter notes document sources of information or opinion. Opinions expressed in this book that are not so designated are those of the author, and I take full responsibility for them.

Acknowledgments

I must first acknowledge the efforts of my wife, Madeline, to make this book a reality. Research assistant, editor, proofreader, cheerleader, sounding board, critic, and cruel taskmaster who denied me leisure activities until "the book" was completed, she is as much responsible for the shape and tone of *Wonju* as I. My gratitude knows no bounds.

Any book that requires extensive research and interviewing could not be written without the assistance of countless individuals. My sincere thanks go to those folks, mostly old soldiers or their widows, who took the time and effort to give another old soldier a helping hand. I wish I had the space to list all of your names.

I am indebted to Colonel Bill Weber for the idea of "the Korean Gettysburg."

Thanks also go to Dr. Phillip West, director of the Maureen and Mike Mansfield Center at the University of Montana, who steered me in the direction of a more in-depth look at Chinese tactics and strategy. That research, I believe, enhanced the scope of my book. I appreciate the efforts on my behalf by retired Lt. Col. Charley S. Heath, secretary/treasurer of the Korean War Veterans Alliance of the Second Indianhead Division. The publications provided by his organization were invaluable tools in my research.

Peter Stewart of Fayetteville, North Carolina, went to extraordinary lengths to obtain for me a copy of his grandfather's memoirs which were unavailable at the National Archives. The written memories of Brig. Gen. George A. Stewart were vital to the completion of this book, and I am grateful for Peter's efforts on my behalf.

A special note of thanks goes to Robin Sorg, the graphics artist at Digital Planet in Kalispell. She converted my crudely drawn sketches and deciphered my arm waving and sometimes incoherent instructions to deliver a first class final product—the maps that appear in this book.

Thanks to my agent, Ethan Ellenberg, who has patiently waited for me to turn my attention again to military history. I also appreciate the opportunity to write for Brassey's Books, and thank my editors for their patience and skill in helping shape the direction of this book.

Abbreviations

AA	antiaircraft
AAA	antiaircraft artillery
ARCT	Airborne Regimental Combat Team
ATIS	Allied Translating and Interrogation Service
BAR	Browning automatic rifle
CCF	Chinese Communist Forces
CG	Commanding General
CP	command post
Divarty	Division Artillery
EUSAK	Eighth United States Army
FECOM	Far East Command
1st Sgt.	first sergeant
FM	frequency modulation
GHQ	General Headquarters (Tokyo)
G-1	personnel officer
G-2	intelligence officer
G-3	operations officer
HE	high explosive
HEAP	high-explosive armor-piercing
JCS	Joint Chiefs of Staff
KIA	killed in action
KMAG	Korean Military Advisory Group
M.Sgt.	master sergeant
MSR	main supply route
NCO	noncommissioned officer
NKPA	North Korean People's Army

ORT	operational readiness test
P&A	Pioneer and Ammunition [Platoon]
Pfc.	private first class
PIO	public information officer
PIR	Periodic Intelligence Report
PLA	People's Liberation Army
POR	Periodic Operations Report
RCT	Regimental Combat Team
Recon	reconnaissance
ROK	Republic of Korea [South Korea]
ROTC	Reserve Officers Training Corps
R&R	rest and recuperation
Sgt. 1/C	sergeant first class
S.Sgt.	staff sergeant
UN	United Nations
USAMHI	U.S. Army Military History Institute
VMI	Virginia Military Institute
VT	variable time
WIA	wounded in action
WP	white phosphorus

Author's Note

All U.S. army divisions that fought in Korea were infantry divisions, including the 1st Cavalry Division, which was configured as an infantry division. After introducing the units, generally they will, thereafter, be referred to by their number, e.g. 2d Division. Republic of Korea units were known as ROK units and they will be identified. Other UN forces will be identified by the country of origin, e.g. French Battalion, Turkish Brigade. Infantry line companies that carry a letter designation—B Company, for instance—will be written in the same way the soldiers of 1951 referred to their units. Company B may be referred to as Company B or as B Company or by the phonetic alphabet in use at that time, e.g. Baker Company.

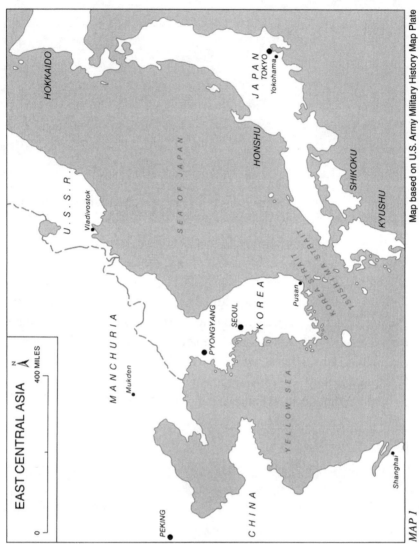

EAST CENTRAL ASIA

N

0   400 MILES

Map based on U.S. Army Military History Map Plate

MAP 1

INTRODUCTION | February 1951– The Month of Destiny

As the winter sun dropped behind the barren mountains of central Korea, the jaws of the bitter Siberian winter bit deeply into soldiers of two facing armies. On one side were soldiers of the Republic of Korea (ROK) Army. Across a no-man's-land of snow and ice were soldiers of the North Korean People's Army, the NKPA.

The South Korean regiments had been advancing slowly over snow-covered ridgelines against sporadic NKPA resistance. With twilight, however, their attack sputtered to a halt. ROK units rarely fought at night. According to operating instructions, the ROK elements were to patrol aggressively in front of their lines and improve their positions. Some of them did, but more did not. Warming fires soon flickered across the entire front.

Elsewhere, unknown to the ROK commanders, critical combat intelligence was starting to wend its way down through the chain of command. For the first time since assuming command of the United States Eighth Army, Lt. Gen. Matthew Bunker Ridgway had been handed some meaningful combat intelligence. His intelligence officer predicted a Chinese offensive in three days, but he could not pinpoint its location. Late that day, Ridgway sent a warning out to the commanders of the American Corps, particularly X Corps on the central front. He did not want the ROK and American units blundering into a trap, but the warning came too late.

Behind the NKPA lines, as the setting sun left deepening shadows, the desolate landscape came to life. Here and there, snow banks stood and moved along ridgelines to join forms that, in daylight, had appeared to be bushes and boulders. Moving quietly, with the

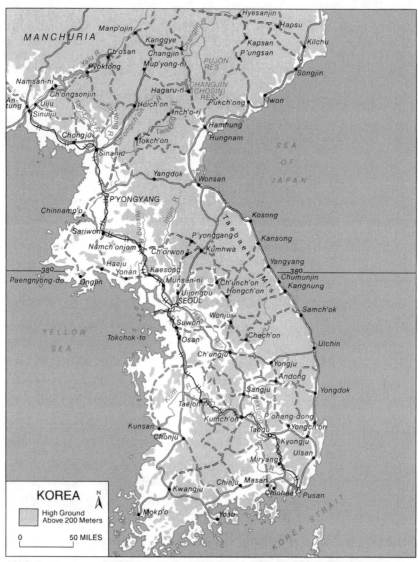

MAP 2   Map based on U.S. Army Military History Map Plate

only trace of their passage being occasional droplets of blood from
poorly protected swollen and frozen feet, were the tough little
peasants of the Chinese People's Liberation Army. They were volunteers all, according to Peking propaganda, which called them the
Chinese People's Volunteer Army. The Americans had fewer

problems with semantics; they simply called the men fighting for Chinese Gen. Peng Teh-huai the CCF—Chinese Communist Forces.[1]

As raindrops become rivulets, then streams, and finally raging torrents, so did the Chinese forces become a torrent. The peasant soldiers moved silently southward and formed into squads, then platoons, and then battalions and regiments. They moved stealthily because even though their enemy had a suspicion that Chinese soldiers were augmenting the North Korean defenders in this sector, they had no inkling of the real strength of the CCF in the rugged central Korean mountains.[2]

The Chinese were from four divisions—the 117th, 120th, 197th, and 198th—of the Thirty-Ninth, Fortieth, and Sixty-Sixth Chinese Field Armies. They were part of the Thirteenth Army Group commanded by Gen. Li T'ianyu. Their first targets were Republic of Korea regiments that had been advancing north in a desultory fashion as part of a limited offensive dubbed Operation Roundup. Four ROK regiments were deployed in an arc north of Hoengsong, a village about 10 miles north of the critical crossroads town of Wonju. North of Hoengsong were also two battalions of the 38th Infantry of the U.S. 2d Infantry Division, plus supporting artillery, but the Americans were not the immediate targets of the Chinese divisions.

The Chinese theater commander, General Peng, and his senior battle commander, General Li, were confident that when their divisions hammered the ROK lines hard, the South Korean formations would dissolve in panic, leaving huge gaps on the mountain ridgelines that the Chinese army could exploit to cut off the roadbound American units. Once the Chinese roadblocks and fire blocks were in place, Peng knew from his earlier experience in North Korea that his soldiers could grind up the American units at their leisure. In nearly every engagement since the CCF entered the war in November, Peng and Li had counted on the American and ROK units to attempt escape by running the Chinese gauntlets of fire. With rare exceptions, the soldiers bunched up near their vehicles, which gave the commanding heights to the Chinese by default.

When the vehicle column was stopped, so was the progress of infantry soldiers.

Chip'yong-ni, another critical crossroads town, was 20 miles west of Hoengsong. Peng dispatched another four divisions, the 115th, 119th, 120th, and 126th, to Chip'yong-ni. Unlike the situation north of Hoengsong, Allied intelligence was aware of the heavy Chinese presence north of Chip'yong-ni. The Allies anticipated that the next CCF offensive thrust would be through Chip'yong-ni and south through the Han River valley.[3]

According to the CCF plan, once the Chinese divisions captured Chip'yong-ni along with Wonju, there was nothing to stop them from making a deep penetration to Ch'ungju, an even larger and more important communications center 50 miles south. Peng and Li envisioned CCF forces spreading both west and east to cut off United Nations forces far behind the main line of resistance.

This was to be a repetition of the deep thrusts in November that had sent American forces into a humiliating, headlong retreat from North Korea. This time, Peng's battle planners believed, the Americans would be decisively defeated and, perhaps, driven back to Pusan.

The night was Sunday, 11 February 1951. The curtain was about to rise on a series of vicious, bloody battles that would transform this part of Korea into the Gettysburg of the Korean War. Wonju and Chip'yong-ni would be the high-water mark of Chinese success in Korea.

As at Gettysburg, when the Confederates tasted victory on Day One and Day Two of the battle, the Chinese had everything going their way during the early stages of the campaign.

Yet, despite some dramatic turns of events on this frozen battlefield, which resulted in ghastly casualties on both sides, these battles have often been forgotten or overlooked. *Forgotten* is a word appearing frequently in histories of the Korean War. Six history books use *forgotten* in their titles. But participants never need be reminded about the war, particularly those who were there when it began.

ONE | **The *Inmun Gun***

At 4:00 A.M., Sunday, 25 June 1950, when even the most determined of the Saturday night revelers in Seoul had at last staggered into their beds, the *Inmun Gun*, the North Korean People's Army, fired the first salvo of artillery at unprepared South Korean positions. The Korean War had begun.

The North Koreans achieved total surprise. If the *Inmun Gun* could have announced the invasion a month in advance, however, it probably still would have been no contest. The Soviet Union commenced arming and training an army as soon as it occupied Korea north of the 38th Parallel. In the South, because the United States was unwilling to give President Syngman Rhee the tools to stage a reunification drive north, it was ambivalent about creating an army. The vacillation finally resulted in the creation of constabulary regiments as an adjunct to the national police. Not until 1 July 1949 did South Korea receive the go-ahead to organize and lightly arm six infantry divisions. The term *lightly arm* was the operative phrase because United States was wary of Rhee's motives and was generally ignorant of the Soviet-sponsored buildup across the 38th Parallel. The U.S. Army organized the Korean Military Advisory Group (KMAG) to train the new divisions.[1]

Some ROK Army officers had been in the Japanese Manchurian Army and had fought the Chinese Communist Eighth Route Army. But many junior officers had no previous military experience and most of the rank and-file soldiers were recruited off the streets of South Korea. Organizing and training this fledgling army was a daunting task for both ROK senior officers and U.S. advisors.

Conversely, the NKPA was an experienced fighting force. The northern army evolved from two groups of Korean expatriates who had fought against the Japanese in Manchuria. One group, later known as the *Yenan Ban* (*Ban* means power-holding group), had joined Mao Tse-tung (Zedong) in the Yenan area during the late 1930s. The Koreans were organized into the Korean Volunteer Army, which eventually numbered 2,500 men and had fought the Japanese with the Chinese Eighth Route Army. After the Japanese surrender, Soviet forces barred the KVA members from returning home and "persuaded" them to remain with Mao's armies to fight the Chinese Nationalists. This permitted the Soviets to install Kim Il Sung as the president of the Democratic People's Republic of Korea.

Kim Il Sung was the leader of a guerrilla band that had fought the Japanese in eastern Manchuria and northern Korea during the mid-1930s. Kim's legend has it that his guerrillas annihilated two companies of Japanese troops near the town of Kapsan in northeast Korea, thus gaining the sobriquet *Kapsan Ban*. The Japanese eventually drove Kim and his followers out of Korea and into refuge in Soviet territory.

In 1946, when the Soviets closed the border between north and south, officer and noncommissioned officer training schools were established to begin the creation of the Korean People's Army.

The Soviets eventually let the *Yenan Ban* troops back into Korea, and these battle-hardened veterans formed three divisions within the NKPA. Two other divisions each had a regiment composed of these veterans of the China wars. By June 1950, the NKPA consisted of a Soviet-trained and equipped force of 135,000 men organized into one army and two corps headquarters with ten infantry divisions, five border constabulary brigades, and one armored brigade. Although the NKPA had only the one armored brigade, it didn't matter much. The ROK Army had nothing to match even a fraction of the north's armored power. The NKPA boasted 120 T-34 tanks mounting 85-mm main guns, in addition to sixteen SU-76 self-propelled guns.[2]

The ROK army had virtually no antitank weapons and those they had proved ineffective against the T-34 armor plate. In the ROK 1st Division, the 57-mm antitank guns had no armor-piercing ammunition, and the projectiles from the 2.36-inch rocket launchers, when they actually detonated, burned only partially through the thick armor. In those first frantic hours after the invasion, desperate South Korean soldiers, acting on their own, charged the lumbering tanks, armed only with satchel charges and grenades. These suicide bombers were able to delay the tank thrusts sufficiently to permit Col. Paik Sun Yup's 1st ROK Division to stage a delaying action that ended only when flanking units collapsed and the Han River bridges were blown behind his unit.[3]

On 30 June, U.S. President Harry S Truman authorized Gen. Douglas MacArthur to commit ground forces under his command in Japan to the developing Korean conflict. In turn, Lt. Gen. Walton H. Walker, U.S. Eighth Army commander, ordered the 24th Infantry Division to fly a battalion to Korea. This was the First Battalion, 21st Infantry Regiment, commanded by Lt. Col. Charles B. ("Brad") Smith. Also known as "Task Force Smith," it was, as MacArthur is alleged to have said, "that arrogant display of strength" that he believed would fool the North Koreans into thinking a larger force was at hand.[4] In any event, arrogance and overconfidence were the prevailing attitudes from General Headquarters (GHQ) in Tokyo through Walker's Eighth Army staff to the privates in Task Force Smith and the other U.S. units following from their soft billets in Japan. "As soon as those North Koreans see an American uniform over here," soldiers boasted to one another, "they'll run like hell."[5]

Smith's mission was to delay until the balance of his division could deploy into Korea. He chose positions just south of Osan, about 35 miles south of Seoul, that were defensible by most standards. His problems were that most standards did not apply here. His men were green, ill equipped, poorly trained, and flabby from soft living in Japan.

The T-34 tanks arrived first and brushed aside the futile efforts of the men manning the 2.36-inch bazookas. Then came the infantry

MAP 3

Map based on U.S. Army Military History Map Plate

troops of the NKPA 4th Division, who were not impressed with American uniforms. Six hours later, the survivors of a shattered Task Force Smith streamed to the rear in near panic. This scenario would be repeated again and again until the Eighth Army finally retreated into the Pusan Perimeter, with nowhere to go but into the sea.

Years later, Army Chief of Staff Creighton W. Abrams spoke to a United States Army Association gathering about the critical need for personnel and materiel readiness in the current Army:

> When the Korean War broke out, the situation was not much different from what it had been in the opening days of the Second World War. We were not prepared. We were not adequately trained. We were not equipped. But we entered the war rapidly, throwing half ready units in to buy time for the Army to get ready. And, again, we paid dearly for our unpreparedness during those early days in Korea with our most precious currency—the lives of our young men."[6]

Abrams was talking about the penchant of the leadership of the United States to erase history—to assume that, because our shores were not under direct attack, we were at peace. After World War II, pinchpenny leadership cut back the armed forces to nearly nothing and permitted the maintenance of an Army where discipline and hard training were virtually nonexistent. A generation of citizen soldiers, who were more civilian than soldier, was sent to Korea to stop the North Korean juggernaut. As the soldiers of the Eighth Army retreated behind the Naktong River, the arrogance of early July had turned into terror and defeatism.

The term *forgotten*, used for the war in Korea, could well have been used to describe the failure of leaders of the armed services to remember the bitter lessons paid for in blood during World War II. The Air Force had forgotten how to provide close air support. The Army had forgotten how to shoot, move, and communicate. Because the men in the ranks never had been taught these lessons, they could not fairly be accused of forgetting that sometimes the lot of the soldier is to be miserable in the mud and, if necessary, to die there.

T. R. Fehrenbach in his classic Korean War book, *This Kind of War*, excoriates the flabbiness of the United States Army in 1950, not only in Japan but everywhere else in the world. At the same time, he lavishes praise on the United States Marines as one organization that never succumbed to American society's post–World War II attempt to push the armed services into an egalitarian social service corps. And it was the 1st Provisional Marine Brigade, probably more than any other unit, that saved the Pusan Perimeter.

Eventually, during those first, desperate sixty days of combat, the American units relearned the rudimentary principles of fighting and surviving. The ROK army, despite taking horrific losses, also learned and survived to plug more than a few holes in the lines around Pusan that frustrated the NKPA desire for a quick victory. The *Inmun Gun* was designed for a blitzkrieg campaign. Protracted warfare against a foe that steadily was increasing its battlefield strength and competence sapped the NKPA of its vitality and led inexorably to its collapse.

Then came the Inchon landing, variously described as a brilliant stroke by an inspired Douglas MacArthur and as an execution of standard Army doctrine for peninsular warfare, the doctrine in World War II that led to landings at Salerno and Anzio in Italy. According to Clay Blair in *The Forgotten War*, the Pentagon, on 19 June 1950, approved a war plan known as SL-17, which assumed a North Korean invasion that would penetrate deep into South Korea, followed by an amphibious landing at Inchon. GHQ in Tokyo urgently requested fifty copies of SL-17 immediately after the NKPA invasion.[7] All of this, of course, poses the question: If the War Plans Division of the Army could assume a North Korean invasion with a penetration to the Naktong River, why was the attack on 25 June 1950 a surprise?

The landing at Inchon put the newly arrived 1st Marine Division in position to outflank the overextended North Korean troops facing the Eighth Army on the Pusan Perimeter. The landing was deceptively easy; the liberation of Seoul was not. The latter required three regiments of Marines and a regiment of the Army's 7th Infantry Division to subdue the fanatical resistance in the city. For political and public relations purposes, Maj. Gen. Edward M. Almond, commander of the newly created X Corps, declared Seoul liberated on

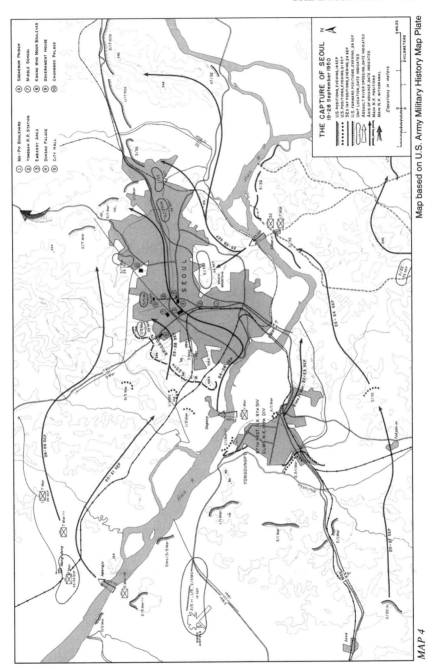

MAP 4

Map based on U.S. Army Military History Map Plate

25 September, exactly three months after the date of the North Korean invasion. Fighting in the city, however, continued for several days after the official proclamation of liberation.

MacArthur flew in from Tokyo, and with rhetorical flourishes, turned the city over to Syngman Rhee, president of South Korea. He also decorated Generals Almond and Walker with Distinguished Service Crosses; the citations for these awards stressed the personal courage of the generals, rather than their management talents. Clay Blair later commented in print that "some who had won DSCs on the battlefield would question whether the awards were appropriate."[8]

As the Marines were making their move on Seoul, another elite fighting unit was air landing on Kimpo Airfield. Fehrenbach overlooked the Army's parachute forces—double volunteers all—when he extolled the martial virtues of the Marines. The 187th Airborne Regimental Combat Team had been scheduled to make a parachute assault on Kimpo in conjunction with the amphibious assault at Inchon, but Typhoon Jane had delayed the unit's ocean transports. As the paratroopers were debarking at Sasebo, Japan, the Marines were overrunning Kimpo. The 187th was supposed to be a reserve for X Corps, but its 3d Battalion was committed almost at once to an attack up the Kimpo Peninsula to provide flank security for the Marine thrust toward Seoul. The battalion won a Navy Presidential Unit Citation for its fight on the peninsula.[9]

With the fall of Seoul and a concurrent breakout of the Eighth Army from the Pusan Perimeter, the North Korean resistance drastically diminished. United States and South Korean forces rapidly moved to the 38th Parallel. And, just as suddenly, their war aims changed from restoring the *status quo ante bellum* to the conquest of North Korea and the unification of the country under South Korean leadership.

The decision to invade the north was made in Washington, D.C., by President Truman, the State Department, and the Joint Chiefs of Staff, abetted in no small way by the relentless hectoring of General MacArthur. The U.S. leadership also believed that Syngman Rhee planned on heading for the Yalu River in North Korea, with or without the consent of the United States. It came as no surprise, therefore, when two ROK divisions on the east coast crossed the 38th Parallel and headed north while the rest of the United Nations (UN) forces waited for official sanction from Washington.

Even as Washington was debating the Korean strategy, Chinese Foreign Minister Chou En-lai publically declared in Peking that the Chinese people would not tolerate their neighbors being "savagely invaded by imperialists." In private, Chou told K. M. Panikkar, the Indian ambassador to Peking, that if UN forces crossed the 38th Parallel, China would send troops into North Korea. Panikkar dutifully reported the exchange to his government, and New Delhi relayed it to Washington, where it was disbelieved. Official Washington believed Panikkar to be anti-American and pro-Chinese. Moreover, just a few days earlier, he had declared that China would not intervene in Korea.[10]

Once Washington issued orders to go north of the 38th Parallel, the primary mission given MacArthur was the destruction of the North Korean Army. The Joint Chiefs of Staff, following guidance from President Truman and Secretary of Defense George C. Marshall, also set limitations on the depth of American penetration into North Korean territory.[11]

MacArthur, as was his usual practice, totally disregarded his instructions and set the stage for an unseemly race for geographic objectives. While still basking in the adulation accorded him following the Inchon invasion, MacArthur, apparently believing that a second amphibious assault would cement his immortality, ordered a meaningless landing of the Marines at Wonsan on the North Korean east coast. According to his plan, the Marines then would attack west to capture P'yongyang, the capital city of North Korea. By the time the Navy cleared the minefields in Wonsan harbor, the ROK I Corps had occupied Wonsan and the 1st Cavalry Division and the ROK 1st Division had overrun the North Korean capital. This bothered MacArthur not a whit. He altered the scheme of maneuver for General Almond's X Corps that eventually put the

Marines and a regiment of the 7th Division adjacent to the Changjin (Chosin) Reservoir.

General Walker and his principal subordinate commander, Maj. Gen. Frank W. ("Shrimp") Milburn of I Corps, smarting from the supply and transport priorities given to the X Corps for its east coast amphibious operation, had determined to get to P'yongyang first. The ensuing pell-mell rush led to incidents that could have been a script for "the gang that couldn't shoot straight." Units were bogged down in traffic jams and ran into each other in the dark, which sparked friendly fire incidents, as their commanders, striving to be the first into P'yongyang, were acting like children on a playground.[12] Fortunately for UN forces, the NKPA resistance was minimal. From the time of the breakout from the Pusan Perimeter, the Eighth Army failed utterly in its mission of destruction of the North Korean units.[13] Many of those units escaped to fight another day, and those that were bypassed became troublesome guerrilla bands behind the UN lines.[14]

On 15 October, General MacArthur and President Truman met on Wake Island to discuss the progress of the war. MacArthur's verdict was that the war was all but over, that he could commence redeploying American troops by year's end. Truman then asked the $64 question—will the Soviets or Chinese intervene?

MacArthur responded that there was very little chance of either occurring. He said that if either power had intervened in the first or second month of the war, it would have been decisive. "But we are no longer fearful of their intervention," he declared. He also confidently predicted that "if the Chinese try to get down to P'yong-yang there will be the greatest slaughter." No one, civilian or military, disagreed.

Fehrenbach wrote that it was not what was said but what was left unsaid that day that would change the course of history.[15]

The needle on the confidence gauge that had started in July pegged on arrogance, and then swung wildly to dark despair and defeatism during the NKPA drive to the Naktong, and now, suddenly, had swung back to arrogance.

Even while the great men had been flying to Wake Island on the night of 14 October, elements of the CCF Thirteenth Army Group, commanded by Gen. Li T'ianyu, were crossing the Yalu River. Night after night, moving only in the dark, exhibiting tough march discipline, and exercising superb daytime camouflage, regiment after regiment of Chinese soldiers melted into the bleak and forbidding North Korean mountains. The Chinese dragon was fully in Korea.[16]

TWO | Bugles, Whistles, and Shepherd's Horns

At 3:30 A.M. 25 October, the sounds of bugles, whistles, gongs, and shepherd's horns floated out of the darkness into the positions of Republic of Korea soldiers. The eerie noises spooked the ROK troops. The follow-on attack by the Chinese assault forces panicked the Koreans, who abandoned their positions and fled to the rear, only to discover that the Chinese had blocked their escape.

The 2d Regiment of the ROK 6th Division had paused for the night in the village of Onjong, some 55 miles from the Yalu River. The 6th Division was part of the ROK II Corps, which had been advancing north in multiple columns virtually unopposed by disorganized NKPA troops. The ROK Corps was on the right flank of the U.S. I Corps, which also was forging ahead in columns to the Yalu River. The entire Eighth Army advance was uncoordinated; each column was free to advance as fast and far as possible without respect to gains made by flanking units.[1]

For the next thirteen days, units of the Eighth Army and X Corps to the east felt the hot breath of the dragon. The Chinese attacks dismantled the 8th Cavalry Regiment of the 1st Cavalry Division, as well as the better part of two ROK divisions. In the X Corps zone, however, the 7th Marine Regiment, advancing toward Changjin Reservoir, met a CCF division, weathered its initial thrusts, and proceeded methodically to chew it up. Then, on 7 November, the Chinese abruptly and mysteriously broke contact.

The infiltration of undetected Chinese forces of field army strength into North Korea indicated a significant American intelligence failure. There were good reasons why aerial reconnaissance failed to detect the Chinese forces; the Chinese moved only at night and exercised superb motionless and camouflaged bivouac discipline during the day. Normal tactical patrolling activity by UN forces, even if carried out aggressively, would not have revealed the strength of the Chinese hidden in the North Korean mountains. Nevertheless, it still was a strategic intelligence failure. The U.S. intelligence services in Washington had failed to recognize the seriousness of the Chinese threats. General MacArthur's Far East Command, nominally a tactical command, had positioned itself much earlier as half tactical and half strategic in nature. Had the UN command recognized the threat for what it really represented and made plans accordingly, the story of Korea would have been entirely different.

The mauling that the ROK divisions received conceivably could be explained away as the result of bad leadership and training, a case where a small but determined band of Chinese had spooked the Koreans into headlong flight. Nevertheless, the damage done to the 8th Cavalry, a decently trained and led American regiment, could not be so readily explained away unless one considered that in Tokyo, the resident of the Dai Ichi Building, General MacArthur, had decreed that the Chinese would not intervene in force. And whatever MacArthur decreed, his sycophantic intelligence officer, Maj. Gen. Charles A. Willoughby, made sure that his intelligence estimates supported.

Clay Blair quotes the X Corps operations officer (G-3), Lt. Col. John H. Chiles, as saying, "Anything MacArthur wanted, Willoughby produced intelligence for. . . . In this case, Willoughby falsified the intelligence reports . . . he should have gone to jail."[2]

Blair was referring specifically to the intelligence estimates before the October 25 attacks by the Chinese. But even after there seemed indisputable evidence of a substantial Chinese presence in North Korea, Willoughby continued to deny the obvious. On 3 November he raised the estimates of Chinese (CCF) strength to somewhere between a minimum of 16,500 and a possible maximum of 34,000.[3] The Far East Command's estimates of Chinese strength continued to inch upwards incrementally until finally, on 19 November, the FEC intelligence report accepted CCF strength in Korea at a maximum of 70,051 and a minimum of 44,851. That strength figure didn't change until after the Chinese unleashed their Second Phase Offensive.[4]

That the FEC intelligence estimates were wildly off the mark is a gross understatement. By the end of the first week of November, the Thirteenth Army Group of the CCF Fourth Field Army, which was arrayed in front of the Eighth Army, consisted of eighteen divisions of infantry, with a total strength of 180,000. On the eastern front, targeted against the X Corps was the Ninth Army Group of the Third Field Army, commanded by General Sung Shih-lun. This army group, which had come from Shantung Province in China, consisted of twelve infantry divisions with a strength totaling 120,000. All together, the CCF mustered 300,000 trained, tough and motivated infantrymen.[5]

The tragedy of the FEC lowball estimates was that the Eighth Army's intelligence officer (G-2), Lt. Col. James C. Tarkenton, tended to mirror Willoughby's erroneous assessments. The same was true for the G-2 of X Corps, Col. William W. Quinn. These estimates, in turn, were reflected in intelligence estimates distributed to all the subordinate commands and begot a recurrence of overconfidence at all levels of command. Moreover, statements from the man in the Dai Ichi Building aided and abetted a burgeoning attitude that the troops would be home for Christmas.

Nevertheless, the Eighth Army G-3, Col. John A. Dabney, believed that a lot more Chinese were north of the Ch'ongch'on River than the intelligence community proclaimed. He pressed his views on his boss, General Walker, who stopped the advance of the Eighth Army and took steps to reduce the vulnerability of some units that were badly exposed. The cessation of the forward movement of the Eighth Army was immediately challenged by MacArthur. Walker, perhaps fearing for his job, didn't tell his boss of his uneasy feeling about the enemy situation. As justification for stopping the Eighth Army's advance, he indicated the shortage of supplies, the collapse of some ROK units, and the need to get his entire command on line. He estimated that he would be ready to resume the offensive by 24 November, the day after Thanksgiving.

Walker moved his IX Corps into the center of the Eighth Army sector, kept I Corps on the western flank, and then made a terrible mistake. He placed the recently mauled ROK II Corps on his exposed eastern flank. There was a 20-mile gap between Walker's extreme right flank and the Marines, the closest X Corps unit to the east. Whether this gap, part of which spanned some of the most rugged terrain of the Taebaek Mountain range, was critical has been debated by historians since the Chinese intervention. Maybe or maybe not, but one point about the so-called gap remains clear. The CCF 124th Division was the one that tangled with the Marines near the Changjin Reservoir in early November. The remnants of this division and two other divisions of the Forty-Second Field Army crossed that forbidding terrain during November to be in a position to confront the ROK II Corps when General Peng kicked off his Second Phase Offensive.[6]

The disposition of the X Corps was even worse than the Eighth Army's alignment. General Almond's scheme of maneuver had all the units, except the Marines, headed north in widely separated columns. In the center of the X Corps sector, the 17th Infantry Regiment of the U.S. 7th Division was already at the Yalu River. Part of a second regiment, the 32d, was to the left of the 17th Regiment and slightly south of the river. The ROK Capital Division, driving north along the seacoast, was separated by nearly 50 miles of mountains from the ROK 3d Division, which, in turn was about 40 miles east of the 17th Regiment.

More than 60 miles to the southwest lay the Changjin Reservoir. There, a cobbled-together regimental combat team known as Task Force MacLean, consisting of two battalions of Col. Allan D. Mac-Lean's 31st Regiment and a battalion of the 32d, was in the process of taking over the 5th Marine Regiment's positions on the east side of the reservoir, thus freeing the 5th to rejoin the rest of the Marine division.

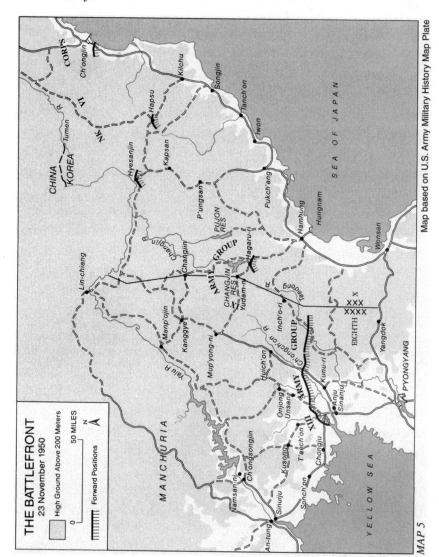

THE BATTLEFRONT
23 November 1950

High Ground Above 200 Meters

0   50 MILES

Forward Positions

N

MAP 5

Map based on U.S. Army Military History Map Plate

The remainder of the Marine division was between Hagaru-ri and Yudam-ni on the west side of the reservoir. Both the Marines and Task Force MacLean had nearly 60 miles of a narrow, ice-covered mountain road between them and the relative safety of Hamhung on the coastal plain. Elements of the 3d Infantry Division were advancing due west from coastal enclaves between Hamhung and Wonsan.

To say the X Corps was scattered would be a gross understatement. On 27 February 1985, long after he had retired and penned his memoirs, Gen. Matthew B. Ridgway reviewed the manuscript of the official Army history of this period. In a written comment to the author, Billy C. Mossman, he said:

> I find it amazing that highly trained professionals with extensive combat experience could have approved and tried to execute the tactical plan of operations for the X Corps in northeast Korea in November 1950. It appears like a pure map exercise put on by amateurs, appealing in theory, but utterly ignoring the reality of a huge mountainous terrain, largely devoid of terrestrial communications, and ordered for execution in the face of a fast approaching sub-arctic winter.[7]

Ridgway's incredulity may be due to the fact that General Almond and his staff believed implicitly in the intelligence estimates of GHQ. There seems to be no other explanation for the comments attributed to Almond on 28 November by Capt. Martin Blumenson, an Army historian. Almond had helicoptered into the perimeter of Lt. Col. Don Carlos Faith, Jr., commander of a battalion on the east side of the Changjin Reservoir that had spent the better part of a night and day beating off powerful attacks by the CCF. After bestowing three Silver Star medals as "impact" awards, Almond declared to a group at the battalion command post, "The enemy who is delaying you for the moment is nothing more than remnants of Chinese divisions fleeing north. We're still attacking and we're going all the way to the Yalu. Don't let a bunch of Chinese laundrymen stop you."[8]

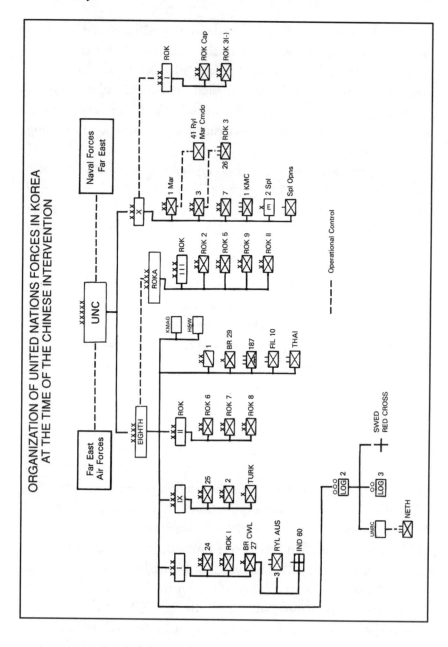

ORGANIZATION OF UNITED NATIONS FORCES IN KOREA
AT THE TIME OF THE CHINESE INTERVENTION

Four days later, Faith was dead, and his battalion, along with another battalion of the 7th Division, had been destroyed by the "laundrymen" of the CCF 80th Division.

In the period between the end of the Chinese First Phase Offensive and the end of November, a plethora of cables and messages had flown back and forth between Tokyo and Washington. The upshot was that MacArthur had been turned loose to pursue the war exactly as he saw fit, the muted murmurs of concern by the Joint Chiefs of Staff notwithstanding. The Dai Ichi tail still wagged the Washington dog, and thousands were about to perish because of it.

The Eighth Army offensive was scheduled to start on Friday, 24 November, the day after Thanksgiving. The X Corps phase of the offensive was slated to kick off three days later, the 27th. On the Chinese side, Gen. Li T'ianyu had set 25 November as the date of his attacks on the Eighth Army, and, to the east, the Ninth Army Group planned to start its offensive on the 27th.

During Thanksgiving week, a new enemy came to North Korea. Sweeping down from Siberia with unimaginable ferocity, the worst winter in a decade laid siege to the battlefield. In the relative low country of the Ch'ongch'on River valley, the temperatures dropped into the low teens at night, but, high in the Taebaek Mountains where the Marines were fighting, daily below-zero readings were commonplace. The weather was an enemy of both armies; the Chinese were not supermen, and their feet and hands froze as quickly as those of the UN soldiers. The UN army was a mechanized army, however, and its machines did not function well in snow, ice, and subzero temperatures, and, in some cases, they failed entirely.

MacArthur flew to Korea on the day before the Eighth Army attack, his presence almost acting as a starting gun for the offensive. His well-publicized visit gave the enemy mildly valuable intelligence, but MacArthur's communique issued after his return to Tokyo provided priceless information.

The communique declared that his three-week air interdiction campaign along the Yalu had "isolated the battlefield" and "sharply curtailed" CCF reinforcements. He said that his X Corps was in a position to cut in two the northern half of what remained of North Korea, and in conjunction with the Eighth Army's offensive, which he announced as being under way, his forces would "close the vise" on the enemy. He concluded that "If successful, this should for all practical purposes end the war. . . ."

Blair commented that, seldom in any war has a commanding general "so foolishly revealed his hand." MacArthur, in effect, told the Chinese that the bulk of their force was still undetected, that UN troop movements were not merely defensive adjustments of the line, and that movements by the X Corps would be part of an overall envelopment plan and not merely feints.[9]

Generals Peng, Li, and Sung didn't really need MacArthur's assistance. Their battle plan, for what they would call the Second Phase Offensive, particularly for the Thirteenth Army Group, was simple and was not, as some historians assert, based solely on Maoist principles of guerilla warfare. Although Mao's principles indeed played a role in the planning, so did the accumulated combat wisdom of Generals Peng and Li dating back to the "Encirclement Campaigns" of 1930–34. These campaigns fought against superior Nationalist forces seeking to encircle the Communist's "soviet" in Kiangsi Province were training grounds for many of the CCF commanders in Korea.

In his book, *The Chinese High Command*, William W. Whitson wrote: "It is virtually impossible to overestimate the importance of the five Nationalist Encirclement Campaigns in Kiangsi in shaping Communist military thought and in stimulating the creation of personal factions that continued to play significant political-military roles in the Chinese Communist polity through the cultural revolution."[10]

The same assertion easily could be said about the battles that the Communist forces fought against the Japanese from 1943 through 1945. Generals Peng and Li gained considerable experience in fighting a modern military force and combined the best of "Mao's thought" with military professionalism learned from USSR advisors.

Peng's and Li's plan—classic Chinese Red Army—combined the principles that had earned victories over the years.

Li deployed his forces so that those facing UN units in the center of the Eighth Army would force UN units to fight desperate defensive battles. But the heaviest blow was to strike in a southwesterly direction at the ROK II Corps hung out to dry on the UN extreme right flank. The Chinese armies planned to shatter the ROK positions and roll up the flank and rear security of the UN forces. The Chinese divisions would then make deep thrusts to the southwest with a goal of eventually reaching the Yellow Sea. According to the plan, they would trap and annihilate the entire Eighth Army.

Two days later, General Sung's Ninth Army Group would strike at the center of gravity of Almond's X Corps—the Marines and Task Force MacLean. Peng and Sung figured that once these units were disposed of, the remainder of X Corps, spread out as it was, would be easy pickings.

Both army groups were confident about the success of the Second Phase Offensive not only because similar plans had worked well against the Nationalists during the civil war, but also because of an analysis of the UN response to the First Phase attacks. Shortly after the First Phase Offensive, the Chinese published a pamphlet titled, "Primary Conclusions of Battle Experiences at Unsan." It revealed that the Chinese were dutifully impressed by the American firepower potential of mortars, artillery, tanks, and aircraft. Conversely, they were contemptuous of the American infantry. The pamphlet said that American soldiers, when cut off from the rear, would:

". . . abandon all their heavy weapons, leaving them all over the place. . . . Their infantrymen are weak, afraid to die, and haven't the courage to attack or defend. They depend on their planes, tanks, and artillery. At the same time, they are afraid of our fire power. They will cringe when, if on the advance they hear firing. They are afraid to advance farther. . . . They specialize in day fighting. They are not familiar with night fighting or hand to hand combat. If defeated, they have no orderly formation . . . they become dazed and completely demoralized. At Unsan they were surrounded for several days yet they did nothing. When transportation comes to a standstill, the infantry loses the will to fight."[11]

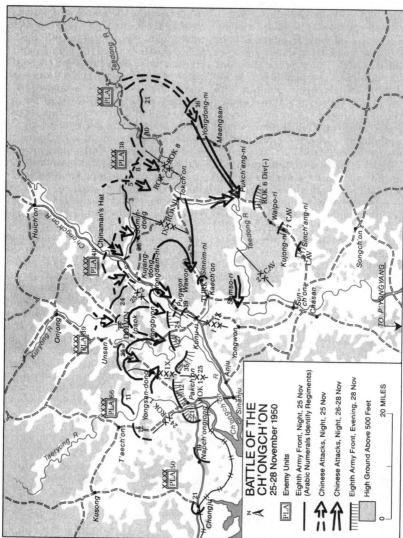

BATTLE OF THE
CH'ONGCH'ON
25-28 November 1950

PLA Enemy Units

Eighth Army Front, Night, 25 Nov
(Arabic Numerals Identify Regiments)

Chinese Attacks, Night, 25 Nov

Chinese Attacks, Night, 26-28 Nov

Eighth Army Front, Evening, 28 Nov

High Ground Above 500 Feet

0   20 MILES

MAP 6

General Walker launched his offensive on the morning of 25 November. The units lurched forward against sporadic resistance and, this time, paid closer attention to keeping abreast of flanking units. Against the North Korean Army, they would have been successful, but the North Koreans no longer were the only ones in the game.

That evening, after dark, the Chinese struck the divisions on the Eighth Army's center and right. Because of the terrain compartments in the Ch'ongch'on River valley, the fights quickly became struggles for survival of companies and platoons on isolated hills, with adjacent units often ignorant of what was happening to other units until it was too late and they, too, became inundated. The odds of survival for those companies led by exceptional commanders were better than most, but they also suffered great numbers of casualties. There were far too few such leaders, and the Eighth Army's IX Corps and the ROK II Corps began dying the deaths of a thousand cuts.

The CCF Forty-Second and Thirty-Eighth Armies[12] quickly demolished the hapless ROK units on the Eighth Army's right flank. In an astonishingly short time, a full CCF division had taken up firing positions for a depth of 6 miles on the Kunu-ri–Sunch'on road. Eventually, the survivors of the many small fights waged along the Ch'ongch'on River by the 9th and 38th Regiments of the 2d Infantry Division would funnel into this gauntlet.

There were far fewer survivors at the southern end of the gauntlet. Two regiments of the 2d Division and most of the division's artillery were destroyed. General Paik summarized the disaster: "That route wound through a valley of sorrow. The God of Death himself hovered with heavy, beating wings over that road."[13]

Fehrenbach eloquently summarized the plight of the Eighth Army on the Ch'ongch'on riverfront: "There were acts of immense courage, and of heartbreaking solicitude, as well as of stupidity and cowardice. . . . These tales have been well told, elsewhere."[14]

On the eastern front, the CCF Ninth Army Group launched its offensive on 27 November. It achieved tactical successes against

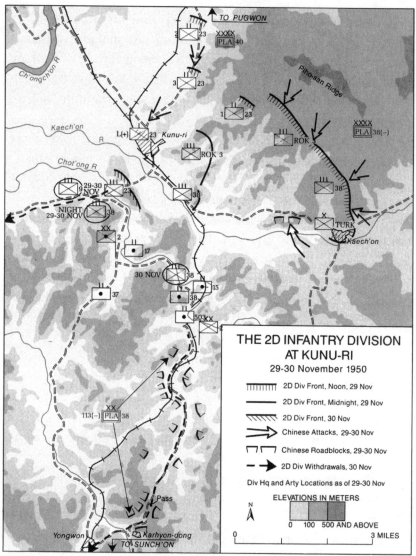

**THE 2D INFANTRY DIVISION
AT KUNU-RI**
29-30 November 1950

⊤⊤⊤⊤⊤⊤⊤	2D Div Front, Noon, 29 Nov
————	2D Div Front, Midnight, 29 Nov
⌍⌍⌍⌍	2D Div Front, 30 Nov
⟶	Chinese Attacks, 29-30 Nov
⎍⎍	Chinese Roadblocks, 29-30 Nov
- - ▶	2D Div Withdrawals, 30 Nov

Div Hq and Arty Locations as of 29-30 Nov

ELEVATIONS IN METERS

0   100   500 AND ABOVE

0 _____ 3 MILES

MAP 7

Map based on U.S. Army Military History Map Plate

the Marine division, but the cost to the CCF was ghastly. Even the isolated Task Force Faith, before it perished, seriously hurt the 80th Division.

The story of the Marines' fight from Yudam-ni to Hagaru-ri and thence on down to Hungnam also has been well told elsewhere. It quickly became clear to General Sung that he had grossly underestimated the Marines' capabilities as infantry, as well as how superbly the Marine Air Wing could provide close-in air support.

When X Corps finally evacuated from Hungnam in mid-December, many of its units were still in reasonably good condition. The same could not be said for the CCF Ninth Army Group. It took until late March before its divisions were rehabilitated to the point that they could join the rest of the Chinese forces facing the Eighth Army.

The massive Chinese intervention changed the tenor of messages issued from the Dai Ichi Building from blustering and arrogant to apocalyptic. The "offensive to end the war" withered in the flames from the dragon and the Truman Administration's war aims instantly changed from unification of Korea to a hope for a negotiated peace along the 38th Parallel.

The Eighth Army was, in MacArthur's phrase, engaged "in an entirely new war."[15]

THREE | **Withdrawal from North Korea**

By 1 December, Walker's Eighth Army had withdrawn from the Ch'ongch'on River. Most historians agree that Walker initially planned to establish a defense line near the North Korean capital city of P'yongyang. Sometime between 1 and 3 December, however, Walker changed his mind and decided that the Eighth Army could not defend the North Korean capital. He apparently based this decision on the condition of his troops. Three of his ROK divisions had disintegrated. The U.S. 2d Division was only about 40 percent effective, and the 25th Division had sustained heavy casualties in two of its regiments. The 1st Cavalry Division, already short its 8th Cavalry Regiment, had sustained heavy casualties in both its 5th and 7th Regiments. The Turkish Brigade had lost about one thousand men and was combat ineffective. Gen. Paik Sun Yup's ROK 1st Division, Walker's strongest South Korean unit, along with the U.S. 24th Division, had been only lightly engaged on the Eighth Army's left flank. They were the only two major combat units capable of mounting any kind of defense at P'yongyang. Although the 187th Airborne Regimental Combat Team and the newly arrived British 29th Brigade were poised just south of P'yongyang, Walker apparently discounted the fighting potential of these units.

There seemed real doubt in Walker's mind whether his army could withstand repeated Chinese assaults on a P'yongyang line where, he believed, his entire eastern flank would be nakedly exposed.

Walker appeared convinced that the only way he could save his army was to withdraw immediately to the Imjin River near the

38th Parallel. He asked MacArthur for approval to commence the withdrawal. Although there is no paper trail about GHQ response, the presence in Walker's headquarters on 2 December of Maj. Gen. Doyle Hickey, acting chief of staff of the Far East Command, and Brig. Gen. Edwin K. Wright, operations officer of the Far East Command, indicates GHQ concurrence. Roy Appleman, in *Disaster in Korea*, indicates that Maj. Gen. Levin Allen, Eighth Army chief of staff, said the two GHQ generals concurred in Walker's decision to abandon P'yongyang.[1]

As units cleared out of the Ch'ongch'on River area and headed south, it became apparent that P'yongyang was not going to be defended at all. The 2d Division had orders as early as 1 December to head directly to Munsan-ni, south of the Imjin River below the 38th Parallel.[2] The 2d Division was merely the vanguard for a rush of units heading south. The Eighth Army issued orders to destroy all food, ammunition, clothing, and petroleum stores in the P'yongyang area, thus reducing the load on the overtaxed road south.

The Eighth Army designated some units to provide defensive lines to the north and east and instructed them to conduct long-range patrols to reestablish contact with the Chinese, but few of the units aggressively complied with the patrol order. Consequently, General Walker had to rely on agent reports and aerial surveillance to provide intelligence about enemy movements. The information was inadequate, and commanders at all levels became apprehensive that the Chinese hordes were just over the next hill.

Some critics have alleged that the entire Eighth Army was afflicted with "bugout fever." Army historian Billy Mossman contends that the term, which implies cowardice and dereliction of duty, was unwarranted. Nevertheless, he did admit that "the hard attacks and high casualties of the past week and the apparent Chinese strength had shaken the Eighth Army's confidence."[3]

The Chinese, of course, were not over the next hill. This was not a highly mobile army, but the CCF, urged on by Kim Il Sung, did make haste to occupy P'yongyang. The Chinese were on its outskirts by 6 December and fully occupied it by 10 December.

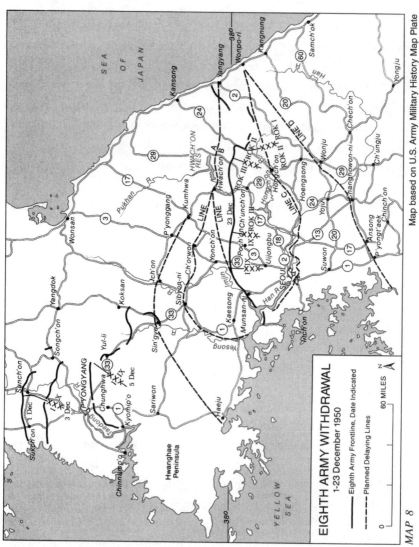

EIGHTH ARMY WITHDRAWAL
1-23 December 1950

— Eighth Army Frontline, Date Indicated

--- Planned Delaying Lines

0   60 MILES

MAP 8

Map based on U.S. Army Military History Map Plate

Walker was not the only commander who had problems with higher headquarters. Peking was euphoric following the victories during the First and Second Phase Offensives and thought the "volunteers" to be invincible. The entire Communist Chinese command structure in Peking believed that the imperialist Americans and their puppet troops could be swept immediately into the sea. In addition, the North Koreans were pressuring the Chinese for a quick recapture of Seoul.

Peng also was convinced that he could win, but he wanted more time for reorganization and resupply. Mao was not willing to wait. Thus, the Chinese made the same error that MacArthur had made earlier, and it, too, would cost dearly.[4]

Orders for the Third Phase Offensive were issued on 19 December, even as columns of the Chinese Thirteenth Army Group were marching south. The U.S. Eighth Army had long since completed its withdrawal and had established a defense line along the Imjin River just south of the 38th Parallel.

The last American combat unit remaining north of the Eighth Army's defense line was the 187th Airborne Regimental Combat Team (ARCT), whose commander, Brig. Gen. Frank S. Bowen, liberally interpreted his mission orders to delay the enemy and protect the main body of the Eighth Army. Once he learned that all American forces were in position to his south, he summoned his commanders and said, "I'm sick and tired of running from a shadow enemy. Tomorrow morning the 187th will turn about and move north until we contact this enemy and give him a real, good bloody nose."[5]

So the regiment moved north on Route 1, the main supply route (MSR) between P'yongyang and Seoul, until the lead battalion spotted Chinese moving south on the road in a column of fours without any advance or flank security.

The ARCT artillery, a battalion of 105-mm howitzers, all of the lead battalion's heavy weapons, and the regimental antitank guns blazed away at the Chinese column. Despite horrendous losses, the Chinese kept coming in column formation. After fifteen minutes of continuous ground fire, Air Force tactical air strikes commenced and Bowen ordered his troops to begin a slow, disciplined withdrawal to the south.[6] That was the last contact with the Chinese that Eighth Army units had in North Korea during 1950.

UN forces were still in North Korea, but X Corps was conducting an orderly withdrawal onto a beachhead at Hungnam and was systematically embarking units for deposit at South Korean ports. The ROK I Corps was sea-lifted on 20 December for Samch'ok on South Korea's east shore almost due east of Seoul. Walker gave it the mission of anchoring the eastern flank of the Eighth Army defense line that was then forming. The remainder of X Corps units sailed in increments for Pusan, where they would come under control of the Eighth Army. MacArthur had decided on 7 December to bring X Corps under Eighth Army control once it extracted from Hungnam. According to Appleman, MacArthur was uneasy about making Almond subordinate to Walker, but when Almond was asked whether he wanted to come back to Tokyo to resume his job as Far East Command (FECOM) chief of staff or to remain as commander of X Corps, he opted to stay with X Corps.[7]

When Walker first received permission to put his army on the defensive, his planners sketched out four phase lines for withdrawal. Line Able was around P'yongyang, Line Baker ran from the Imjin River on the east across the peninsula to a point just above the 38th Parallel, Line Charlie was just south of Seoul, and Line Dog was forty miles farther south. Eighth Army planners also had phase lines farther south to the old Naktong River line, which was being prepared for a last-ditch defense before evacuation of UN forces from Korea.

Walker, of course, never stopped at Line Able, and most members of his command believed that the defenses at Line Baker would be only a temporary halt on their way out of Korea.

What was it about this enemy that had so badly spooked soldiers who had participated in the triumph over the Wehrmacht and the Japanese Imperial Army just a half-dozen years earlier? Appleman, who calls the abandonment of P'yongyang one of the most "serious tactical errors of the war," provides a concise summary of the strengths and weaknesses of the CCF. The Thirteenth Army Group of the People's Liberation Army (PLA) had been in an attack mode for five days and nights without respite. They had advanced entirely by foot, usually over mountains and ridges. They carried on their backs what food they ate, and there was no ready resupply. While they had warm quilted uniforms, their footgear was a type of canvas and rubber sneaker ill suited for the vicious Siberian winter. Frostbite and frozen feet exacted a tremendous toll.

No westerner could know for certain, but it is believed that the composition of the PLA in 1950 was a mix of communist soldiers from World War II or earlier (15 percent), communist soldiers who were veterans of the civil war (25 percent), former nationalist soldiers (30 percent), and 30 percent conscripts since 1948. Most of the soldiers were of peasant origin, and few could read or write.

Appleman notes that the major weakness of the Chinese army was the miscellaneous origin of its weapons. Although it had a smattering of weaponry from Soviet bloc forces, mostly submachine guns, recoilless rifles, and mortars, a fair number of rifles were of Japanese origin. The Red Army had captured large quantities of American arms at the conclusion of the civil war, and many Chinese in Korea were armed with Thompson submachine guns, M-1 rifles, and 60-mm mortars. Altogether, the supply of ammunition for this motley collection of hardware was a logistician's nightmare. Complicating the supply problems for the CCF were a shortage of transport and the necessity of moving vehicles only at night to avoid allied air strikes.[8]

This was the army that, in late December, had arrayed itself north of the Eighth Army's Line Baker, with the preponderance of strength aimed down the historic invasion corridors to Seoul.

Saturday, 23 December, was the first day of *Tung Chih*, the twelve-day period of the winter solstice, and an inauspicious day for a journey according to ancient Chinese legend. That morning, General Walker left Seoul by jeep to visit units above Uijongbu. Ten miles into the journey, his speeding jeep, rolling with red lights flashing and sirens blaring, had a near head-on collision with a South Korean 3/4-ton truck. The sideswipe impact threw Walker's vehicle off the road and into a ditch, where it overturned. Walker was beneath the jeep and sustained severe head injuries, as well as a broken neck. He was pronounced dead at a nearby 24th Division clearing station.

General Walker had, at times, fought his Eighth Army very well under difficult circumstances, but his fear of his boss in the Dai Ichi Building sometimes led to questionable tactical decisions. His death denied him an opportunity to prove that the withdrawal from the north was a skillful maneuver designed to save his army rather than a disgraceful bugout.

FOUR | Ridgway Takes Command

When Lt. Gen. Matthew Bunker Ridgway stepped down from the B-17 that brought him to Kimpo Airfield just outside Seoul, his greeting party saw a man who flat out looked like a soldier. He was clad in field gear and wore what became his trademark—a .45-caliber pistol on a web belt with shoulder harness containing a grenade on the right-side D ring and a special paratrooper's first aid kit on the left shoulder strap. He stood ramrod straight, nearly 6 feet tall, with a trim 180 pounds on an athletic build that he worked hard to maintain. High cheekbones, a slightly hooked nose, and dark eyebrows framed wide-set piercing hazel eyes. Clay Blair quoted associates who said that the most striking thing about Ridgway was the aura of force or determination—a very powerful presence—that he radiated.[1]

Ridgway was the Army's assistant chief of staff for operations and administration when he was ordered to Korea. His only previous experience in Korea had been in August when he accompanied White House National Security advisor William Averell Harriman on an inspection trip to Japan and Korea. During World War II, Ridgway had commanded the 82d Airborne Division, which he led during the invasions of Sicily, Italy, and Normandy. Later, he was promoted to lieutenant general and given command of the XVIII Airborne Corps.

After Ridgway met with Syngman Rhee and reassured him of American intentions to stay and fight in Korea, he had a productive meeting with U.S. Ambassador John J. Muccio. Ridgway at once appreciated Muccio's knowledge, and when the ambassador told him that the gravest danger to the UN lines was in the central front, Ridgway acted decisively. He immediately ordered the 2d Infantry Division, which was still rebuilding, north from its positions near Ch'ungju, about 65 miles southeast of Seoul, into the Wonju and Hoengsong areas to back up ROK formations that were starting to show signs of crumbling. The division covered the 40-mile journey just in time to slow a North Korean offensive on the central front.[2]

About 70 miles northwest of Seoul in the North Korean town of Sariwon, senior Chinese and North Korean commanders and staff were reviewing final plans for the forthcoming Third Phase Offensive. Maj. Han Liqun, aide to General Peng, was one of the sources interviewed by Russell Spurr for his book, *Enter the Dragon*. Han told Spurr that an enormous feeling of optimism was apparent throughout the conference. Peng had started talking about this offensive being the one that would end the war. P'yongyang radio carried news of Walker's death and claimed that he had been killed in a guerrilla ambush. As far as Peng and his cohorts were concerned, Ridgway was a little-known airborne general with no Asian experience who would barely have time to study his maps before his army was overwhelmed by the Chinese. The situation was so favorable that the generals were debating whether to swing more strength toward the central front instead of concentrating their main thrust on Seoul. Peking quickly vetoed that notion, and Seoul remained the prime target of Gen. Li's Thirteenth Army Group.[3]

With the reconstituted North Korean Divisions exhibiting strength and confidence, however, it was decided to start the two NKPA Corps, the Fifth and the Second, south against the lightly defended central front four days in advance of the main Chinese assault against Seoul. Starting on the day that Ridgway arrived in Korea, the NKPA assaults were aimed at the ROK 8th and 9th Divisions which were defending a portion of the Eighth Army's Line Baker just south of the Hwach'on Reservoir. Ridgway's decision to move the U.S. 2d Division, reinforced by a regiment of the U.S. 7th Division, into blocking positions in the vicinity of Wonju turned out to be one of the most timely decisions of the war.

Meanwhile, on 27 and 28 December, Ridgway visited commanders and units all along Line Baker. He was keenly disappointed in the defeatist attitude that he found in officers and men in nearly every unit. He later wrote:

> The leadership I found in many instances sadly lacking and I said so out loud. The unwillingness of the army to forgo certain creature comforts, its timidity about getting off the scanty roads, its reluctance to move without radio and telephone contact, and its lack of imagination in dealing with a foe whom they outmatched in firepower and dominated in the air and on the surrounding seas—these were not the fault of the GI but of the policymakers at the top. I'm afraid my language in pointing out these faults was often impolite.
>
> What I told the field commanders in essence was that their infantry ancestors would roll over in their graves could they see how roadbound this army was, how often it forgot to seize the high ground along its route, how it failed to seek and maintain contact in its front, how little it knew of the terrain and how they seldom took advantage of it.[4]

Ridgway had met with the corps commanders within hours of his arrival at the Eighth Army forward command post in Seoul. He quickly decided that the IX Corps commander, Maj. Gen. John Coulter, who had dithered on the Ch'ongch'on while the Chinese destroyed his command, would be the first to go. His replacement would be Maj. Gen. Bryant E. Moore, Ridgway's classmate from the West Point Class of 1917 and, at the time, superintendent of the U.S. Military Academy. Ridgway knew that neither Maj. Gen. Frank Milburn, I Corps commander, nor Maj. Gen. Edmund Almond, X Corps commander, fully met his high professional standards, but Milburn was an old friend and he could be prodded into action. Almond, though, was a different story. While Milburn lacked what Ridgway termed "the spark of initiative," Almond was the opposite, bold to the point of recklessness. Ridgway wrote that Almond was one of the few commanders whom he did not have to push but one whom he had to watch closely to ensure that his recklessness did not jeopardize his command.

Following his introductory visits to the units, Ridgway also knew that he had to do a general housecleaning of commanders. He had to operate under some constraints. Too many firings would create unfavorable press and cause an uproar in Washington, and there also could be a counterproductive backlash within the units whose leaders were sacked. So he decided to do his housecleaning over a period and to use rotations and promotions to soften the blow. A prime example was the mid-January promotion of General Coulter to three stars and an appointment as deputy commander of the Eighth Army with duties as senior liaison officer to the ROK Army and President Syngman Rhee.[5]

Ridgway had arrived in Korea fully prepared to order limited attacks. In his interview with General MacArthur, Ridgway had asked that, if he found the situation to be favorable, would MacArthur object to a decision to attack. MacArthur had answered, "The Eighth Army is yours, Matt. Do what you think best." On the ground, however, Ridgway found units so dispirited that any kind of offensive action was out of the question. Whether he had enough time also was questionable. Despite the lack of good intelligence—at briefings, he was confronted with maps showing a large red goose egg containing the number 174,000 scrawled in the middle of it—there still was evidence of an imminent enemy offensive. The coming New Year holiday seemed to be a logical date on which to expect the opening assault.[6]

Unit dispositions along Line Baker had not changed since General Walker had established the line. The reconstituted Turkish Brigade garrisoned the Kimpo Peninsula near the mouth of the Han River. U.S. I Corps, with the U.S. 25th Division and the ROK 1st Division, had the line that ran northeast along the south bank of the Imjin River. The British 29th Brigade was in I Corps reserve south of Munsan-ni on Route 1.

U.S. IX Corps was responsible for the line where it straightened out and followed the 38th Parallel. The ROK 6th Division, on the left of IX Corps, was tied with the ROK 1st Division and astride Route 33. Inexplicably, Walker had placed two ROK divisions side by side, divided by a corps boundary, and made them responsible for defending the historic invasion corridor to Seoul. It appeared that the Eighth Army commander and his subordinate commanders had learned nothing from the Chinese attacks in November.

Next on line to the east was the U.S. 24th Division. In reserve for the IX Corps was the British 27th Brigade, assembled near Uijongbu, the junctions of Routes 3 and 33. The U.S. 1st Cavalry Division, now with a Greek battalion and a Filipino battalion attached, was in reserve but oriented to protect the right flank of IX Corps.

Three ROK corps defended the remainder of Line Baker to the east. ROK III Corps, with the ROK 2d, 5th, and 8th Divisions, guarded the critical central sector below the Hwach'on Dam and Reservoir. To the east, the ROK 3d Division of the ROK II Corps already was showing signs of buckling in the face of renewed NKPA thrusts, as were units of the ROK 9th Division, which belonged to ROK I Corps. The capable ROK Capital Division anchored the eastern flank of Line Baker.

Once Ridgway moved the U.S. 2d Division, with its newly attached French and Netherlands battalion, into the Wonju–Hoengsong area, his only immediately available reserve for strengthening the front was the 187th Airborne RCT. The 187th, with a Thai battalion attached, was at Suwon, south of Seoul, and thus not close enough to the vulnerable central sector. Ridgway's main reserve consisted of the three divisions of X Corps, still reassembling near Pusan after the evacuation from Hungnam, but it was a reserve in name only.[7]

The 1st Marine Division had moved into a training area at Masan on the southern tip of the peninsula, to recover from its recent ordeal. On 27 December, Ridgway met with Maj. Gen. Oliver P. Smith and his G-3 at X Corps headquarters at Kyongju in southeast Korea. Ridgway impressed the Marines. He told them to pitch the withdrawal plans that the Eighth Army staff had given them because there wasn't going to be any withdrawal from Korea. Ridgway also was impressed by Smith. In his oral history, he remembered: "Smith was top flight, a splendid commander. If it had not been for his moral courage and doing some of the things he did, which were not in full accord with the instructions he had received (from Almond) he'd have lost a great part of that division."[8]

After his experience of working for Almond at Inchon, Seoul, and the Changjin Reservoir, Smith did not want his Marine Division ever again to serve under X Corps. According to Clay Blair, Smith definitely conveyed his feelings to Ridgway without actually saying so. Although it complicated his planning, Ridgway sympathized and assured Smith that his Marine division never again would be placed under command of X Corps.[9]

Almond, in his own right, probably was relieved. In his oral history, Almond was asked if the two men instinctively distrusted or disliked each other from the start. Almond responded, "Not at all. I got the impression initially, and it was fortified constantly later, that General Smith always had excuses for not performing at the required time the tasks he was requested to do."[10] Almond clearly wanted subordinates who were as responsive to his orders as he was to MacArthur's.

The 17th Regiment of the U.S. 7th Infantry Division, the only U.S. formation that actually reached the Yalu River, had escaped from northeast Korea in good condition and was hurried north to reinforce the 2d Division. The other regiments of the 7th Division—the 31st and the 32d—had been hurt badly; although their complete rehabilitation would take a little longer, they still were pushed north to reinforce the 17th Regiment in the Chech'on area. X Corps had been given the mission of developing Route 29 from Wonju south to Andong and Taegu as a main supply route for the central sector of Korea. North Korean guerrillas were still in the area of the rugged mountain passes between Chech'on and Tangyang, and the 7th Division regiments were needed to keep the road open.

Ridgway was offensive minded and deplored the withdrawal mind-set of the Eighth Army, but he was realistic about his chances of holding Line Baker. He instructed the two U.S. corps commanders holding the line north of Seoul to establish bridgehead defensive positions above Seoul. This defensive line would be deep enough to keep the Han River bridges below Seoul free of enemy artillery fire. He refused to let subordinate commanders issue "hold at all costs" orders, and reserved that prerogative for himself. He authorized his corps commanders to withdraw on their own initiative at any time that they concluded it was necessary. But Ridgway was emphatic that, no matter who issued a withdrawal order, the retrograde must be more than a simple movement from one line to another. Both corps were to use infantry and armor units to punish the advancing Chinese.

Despite the North Korean attacks north of Hoengsong, all available intelligence evidence pointed to the main Chinese effort as being directed against the South Korean capital down the Uijongbu–Seoul corridor. Although the Chinese maintained excellent concealment of assault units, aerial reconnaissance revealed significant artillery units generally positioned near the I and IX Corps boundary were it to be extended north into enemy territory. Air observers also noted a buildup of bridging material near the Imjin River.[11]

When Ridgway flew into Seoul on the afternoon of 31 December and toured the western front, the 116th Division of the Thirty-Ninth CCF Field Army was in the final stages of preparation for an assault on the 1st ROK Division. Ridgway returned to his quarters at his advance command post in Seoul just after dark. Two hours later, the Chinese artillery opened up to signal the start of the Third Phase Offensive.

FIVE | **The Third Phase Offensive**

In March 1951, the CCF Thirteenth Army Group prepared a remarkable document for the Nineteenth Army Group, which was preparing to move on line against UN forces. This document was mimeographed and became required reading for the Chinese officer corps. It contained an exhaustive study of the planning, preparation, and conduct of the Imjin River assaults. A copy of the document was captured, translated, and made available to UN forces for study. The document was valuable in that it showed that Chinese attacks were meticulously planned and violently executed. In its preamble, the document stated:

> As we had been preparing for over a month for the attack, we had plentiful information on the enemy situation and terrain and knew that artillery cover was available. The battle we fought was an attack from comparatively well prepared positions. The 116th Division broke through the ROK Army front in less than two and a half hours with only two of its regiments.[1]

The Chinese were adept at reconnaissance that revealed defensive weaknesses, as well as unit boundaries. The CCF planners chose the boundary between the 11th and 12th Regiments of the ROK 1st Division as the point of penetration for the CCF 116th Division. General Paik's 1st Division arguably was the best unit in the ROK Army, but every unit had its vulnerabilities. The boundaries between regiments were among those vulnerabilities.

After full darkness on 31 December and following a thirty-minute artillery preparation, the assault battalions of the 116th Division crossed the frozen Imjin River and penetrated the ROK 1st Division defenses. From this opening on the extreme right of the U.S. I Corps, General Li broadened his attack eastward. At around midnight, the 113th Division, CCF Thirty-Eighth Army, struck the ROK 6th Division on the IX Corps left, while the 114th Division of the Thirty-Eighth Army conducted smaller attacks on the U.S. 24th Division. The Chinese had designed these attacks on the right of IX Corps more to freeze the 24th Division in place than to effect a penetration, although they were prepared to exploit a penetration if one developed. Farther east, the CCF Sixty-Sixth Army sent a pair of divisions against the two ROK divisions of the ROK III Corps. Here, the aim of the Chinese seemed to be a replication of their Second Phase Offensive where a violent thrust at the flanks of the two American Corps through easily defeated ROK units caused the entire Eighth Army structure to crumple.[2]

The night attack by the CCF 116th Division routed the ROK 12th Regiment. General Paik tried to plug the gap with his reserve, the 15th Regiment, but it was hit hard. With the ROK 11th Regiment on the left of Paik's division being forced back, this effort was futile.

The preparation of the 116th Division for the assault was impressive. The men constructed scaling ladders 5–10 meters in length to use in climbing the riverbanks. The Chinese planners had deliberately chosen the most difficult part of the Imjin River for the assault. The ROK commanders, believing the banks were too high and steep, had prepared stronger defenses at more logical crossing sites. The CCF's intensive preassault training program had included techniques of grappling and neutralizing mines, map reading to eliminate the need for guides, and techniques for attacking bunkers and communication trenches. The assault regiments broke through on a 1,500-meter front.

Though the presence of CCF on the north bank of the Imjin was well known to UN forces, they did not know the precise disposition of troops because of the CCF's stringent concealment discipline during daylight hours. The Chinese report said:

Closest attention was paid by officers of all grades to the strict maintenance of antiaircraft discipline. The divisional commander personally inspected the condition of the troops at dawn. All personnel took cover in underground shelters and did not leave them for any reason before the attack began. Not a single man, horse, rifle or one round of ammunition was exposed. Enemy planes circled at low altitude all day long, but were unable to detect our intentions. We were thus able to achieve complete surprise.[3]

That first night, the two assault regiments of the 116th Division penetrated about 10 miles, far enough so that a battery of U.S. artillery supporting the ROK 1st Division was caught in a CCF ambush about 8 miles south of the Imjin. It lost four 155-mm howitzers while trying to escape the trap. To the right of Paik's division, the ROK 6th Division was doing better in resisting Chinese assaults, but the sudden loss of its left flank forced it to give ground rapidly.

By dawn on New Year's Day, when Ridgway started by jeep toward the ROK 1st and 6th Division sectors, he began to see evidence that justified his overnight fears. Apparently, the Chinese advance toward Seoul was more than his committed forces could handle. No more than three Chinese divisions had been identified in the attacks north of Seoul, but Ridgway knew that there were many more divisions poised to exploit the rupture in the ROK 1st Division lines. He was also aware of Chinese attacks on ROK Army formations to the east, but reports from those sectors were slim. In addition, the troublesome North Korean offensive was threatening Wonju on the central front.

The Eighth Army commander's concerns grew rapidly to alarm when he met trucks packed with South Korean troops. Jumping from his jeep, he futilely tried to flag them down. He ordered straggler collection points established so that retreating troops could be stopped and held for reassembly into units.

Despite the appearance of panic among the fleeing South Korean soldiers, both the ROK 1st and 6th Divisions had reoriented their

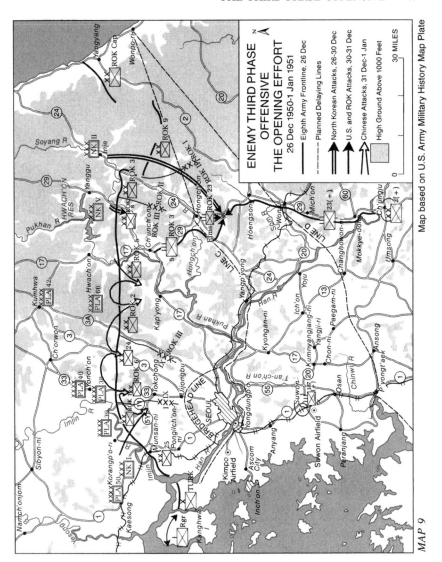

ENEMY THIRD PHASE
OFFENSIVE
THE OPENING EFFORT
26 Dec 1950-1 Jan 1951

Eighth Army Frontline, 26 Dec
Planned Delaying Lines
North Korean Attacks, 26-30 Dec
U.S. and ROK Attacks, 30-31 Dec
Chinese Attacks, 31 Dec-1 Jan
High Ground Above 1000 Feet

0   30 MILES

Map based on U.S. Army Military History Map Plate

MAP 9

remaining forces to defend against Chinese exploitation of its 10-mile salient. As reports came in from ROK units to the east, it became clear to Ridgway that he would be forced to withdraw and give up Seoul to the Chinese. At noon on 1 January, he ordered the I and IX Corps back to the Seoul bridgehead line and directed all South Korean forces in the east to pull back to Line Charlie.[4]

Line Charlie followed the south bank of the Han River to Yangp'yong, then along a northeasterly course through Hongch'on in central Korea to Wonpo-ri on the east coast. Line Dog, the next withdrawal phase line, extended from P'yongt'aek on the west coast, about thirty-five miles south of Seoul, and northeast through Wonju in central Korea to the same east coast anchor of Wonpo-ri.

Chinese forces took two days to consolidate the conquered territory. Early on the morning of 3 January, elements of the CCF Fiftieth Army struck the U.S. 25th Infantry Division on the extreme left of the Seoul bridgehead line. The Thirty-Ninth Army attacked the British 29th Brigade, and, to the west, the U.S. 24th Infantry Division was hit hard by units of the Fortieth and Thirty-Eighth Armies. By noon that day, the ferocity of the attacks and the uncertainty of the situation in the ROK sectors east of Seoul persuaded Ridgway that a withdrawal of his units to south of the Han River would have to commence soon. He had the responsibility of informing the South Korean government of the necessity of moving government officials, along with countless civilians in the city, to safety.

Complicating the evacuation problem was the condition of the Han River bridges. All permanent bridges had been destroyed when the North Koreans occupied the capital city. The three temporary structures built by engineers were floating bridges that could be destroyed by shifting ice caused by the tidal surges on the Han. There were five floating footbridges across the river to handle a potentially huge refugee exodus. At points where tidal forces did not buckle the ice, the Han was frozen sufficiently to permit pedestrian crossings.

Ridgway was confronted with two problems. He had to extricate his forces from the bridgehead line while they still were in contact, and his Line Charlie positions just south of the Han no longer seemed all that secure. The Chinese Sixty-Sixth Army had penetrated past Kap'yong, and the head of a CCF column was only 15 miles west of 1st Cavalry Division positions on the right flank of IX Corps. Ridgway feared that the CCF could bypass the 1st Cavalry outposts and continue driving toward the rear of the Eighth Army well south of Seoul.

Ridgway therefore believed that the only way to avoid undue risk to his command was to evacuate Seoul as quickly as possible. Putting his instructions in writing, he stressed two points: (1) no usable equipment was to be abandoned and all sick, wounded, and dead were to be evacuated; and (2) withdrawals should be conducted with maximum losses inflicted on the enemy. Ridgway also canceled Walker's "scorched earth" demolition policy, which stated that "the execution of demolitions and necessary, military destruction in South Korea shall be such to combine maximum hurt to the enemy with minimum harm to the civilian population."[5]

The withdrawal from the bridgehead line went smoothly, marred only by the entrapment of a company and a half dozen tanks of the Royal Ulster Rifles. Ridgway sent orders that the 25th Division should attempt to extricate this force, but its commander, Brigadier Thomas Brodie, would not permit Col. John H. Michaelis to send a rescue force from his 27th Regiment, nor would Brodie send any of his forces. Some of the trapped men got out, but more than 250 men and ten tanks were lost to the Chinese.[6]

Ridgway had planned to maintain a strong force along the north bank of the Han so that he could give the pursuing Chinese bloody noses as they tried to cross the river. But the CCF, apparently in no hurry to begin assaults south, seemed content to occupy Seoul after the pro forma raising of a North Korean flag over city hall in the heart of the city.

A strange lull in the fighting set in along the Han River. Ridgway's estimate of the situation was that once the Chinese had wrested Seoul from the Americans for political purposes, the CCF would be more cautious about close pursuit of the Eighth Army on the relatively flat terrain of the Seoul–P'yongt'aek corridor. This was country where armored units could create havoc among Chinese infantry formations and air strikes would be more successful than in the mountains. So, he believed, the CCF would shift the weight of its attack toward the east and the protective mountains.

An intelligence report on 4 January seemed to confirm Ridgway's estimate. CCF forces were identified just north of Yoju, a village about 30 miles due east of Suwon, which itself was 15 miles south of Ridgway's main forces arrayed along the Han River. The threat of Chinese forces driving a wedge between I and IX Corps in the west and X Corps farther east and then flanking and trapping either force caused Ridgway to rethink his plan to bloody Chinese noses at the Han. On 4 January, he issued a series of orders that would consolidate his forces on Line Dog and buy his army time to undergo the physical and psychological changes that it would need to conform more closely to his idea of an American field army.

Ridgway directed I and IX Corps to commence withdrawal from Line Charlie at 8:00 P.M. that day and fall back toward Line Dog, with a temporary stop on a phase line at Suwon to permit evacuation of sixteen trainloads of supplies parked there. He called off the advance of the 2d Division north of Hoengsong and instructed X Corps to establish a defense in the Wonju area. Also, Ridgway hurriedly deployed the 187th Airborne RCT from Suwon toward Ichon and Wonju to block any kind of Chinese flanking movement toward the Eighth Army rear. He directed the U.S. 3d Infantry Division, which had been in Eighth Army reserve near the southern tip of Korea, to move forward immediately and join Milburn's I Corps on Line Dog.[7]

Drawn on map acetate, Line Dog looked nice, but, in reality, it could be called a defensive line only as far as Wonju, and, even then, there were gaps between the IX Corps boundary and Wonju. East of Wonju, only a loose and disorganized amalgamation of ROK units covered the vastness of the Taebaek Mountains, and North Korean forces could easily penetrate them.

Now that the bulk of his army was relatively safe, Ridgway could vent his anger. The Chinese New Year's offensive had forced the bulk of his Eighth Army to withdraw about 60 air miles in seven days, forcing Ridgway to give up Seoul as Walker had yielded P'yongyang. Ridgway was prepared to accept the notion of a withdrawal to protect his flanks, but what he could not accept was the inability of Eighth Army units to inflict punishment on the CCF as they were withdrawing. His displeasure was revealed in a 7 January message to his corps commanders:

> Reports so far reaching me indicate your forces withdrew to D line without evidence of having inflicted any substantial losses on the enemy and without material delay. In fact some major units are reported as having broken contact. I desire prompt confirming reports and if substantially correct, the reason for non-compliance with my directives.[8]

Ridgway was also disgusted with the performance of the South Korean formations. On 2 January, he had called on Syngman Rhee in the company of Ambassador Muccio and bluntly demanded a housecleaning. Knowing that Rhee had sent requests to MacArthur for more equipment and arms to increase the size of his army, Ridgway told Rhee that until he got rid of the incompetents and his army demonstrated that it had an officer corps worthy of the name, the South Koreans would get no additional equipment nor would their overall strength be increased.

Arguably, the best combat leader in the ROK army was General Paik, who had been mortified over the failure of his 1st Division to make a better showing on the Imjin. Paik ordered an investigation into the conduct of his regiments. The results were court-martial convictions of a battalion commander and a company commander for cowardice. Both were executed, and law and order were restored in the ROK 1st Division.

Gen. Chung Il Kwon, ROK Army chief of staff, reacted to the problem of bugout fever among his troops by delegating to all commanders the right of summary trial. This discretionary wartime authority to punish without resort to the usual court-martial process devolved all the way from corps commanders down to squad leaders.[9]

Ridgway felt reasonably comfortable about the situation in the west now that the U.S. 3d Division was on line in the I Corps sector, but he was decidedly uneasy about the situation to the east. The central corridor of Korea, perhaps 30 miles wide at the most, reaching from the Hwach'on Reservoir just north of the 38th Parallel and south past Taegu, was the most critical terrain in Korea. It was dominated by the high Taebaek Mountains on the east, with numerous subordinate ranges creating terrain compartments running off to the west. In these compartments were found the only improved roads available in Korea at that time, in addition to railroads, the most reliable mode of transportation for supplying armies. In areas where the terrain compartments intersected, crossroads towns were of importance to military planners far beyond the value of the handful of houses that made up each village.

The central corridor was a prize waiting to be seized. General Peng had realized this when he planned the Third Phase Offensive. He wanted to reinforce the center at the expense of the assault in the west, but he was overruled by Peking. In his headquarters in P'yongyang, Peng must have been gnashing his teeth in frustration. His volunteers had made excellent progress on the western edge of the central corridor, and they reached the outskirts of Yoju by 4 January. But the central and east sectors of Korea, for political reasons, had been given to the reconstituted North Korean army. North of Wonju, the U.S. 2d Division was putting up more resistance than the North Koreans had anticipated or could immediately overcome.

The mission of bringing order out of the chaos of broken ROK formations and under-strength American divisions fell to Maj. Gen. Almond, X Corps commander. Appleman, probably the only historian who was an unabashed admirer of Almond, wrote:

For General Almond it was to be a test of his leadership and generalship. On the outcome rested no less than the decision whether the UN could remain in Korea. The fight for the central corridor demanded a decisive and aggressive commander. In Almond it had one.[10]

six | **Rekindling the Offensive Spirit**

As the Eighth Army settled down into defensive positions on Line Dog, Ridgway had no intention of allowing the units to get too comfortable in their present posture. He entrusted X Corps with the task of securing the central corridor, which included giving Almond operational control of ROK units in the sector. In the western sector, manned by I and IX Corps, units had lost contact with the CCF during the withdrawal. Ridgway's combat intelligence was woefully scant. The Chinese had halted their advance somewhere south of Seoul, but Ridgway did not know exactly where they had stopped and how many there were. He knew that he must take action to satisfy three objectives, (1) to rekindle an offensive spirit, (2) to reestablish contact with the enemy, and (3) to begin crystalizing a fuzzy intelligence picture.

He ordered both corps commanders to begin aggressive patrolling in front of their positions. For most units, that meant quick out-and-back infantry patrols. Not surprisingly (the Chinese were nowhere close), they made no contact. Ridgway wanted a deeper probe. I Corps chose Colonel Michaelis's 27th Infantry, reinforced by tanks from Lt. Col. Welborn G. "Tom" Dolvin's 89th Tank Battalion to conduct the deep reconnaissance in force.

Dubbed Operation Wolfhound, the probe kicked off on 15 January and reached Osan, 10 miles north of Line Dog, without incident. After traveling 10 more miles, the task force ran into Chinese opposition on the outskirts of Suwon. At that point, the task force broke contact and withdrew. It established a corps outpost line on the banks of the Chinwi River, about 7 miles north of Line Dog. Although the probe did not produce much usable intelligence, it did indicate that the Chinese were not in hot pursuit of the Eighth Army. Ridgway also was pleased because it rekindled the men's offensive spirit, and he believed that it presented enough threat to the Chinese to prevent them from siphoning forces away from the western sector to reinforce the central corridor.[1]

Meanwhile, to the east, X Corps had created a line of sorts from Wonju to Chech'on with the 2d Division and 17th Regiment of the 7th Division. The two other regiments of the 7th manned outposts along Route 29, the main supply route for X Corps. In his oral history, Col. Herbert B. Powell, commander of the 17th Infantry Regiment, said that General Almond initially thought that he would make this line "impregnable by stationing a brigadier general every 5,000 yards and he took all the assistant division commanders and other brigadier generals that he could find and gave them a spot on the map to go and occupy."

Brig. Gen. Henry Hodes, assistant division commander, dutifully moved into Powell's command post, thus bleeding off staff assistance in the regimental headquarters. Powell said that Almond also insisted on sending out artillery task forces escorted by an infantry battalion to conduct infiltration interdiction fire missions. "They would fire indirect fire to a position maybe ten miles away, at a crossroads or something else. In this way we ran up a tremendous expenditure of ammunition. Whether we really interdicted enemy movement, I don't know," Powell added.[2]

The 7th Division's foe in January was the NKPA Second Corps, consisting of some fourteen thousand troops organized into four understrength divisions. This was not the well trained and equipped *Inmun Gun* that had dominated combat on the peninsula six months earlier. These troops were survivors of earlier battles who had been scattered in the wake of advancing UN forces, then had been collected, and, along with new conscripts, hastily fed into freshly reconstituted units. The mission of the Second Corps, after it broke through desultory resistance by the ROK 3d and 9th Divisions in the Taebaek Mountains, was to move south and link up with North

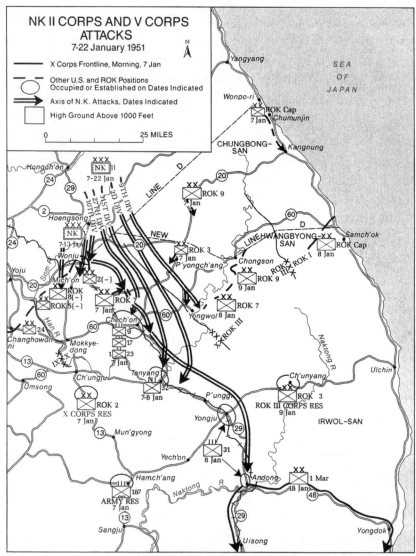

MAP 10

Map based on U.S. Army Military History Map Plate

Korean guerrilla units operating in the mountains south of Che-ch'on. From there, the North Korean units were to continue south to hit communications centers, transportation hubs, and, ultimately, attack Taegu.

NKPA Lt. Gen. Choe Hyon had instructed his troops to avoid

engagements, if possible, during this infiltration. This presented the U.S. 7th Division with an exceedingly difficult task.

The U.S. 2d Division had an even tougher assignment. North Korean Fifth Corps, under Maj. Gen. Pang Ho Song, had more men and those he had were better trained and equipped than those in the Second Corps. Still, none of his seven divisions were close to full strength, and most of them were equivalent to an American regiment in size. Early in January, the U.S. 23d and 38th Infantry Regiments had attacked north of Hoengsong to help extricate ROK elements that had been overrun and trapped by NKPA Fifth Corps.

That thrust put the two regiments into an untenable position with zero flank security, so X Corps directed Maj. Gen. Robert B. McClure, commander of the 2d Division, to pull back to Wonju and establish a defense there with the 23d and 38th Regiments. Col. Edwin J. ("Ed") Messinger's 9th Regiment, 2d Division, was deployed along Route 29 that ran southwest from Wonju to Chech'on. Wonju itself could not be easily defended. It sits in a bowl that is surrounded by mountains. Almond did not have sufficient forces to garrison the mountains, and there was a 20-mile gap to the west between Wonju and IX Corps positions at Yoju. This gap was manned by some disorganized ROK forces on which X Corps was desperately trying to get a handle. On the east, aside from Messinger's thin screen along Route 29, there was no security. McClure, who had assumed command of the 2d Division on 7 December after Walker sacked Maj. Gen. Lawrence Keiser, was concerned that the safety of his regiments was jeopardized.

McClure's alarm grew when his positions were assaulted in force by the NKPA 6th and 27th Divisions while, simultaneously, the NKPA 12th Division drove the ROK 10th Regiment out of position on McClure's left. He sought Almond's permission to withdraw from Wonju and received authority to move back 2 miles to a more defensible position on the hill mass south of the town. Instead, McClure pulled his regiments back nearly 10 miles. Almond was furious. He ordered McClure to attack back north, and the 23d and 38th regiments had a bloody struggle on Hill 247 about 2½ miles south of Wonju before finally wresting control from the North Korea. Despite the success of this attack, Almond wanted Mc-Clure's scalp and got it. On 14 January, Maj. Gen. Clark L. Ruffner, X Corps chief of staff, was dispatched to command the 2d "Indianhead" Division.[3]

Ridgway had planned an orderly relief of division commanders, with rotation back to training centers in the States, where their combat knowledge would be useful. But McClure's sacking, coming just thirty-seven days after he had assumed command of the 2d Division, could not be disguised as a routine rotation of a combat-weary general. His professional career in tatters, he was reassigned to the 6th Division at Fort Ord, California.

Blair wrote that the appointment of Ruffner and the new assistant division commander, Brig. Gen. George Craig Stewart, placed the 2d Division in the hands of two generals who were "strangers" to the division and who had never led troops in combat. He quoted Lt. Col. John H. Chiles, X Corps G-3: "But that was no problem. Tactically Almond ran the division, the regiments and the battalions. All Ruffner had to do was simply obey Almond's orders." Blair also provided an insight into general officer politics when he quoted Lt. Col. Maurice Holden, the former 2d Division G-3, about the irony of the relief of McClure and Keiser. "They were not working for the right bosses at the right time," Holden told Blair. "If the command sequence had been the reverse, all would have been rosy. McClure was a Collins [Army Chief of Staff Joseph ("Joe") Lawton Collins] man and Walker's drinking buddy. If McClure had commanded at Kunu-ri, Walker would not have relieved him. Keiser was an Almond man; they'd served together in Italy. If Keiser had commanded at Wonju, Almond would not have relieved him."[4]

While I Corps' 27th Infantry was pushing north in Operation Wolfhound, the Joint Chiefs of Staff (JCS) sent two of their own, General Collins, and Air Force Gen. Hoyt S. Vandenberg, to Tokyo and Korea to ascertain the facts about the situation in Korea. The visit followed nearly a fortnight of cable messages between Mac-Arthur and the Joint Chiefs. The tone of the messages was uniformly pessimistic—the Eighth Army would be forced to withdraw into the old Pusan Perimeter and would be ultimately evacuated from Korea. MacArthur wanted approval of punishing strikes against the Chinese mainland, as well as approval of unleashing the Nationalist Chinese for an invasion of the mainland.

The meeting in the Dai Ichi Building on 15 January was inconclusive. MacArthur was unbending, but neither Collins nor Vandenberg was as much in awe of the great man as they once had been. Increasingly, the Joint Chiefs were turning to Ridgway for accurate assessments of the situation in Korea. Both chiefs flew on to Korea the same day and arrived in Taegu around noon. There, the two split, Vandenberg to inspect the air forces and Collins, with Ridgway as escort, to look at the ground forces. In order to keep excessive pressure off General Milburn, who was running Wolfhound, the visitors headed for Almond's X Corps command post. Collins had good news for Almond. In response to lobbying by MacArthur, Collins had approved a third star for Almond with White House and Senate confirmation probably coming within a month.[5]

Collins also had a private conversation with Almond to seek the reasons for the relief of McClure. In his personal diary for 15 January, according to Appleman, Almond wrote that he explained the reasons to Collins and that he had also given a full account of his rationale in a three-page letter to General MacArthur. Almond wrote that Collins made no further comments.[6]

Next, Collins visited IX Corps, where he informed General Coulter that his third star would be on the same order as Almond's and Milburn's. It was bittersweet news to Coulter, who knew that he was being gently relieved and given a consolation-prize job in Eighth Army Headquarters. When Collins and Vandenberg returned to Tokyo, Collins cabled Gen. Omar N. Bradley, JCS chairman, with an upbeat report on their findings. Upon their return to Washington, both generals briefed President Truman, his cabinet, and the JCS. Collins said that morale in the Eighth Army was improving rather than worsening. He praised Ridgway for having taken command of the UN forces with "great confidence and energy," and said he "was doing a magnificent job." There had been a dramatic change in the Eighth Army, and, Collins stressed, "Ridgway alone was responsible."[7]

The fight with the U.S. 2d Division units in the Wonju area had exhausted the NKPA Fifth Corps. Short of men, ammunition, and food, and with troops suffering from a renewed Siberian winter that had blasted central Korea with subzero temperatures, General Pang gradually broke contact and withdrew north to the hills overlooking Hoengsong. Farther east, however, the NKPA II Corps had been mostly successful in sidestepping contact with American and ROK units and the majority of its force was south and east of Chech'on.

Ridgway successfully prodded the new ROK III Corps commander, Maj. Gen. Yu Jai Heung, to organize his 7th and 9th Divisions on a line that would close the gaps between X Corps and the ROK Capital Division, which had pulled back to Samch'ok on the east coast. This action bent Line Dog at Hoengsong to run more directly west to east and sort of tidied up the situation east of Wonju. The withdrawal of the North Korean Fifth Corps also gave the ROK 5th and 8th Divisions an opportunity to regroup and rehabilitate themselves and, at the same time, to establish a defensive line from Yoju east to Wonju.

The fight against the NKPA II Corps units became a series of battles along Route 29, the MSR. The 187th Airborne RCT was moved from Eighth Army reserve to the mountain pass between P'unggi and Tanyang and placed under operational control of X Corps. On 13 January, the RCT, with the 3d Battalion leading, attacked and occupied the ground on all sides of the pass. The following day, the 2d Battalion had a firefight with an estimated five hundred North Koreans. By the end of the week, despite battling constant below-zero temperatures, the 187th had almost eliminated the enemy threat to Tanyang and P'unggi. In the process, the paratroopers destroyed much of the North Korean 2d Division, severely damaged the NKPA 10th Division and ran the remnants of both south where they were engaged by the U.S. Marines. Ridgway had given the 1st Marine Division the mission of cleaning out guerrilla forces in the southeastern quadrant of the peninsula.[8]

With his east flank now reasonably secure, Ridgway could begin expanding the reconnaissance-in-force missions in the western sector, but he first had to deal with another series of purges in X Corps. When Ridgway contemplated the eventual rotation of division commanders, he planned on a "first in, first out" principle. Almond upset the plan by demanding the immediate sacking of the 7th Division commander, Maj. Gen. David G. Barr. Almond had often clashed with Barr. On 13 January, the 3d Battalion, 17th Infantry, was on patrol and ran into about two hundred North Koreans dug into a defensive position at Yongwol, about ten miles east of Chech'on. The 3/17 broke contact and called in artillery fire and air strikes on the enemy force. Aerial observers reported a concentration there of approximately two thousand troops. Two days later, the 1st and 2d Battalions of the 17th Infantry sent patrols into the Yongwol area. When they drew heavy fire, the patrols withdrew and also called in artillery fire and tactical air strikes. On 17 January, Almond ordered Barr to enter Yongwol immediately.[9]

That order led to a confrontation between Almond and Barr, according to Colonel Powell, when Almond visited the 7th Division's command post. "General Almond was directing that a certain operation be done," Powell remembered. "He wanted to send us over to a place about twenty miles away and occupy some high ground where we knew there'd been enemy. General Barr kept objecting to this, saying that it was dangerous and some of his men were going to get killed. The room was full of the staff and enlisted men that worked on maps and other things. I thought General Almond made one of the poorest mistakes in leadership that I heard in that war when he said, 'I don't care if your men get killed; you go and do this.' Now you can maybe say this privately to another commander—buck up—but you can't say it in front of the men you command."[10]

Barr's sacking brought Maj. Gen. Charles B. ("Buddy") Ferenbaugh to the 7th Division and set off a chain reaction of reassignments. Hodes, the assistant division commander, a fighter who also had clashed loudly and often with Almond, was rescued by Ridgway, promoted to major general, and installed as deputy chief of staff of the Eighth Army. Powell, who was well known to Ferenbaugh, became chief of staff of the division.[11]

During the first three weeks of January, IX Corps had not staged any reconnaissance in force comparable to I Corps' Operation Wolfhound. Responding to Ridgway's prodding, IX Corps' General Coulter, in one of his last acts before being replaced by Maj. Gen. Bryant Moore, finally scheduled a deep probe for 22 January. The 8th Cavalry Regiment, commanded by Col. Harold K. Johnson, provided the infantry element for the task force. Elements of the 70th Tank Battalion supplied the heavyweight punch. The task force made it to the town of Yangji-ri, the crossroads of Routes 20 and 55, before hitting Chinese resistance.

These reconnaissance forays did not yield a great deal of intelligence, other than learning that the Chinese were not in strength in proximity to Line Dog. Their real value, however, was the knowledge among the rank and file that American forces were advancing and not retreating. It did wonders for the morale of the Eighth Army, although some malcontents, who had hoped soon to be on board ships at Pusan, insisted on calling the Eighth Army commander "Wrong Way Ridgway."

Determined to resolve the ambiguities of the intelligence picture, Ridgway directed a broad reconnaissance in force by both corps. If it were possible, units could advance all the way to the Han River. Ridgway named this probe Operation Thunderbolt.[12]

SEVEN | Thunderbolt and Twin Tunnels

Ridgway was desperate for solid combat intelligence. He had moved his forward command post to the I Corps command post. Although other commanders might have been satisfied with a big red goose egg on a map with a large number inside, Ridgway decidedly was not. According to Lt. Col. Norwood G. Read, a member of the I Corps G-2 staff, Ridgway wanted precise information on men, weapons, vehicles, kinds of mines, and terrain covered by fires.[1]

With the state of intelligence in the Eighth Army, however, he did not often receive information of value. Two days before Thunderbolt kicked off, the Eighth Army G-2 reported the bulk of the CCF Thirteenth Army Group to be below Seoul in the area bounded by Route 20 on the south and the Han River on the east and north. Although air reconnaissance reported troop movements south of the Han, there was no real confirmation of such a large force in that region. In a personal effort to develop the intelligence situation before the operation, Ridgway and Gen. Earle E. ("Pat") Partridge, commander of the Fifth Air Force, flew their own reconnaissance mission.[2]

Ridgway learned firsthand what aerial observers had begun to understand in November—when the Chinese chose to remain invisible, aerial eyes and cameras were useless. He said of this mission:

> Dissatisfied with the meagerness of the intelligence that reached me, I felt I must make a determined effort to detect the presence of large concentrations of hostile forces, if they existed, before I ordered the Eighth Army into its first offensive operations since its setback.

Pat Partridge offered me a slow AT-6, an old advanced trainer, with himself at the controls and a seat for me in back. We proceeded then to search the area from our own advance elements to a point some twenty miles deep in enemy-held territory. We flew at times at tree top level and frequently below the barren ridge. Hardly a moving creature did we spot, not campfire smoke, no wheel marks, not even trampled snow to indicate the presence of a large number of troops. Obviously, the only way we were ever going to remove the question mark from the goose egg was to advance into it."[3]

The deficiencies in combat intelligence had plagued all Eighth Army units since the beginning of the war. Too often, assignment to an S-2 position in battalion or regiment or a G-2 position in division or corps was considered either a demotion or a career-damaging move. In describing the purge of staff officers in the 7th Division, Blair comments, "Ferenbaugh also relieved the 7th Division chief of staff, Louis T. Heath, and the G-2, Irwin A. Edwards . . . and 'demoted' the G-3, Bill Paddock, to G-2."[4]

Little by little, however, the peacetime bias against intelligence duty dissipated. A notable early exception to this avoidance of G-2 duty by promising officers was in X Corps. Almond had the pick of the litter when he selected his staff for the Inchon landing. He chose as his G-2, Colonel Quinn, a 1933 West Point graduate. The only blot on Quinn's intelligence record with X Corps was that he, along with all the other intelligence officers in Korea, had been taken in by the bad intelligence on the Chinese that came from MacArthur's headquarters. Quinn earned a slot as regimental commander and took over Powell's 17th Infantry in mid-January. He went on to three stars before retiring.

Quinn's replacement as X Corps G-2 was his West Point classmate, Col. James H. Polk, who came to Korea from General Willoughby's staff in Tokyo. Polk immediately initiated a program of line crossers, whom he called the "Blue Boys." Polk remembered, "We sent all these natives north and when they came back, they would tell us these stories. When only one gave us a story, we weren't about to believe it. But when five told you the same tale, and you could confirm the story, you believed it."[5] Polk went on to become the Eighth Army G-2 and ultimately wore four stars, a clear indication that intelligence assignments did not hinder his career.

Operation Thunderbolt kicked off on the morning of 25 January. Ridgway had established five phase lines between Line Dog and the Han River, each about 5 miles apart. Ridgway made Milburn responsible for ordering the advance from each phase line for both corps, thus ensuring a fully coordinated operation. In I Corps, Milburn chose the U.S. 25th Division, reinforced by the Turkish Brigade, to make the advance. To the east in IX Corps, the 1st Cavalry Division would spearhead the probe. In both corps, the divisions had screening elements on both flanks to preclude bypassing an enemy force. The 1st Cavalry had some sharp skirmishes just shy of the first phase line, but, in all instances, the Chinese were the ones who broke contact. Captured CCF soldiers identified two divisions of the CCF Fiftieth Army. This information persuaded Eighth Army planners that the CCF Thirteenth Army Group had set out a counterreconnaissance screen to shield defenses or assembly areas farther to the north. Meanwhile, Ridgway, growing more confident that his reconnaissance in force would reach the Han River and that his army could hold the ground, directed both corps commanders to develop plans for holding on to territory regained.[6]

On 26 January, Milburn permitted his I Corps columns to move forward to the second-phase line, while IX Corps continued to clear the area around the first-phase line in its zone. Advances in both corps areas became plodding affairs with enemy resistance strongest in front of the 1st Cavalry Division. In consonance with Ridgway's intention to retain ground gained by the probes, both Milburn and Moore each added another division to their attacking forces. The newly arrived U.S. 3d Division joined the I Corps thrust on its right flank, and Milburn also added a South Korean regiment to the mix in his zone. To the east, Moore started the 24th Division north from Yoju on the corps' right. Thunderbolt, originally a two-corps

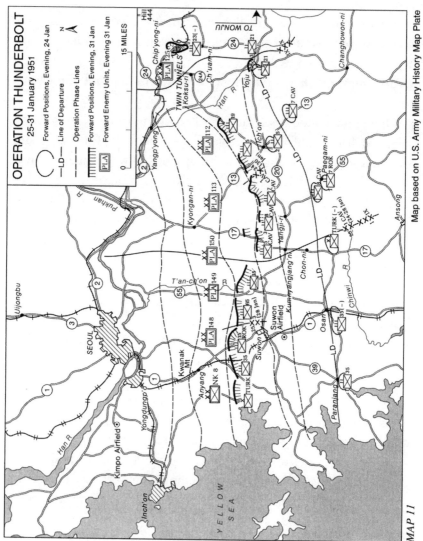

OPERATION THUNDERBOLT
25-31 January 1951

Forward Positions, Evening, 24 Jan
—LD— Line of Departure
Operation Phase Lines
Forward Positions, Evening, 31 Jan
PLA Forward Enemy Units, Evening 31 Jan

0   15 MILES

Map based on U.S. Army Military History Map Plate

MAP 11

reconnaissance in force had, without fanfare, turned into a general offensive, but this one differed greatly from previous forward thrusts by the Eighth Army. It was a shoulder-to-shoulder, yard-by-yard, grind-it-out advance, with maximum use of artillery, tanks, and other firepower.

Ridgway also wanted to widen his offensive. On 30 January, he asked Almond and ROK Army Chief of Staff Maj. General Chung for recommendations on sending the X Corps and the ROK III Corps forward in the fashion of Thunderbolt. The purpose of the advance primarily would be to disrupt any offensive notions of the North Koreans in the central zone. Ridgway also ordered the ROK I Corps to begin an advance on the east coast to the town of Kangnung, about 25 miles north of the ROK Capital Division's position at Samch'ok.[7]

X Corps was tasked to provide security for the right flank of IX Corps, as well as to conduct some diversionary probes north of Route 20, the Yoju–Wonju road. To cover the IX Corps flank, the 2d Division moved Col. Paul W. Freeman's 23d Regiment, with the French battalion attached, to Iho-ri, a town just east of Yoju. One of the first moves was a motorized patrol north from Yoju and Iho-ri in the direction of Chip'yong-ni. It was a joint affair of troops from the 19th Infantry of the 24th Division, the right-flank unit of IX Corps, and the 23d Infantry, the extreme left-flank unit of X Corps.

Army historian Russell A. Gugeler, in his story of this patrol, wrote that of the four officers and fifty-six men in the combined patrol, forty-four of them were from Charlie Company, 23d Infantry. Of the forty-four, twenty were embarking on their first combat action; they had joined the company only four days before. Most were specialists—draftsmen, mechanics, radar repairmen, technicians, and the like—and had received little training as infantrymen.[8] In fact, many of these men were enlisted reservists called back to active duty, and their depths of despair knew no bounds as they became fodder for the insatiable appetite of the replacement pipeline.

About 3 miles southeast of Chip'yong-ni, the railroad from Seoul to Wonju passes through two tunnels, positioned end to end through two ridges with a small valley between the interior portals. Route 24 from Yoju to Chip'yong-ni crosses the tracks in this valley. A patrol had reached the twin tunnels the previous day without making contact with the enemy. The joint-force patrol, commanded by Lt. James Mitchell, a Charlie Company platoon leader, went as far as the twin tunnels and found Chinese in abundance. Under heavy fire, the patrol abandoned its vehicles on the road near the railroad crossing between the tunnels and clambered up the snow-covered side of the hill to the east of the road. Seven of the new members of Charlie Company refused to leave the ditch by the vehicles and subsequently were killed by the Chinese.[9]

The patrol made a last-ditch stand on a tiny knob. A spotter plane noted their predicament and notified 23d Regimental headquarters. Freeman ordered air strikes and dispatched his Fox Company under Capt. Stanley C. Tyrrell, to reinforce the platoon. The air strikes in the fading light of the day bought the beleaguered patrol some time. Tyrrell's company arrived at nightfall and immediately assaulted the Chinese and rescued the survivors of the patrol.[10]

Although the patrol was badly hurt, it developed vital intelligence confirming that the Chinese appeared to have occupied the critical crossroads town of Chip'yong-ni in some strength. The Eighth Army G-2 believed that the CCF in the area were elements of the Forty-Second Army, whose claim to fame was the attack on the ROK II Corps at Ch'ongch'on that turned the Eighth Army's right flank. Ridgway immediately directed Almond's X Corps to develop the situation by placing a strong blocking force at the twin tunnels.

Freeman's 23d Regiment, organized by 2d Division Headquarters as a regimental combat team, drew this assignment. An RCT commander had under his direct command a representative slice of all division support assets—artillery, armor, engineer, signal, and so on. Freeman planned to attack on 31 January with his 3d Battalion and the French Battalion, supported by the 37th Field Artillery Battalion. Freeman also took Triple-A weapons—the M-16 quad-

50 and the M19 dual-40. The quad-50, with its four .50-caliber machine guns, and the twin forty, with its two 40-mm Bofors guns, provided an incredible volume of fire and were the infantrymen's favorite fire-support weapons. Freeman's two other battalions had security missions along the Yoju–Wonju road, the 1st Battalion at Iho-ri, located on the Han River just east of Yoju, and the 2d Battalion in the vicinity of Munmong-ni, about halfway to Wonju.

The French battalion was a story in itself. Made up mostly of French Foreign Legionnaires from garrisons in Africa, Madagascar, Indochina, and elsewhere, this tough aggregation was led by an amazing legionnaire, Ralph Monclar (a nom de guerre). At fifty-nine years of age, Monclar bore the scars of numerous battle wounds from World War I and Legion battlefields around the world and had won all the decorations for valor that the French government could bestow on a soldier. He had risen to the three-star rank of *général de corps d'armée* but had voluntarily taken a reduction in rank to lieutenant colonel so that he could have the honor of leading the French in Korea. He wore a black beret and steel-rimmed spectacles and, in battle, was often seen limping with a cane among his men.[11]

Freeman's force reached the twin tunnels in late afternoon without opposition and, indeed, without seeing a single enemy soldier. Freeman used the remaining light of the day to establish a perimeter defense that utilized the available high ground. He put the 1st Company of the French battalion on the crest of Hill 453, the dominant terrain feature in the area; the other two French companies occupied the high ground to the north on the west side of the MSR. There was a valley between the French 1st and 2d Companies. This relatively flat, rice paddy zone was covered by fire and by the ROK company that had become the 4th Company in the French battalion. The 3d Battalion of the 23d Regiment organized the high ground on the west side of the road, including the top of the ridge, where the patrol had fought for their lives two days before. The road itself was covered by tank and automatic weapons fire. Freeman had a rifle company from his 1st Battalion protecting his artillery base, and the regimental 4.2-inch mortars were inside his perimeter with a fire plan for coverage of the artillery base.[12]

General Stewart, 2d Division assistant division commander, who had accompanied the force, remembered that General Almond was displeased that the force had not progressed farther. "General Almond arrived [by helicopter] and told me he wanted a village two or three miles to the north to be taken before we stopped. I explained it was near dark and that the security of the unit required immediate preparations for the night. He reluctantly agreed, but ordered me to personally see that the village was fired upon." Stewart believed that these orders were probably wrong, but if he refused to carry them out, he thought that Almond would relieve him so he complied. He went north by tank to the village. Although he found no Chinese, Stewart fired several bursts of machine-gun and cannon fire, as Almond had ordered. He took care to aim high and wide to avoid unnecessary civilian casualties within the village. On returning to the perimeter, Stewart reported to Almond by radio that he personally had fired on the village.[13]

Freeman was furious at this action. If CCF troops were in the area, firing on the village was certain to alert them and provoke an attack. That night, Freeman had to contend with another matter that could have been a tip-off to the Chinese. Freeman remembers that he had the embarrassing task of chiding Monclar about the warming fires that sprang up all over the French positions. He called Monclar on the field telephone, "Tell your men to get those fires out."

"Yes, sir," the old warhorse replied. "In the morning, I will tell them."

"Tell them now," Freeman demanded.

"But, *mon colonel*, they are such little fires."

"Big fires or little fires, get 'em out, damn it, and do it now! You've already given away your positions to every Chink within a hundred miles!"

Monclar waited a beat or two before replying, "Ah, *mon colonel*. It is, as you say, without doubt. But if they know where we are, they will attack us. Then we will kill them."

The crusty regimental commander had absolutely no response to this and hung up. All of the fires were extinguished within an hour.[14]

Two hours before dawn, the CCF attacked the perimeter. Freeman was right to be furious about Almond's interference. His mission was to develop the situation in the twin tunnels area. Stewart's foray by itself, however, did not spawn a Chinese reaction nor did the fires in the French positions. The attack by the CCF just before dawn was not an impromptu or ad hoc affair. In the aftermath, the body of a dead Chinese officer yielded a written attack order, and the regiments of the CCF 125th Division had marched south from positions near Chip'yong-ni. All of this indicated that the Chinese had observed Freeman's force since its arrival at the twin tunnels and had a rather good handle on the positioning of perimeter defenses.[15]

At 4:40 A.M., the Chinese 374th Regiment, with the usual accompaniment of bugles, whistles, and shepherd's horns, assaulted straight down the road from Chip'yong-ni. The volume of fire from the defenders at that point was awesome, and the stunned attackers withdrew to regroup. At 6:00 A.M., the Chinese 373d and 375th Regiments, which had marched all night from a position west of Chip'yong-ni, arrived and began attacking the French 1st Company on Hill 453, along with other French positions. Two battalions of the 375th continued south to establish roadblocks and fire blocks on the road south of the perimeter, as well as to make a company-sized assault on the artillery base. Concurrently, the 374th Regiment slid to its left and began an assault on the hill mass occupied by the 3d Battalion of the 23d Infantry. There was a gap of perhaps 400 yards between the right flank of L Company and I Company. The squad leader of the L Company's right flank squad sent his BAR (Browning automatic rifle) man, Cpl. Larry Hauck, and two other soldiers to make contact with I Company. When he made visual contact, Hauck sent a rifleman back to his squad leader. The Chinese attacks swept over parts of L and K Companies. Hauck was wounded and narrowly escaped death when Chinese soldiers swept past his position, looted bodies, and occasionally bayoneted men on the ground.[16]

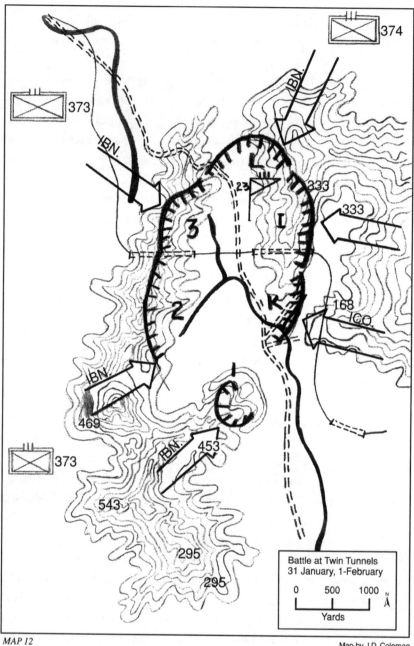

MAP 12

Battle at Twin Tunnels
31 January, 1-February

0   500   1000

Yards

Map by J.D. Coleman

Soldiers of both companies counterattacked and regained ground, and, in some sectors, positions changed possession repeatedly during the day. On Hill 453, the French 1st Company was pushed out of its positions by overwhelming Chinese assaults. But, just as it appeared that the situation was lost, the Legionnaires, screaming "Camarón" like madmen, made a bayonet charge and restored their lines. The battle cry "Camarón" is how the Legion remembers the town in Mexico where Legionnaires had fought to the last man. Fights like this one took place all around the perimeter.

Freeman and Stewart, writing about the battle later, said that their force, even with superb artillery support, faced almost certain annihilation. Ammunition was running out. Ground reinforcements were still hours away and had to fight through Chinese roadblocks to get there.

Stewart said that the machine guns on his jeeps and his ammunition had been taken to strengthen the perimeter. About every thirty minutes, General Ruffner called on the radio and asked how things were going. About midday, during a Ruffner inquiry, Stewart overcame Ruffner's skepticism when he said, "I am at the moment standing in a pool of blood from the wounded radio operator who has just been shot." Then Stewart held the microphone out so that Ruffner could hear the firing. Stewart's party dug a circle of foxholes around the jeeps and gathered all the hand grenades that they could find.

An air liaison officer, who was with Stewart in their little bastion, asked, "General, I don't like this. What is going to happen?" Stewart's answer unsettled the young aviator. He said that, in about twenty minutes, they all would be dead. Stewart again asked the liaison officer about air support, and he said that several flights were stacked up above them, but because of the cloud cover, the pilots could not see the ground. At that moment, they looked up and saw a narrow break in the clouds directly above their position. The air controller immediately contacted the leader of the lowest flight and asked if he could see the ground through the break in the clouds. The flight leader replied in the affirmative. The air controller then said, "We are directly below that break and we need help badly."

Stewart wrote of that moment: "Down through the cloud opening came a flight of Marine fighter-bombers. It was a very brave action, for there were hills and peaks all around, and the flight leader could not see them as he came down."[17]

Freeman was delighted that the first flight were Marines, who immediately recognized the hand-to-hand fighting situation and how tight it was. The Marines laid ordnance right on the most critical Chinese positions. Then, like a scene from a motion picture, the dense cloud cover suddenly lifted and Air Force fighter-bombers roared in. Twenty-five strikes from the air devastated the Chinese forces massing for one final assault. As the enemy broke and began to run, Freeman quickly ordered counterattacks to punish the remnants of the fleeing Chinese. By nightfall, Freeman wrote, the CCF 125th Division of the combat-tough Forty-Second Field Army, "could be eliminated as an effective unit."[18]

What had started out as a probing attack had developed into an important victory for the U.S. Eighth Army. For the first time in the war, a UN force had stood fast in the face of an initial CCF assault. The Chinese planned, as usual, to strike hard and then ambush the defenders as they attempted to escape. Clearly, the 125th Division commander never expected a two-battalion perimeter to defend its ground with such determination. It is also clear that the Chinese high command had plans for the Chip'yong-ni area that justified its expenditure of a full division of experienced troops; plans that had to be revised after the Twin Tunnels fight.

EIGHT | **Thrusts, Counters, Deceptions, and Plans**

As January turned into February, the commanders of the combatants in Korea indulged in some serious reading of tea leaves regarding the intentions and capabilities of their opponents. Both Generals Ridgway and Peng got them partly right and partly wrong. Each general was planning an offensive against the other, but both of them based the offensives partly on faulty intelligence and a lack of understanding of each other's real intentions and capabilities.

Ridgway was keenly aware that he did not have access to first-rate intelligence from either American or ROK units. On 1 February, he asked President Rhee to use every means at his disposal to have ROK units improve this vital commodity.[1] Moreover, Ridgway constantly drummed into subordinate commanders the importance of collection and analysis of usable combat intelligence, but he might have been further hampered because he was not even aware of his counterpart's identity. When he had arrived in the command, he was informed that Lin Piao was the commander of Chinese forces. None of Ridgway's writings suggests that he was even aware of the existence of General Peng. Moreover, his background and training had been oriented toward a European war. Ridgway doubtless could have conducted lectures on European battlefields and had a good knowledge of Soviet tactics and doctrine. About the Chinese, however, he was still learning.

Within the Eighth Army, there had been no real examination of what had happened in November along the Ch'ongch'on River. A general feeling prevailed throughout the Eighth Army that the Chinese triumphed in November and again in January because of

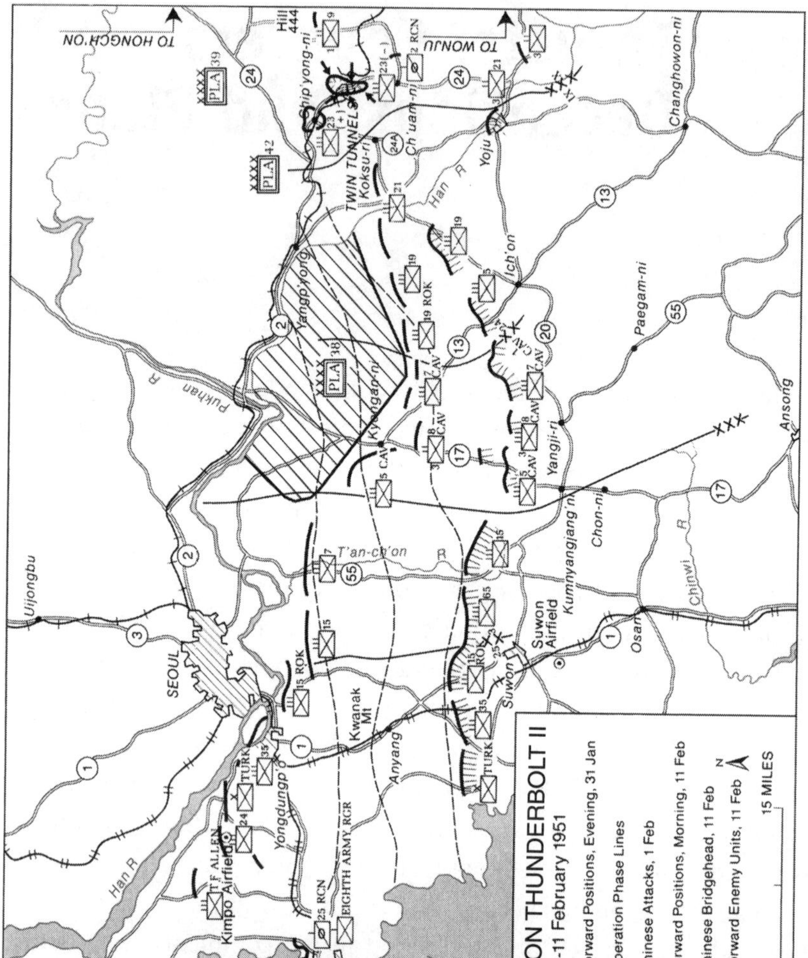

OPERATION THUNDERBOLT II
1-11 February 1951

Forward Positions, Evening, 31 Jan

Operation Phase Lines

Chinese Attacks, 1 Feb

Forward Positions, Morning, 11 Feb

Chinese Bridgehead, 11 Feb

PLA Forward Enemy Units, 11 Feb

0   15 MILES

Map based on U.S. Army Military History Map Plate

MAP 13

the application of overwhelming manpower. There was no systematic study of Chinese strategy and grand tactics. To be sure, units down to battalion level produced documents on lessons learned, but these tended to deal with small unit tactics, which was good. At this stage of the war, however, no documents had analyzed Chinese field army tactics.

With the forward movement of I Corps and IX Corps, the morale of American soldiers began to improve. Once fearful at the very thought of contact with the Chinese, they began making jokes about the so-called Chinese manpower superiority. Blair reported a couple of wisecracks: "How many hordes in a platoon?" "I was attacked by two hordes and killed both of them."[2] Then, too, Americans were afflicted by attitudes that later in the twentieth century would be termed racist. These prejudices were not recognized in 1951, but there unquestionably was racism within the Army, both in terms of attitudes toward some of its own people and institutional biases against Oriental foes.

The Chinese, of course, were not exempt from the sin of underestimating the capabilities of one's opponents. Peng and his chief lieutenant, General Li, were disdainful of Ridgway.[3] Further, Chinese elites had always considered westerners to be barbarians. Peng's forces had routed the Americans in November and again in January. Because no American general apparently had properly appreciated Chinese tactical planning thus far, Peng and Li had every reason to believe that nothing had changed.

In early February, the two western corps of the Eighth Army were slowly moving north from phase line to phase line as Operation Thunderbolt continued. The CCF Fiftieth Army was in contact with Milburn's I Corps in the western flank of the Eighth Army. The Fiftieth Army had steadily given up enough ground so that Eighth Army intelligence believed that the mission of the Fiftieth was merely to provide a counterreconnaissance screen for other CCF units, north of Seoul, that were completing the process of resting and refitting.

IX Corps, however, faced the CCF Thirty-Eighth Army, which had dug in and stoutly defended a salient 20 miles wide and 10 miles deep. Salients, which were deep bulges into enemy territory, by their nature provide danger and opportunity for both sides. The Thirty-Eighth Army's back was on the Han River where it generally flowed from east to west. Because the Han curved at Yangp'yong to a north-south orientation, the Thirty-Eighth Army's left flank was somewhat sheltered by the river. Its right flank, however, was unprotected. Simultaneously, UN units outside the bulge had a degree of vulnerability because a salient can be a great place from which to originate an offensive.

Nevertheless, there was an opportunity for the Eighth Army to push forward with Thunderbolt, flatten out the bulge, and drive the Chinese back north of the Han River. The danger in this move was that, in so doing, the IX Corps' right flank would be exposed. To provide some degree of flank security for the IX Corps, as well as to pose a threat to the base of the Thirty-Eighth Army's salient, Ridgway directed X Corps to give the mission of attacking and occupying Chip'yong-ni to the 23d RCT. The town was important because the force occupying it could control movements over three major roads and a railroad. An American force there could pose a potential threat to CCF-occupied Yangp'yong, just 10 miles to the west.

The 23d RCT moved into Chip'yong-ni two days after the twin tunnels battle and, other than sporadic resistance from some high hills to the northeast of the town, encountered no organized Chinese defense. Curiously, no American intelligence analyst questioned why the Chinese, after battling so furiously at the twin tunnels, were willing to give up a vital terrain feature such as Chip'yong-ni without a fight. Nor do any intelligence documents discuss the location of the rest of the CCF Forty-Second Army. A U.S. Army historian wrote in 1988 that, judging from the sharp actions at the twin tunnels, the Chinese were determined to retain control of Chip'yong-ni.[4] No one saw the parallels between the twin tunnels fight and the battles at Unsan back in October, when the CCF struck, drew blood, and then broke contact for three weeks. Freeman's 23d RCT had put a hurt on the CCF 125th Division, but enough forces remained in that division alone to have made the occupation of Chip'yong-ni very costly. Because the Chinese rarely split their divisions far from the parent field army, it was likely that two more divisions, the 124th and 126th, were lurking somewhere nearby.

Freeman established a perimeter defense based on lower hills immediately surrounding the town. There was more desirable high ground farther out, but Freeman didn't have enough troops for a perimeter that large. A defense based on mutually supporting outposts was out of the question for an isolated regimental combat team located at least a dozen miles from the nearest friendly unit. Its exposed position dictated a tight perimeter defense, and that's what the 23d RCT established. All of the line companies, except one, deployed into carefully selected positions. Freeman designated B Company and the 1st Ranger Company as regimental reserve.[5]

The Chinese now had a juicy plum hanging from the vine at Chip'yong-ni.

The posting of Freeman's RCT at Chip'yong-ni was a part of Ridgway's plan for a general limited-objective offensive, dubbed Operation Roundup, that would involve units across the entirety of the peninsula. Ridgway wanted his IX Corps to reduce the CCF salient south of the Han in coordination with I Corps moving north and reoccupying the Kimpo Peninsula. For the remainder of UN forces, Ridgway's directives reflected intelligence obtained by the Eighth Army and X Corps. Intelligence reports indicated a strong North Korean buildup around Hongch'on, about 15 miles north of Hoengsong. Eighth Army intelligence also believed there was a possibility of an enemy attack on 8 February, in conjunction with the start of the Chinese New Year on 6 February or with the North Korean Army Commemorative Day celebrated on 8 February.[6]

Ridgway wanted X Corps to stage a spoiling attack to the north toward Hongch'on. He also directed that ROK I Corps and III Corps in the Taebaek Mountains and on the east coast begin an advance coordinated with X Corps.

At X Corps Headquarters on 1 February, General Almond held a planning conference to brief participants in the X Corps part of Roundup. Attending were all of the ROK division commanders who would participate—Col. Min Ki Shik, 5th Division; Brig. Gen. Choi Suk, 3d Division; and Brig. Gen. Choi Yong Hee, 8th Division. Maj. Gen Yu Jai Heung, commander of the ROK III Corps, which would be responsible for security of X Corp's right flank, was also there. Brig. Gen. Frank Bowen, commander of the 187th Airborne RCT, was invited to the conference because his paratroopers were scheduled to move to the Wonju area.

Gen. Almond unveiled the X Corps Roundup plan, which envisioned a two-division attack north from Hoengsong to seize the town of Hongch'on. The attack was to be a double envelopment maneuver, with two regiments of the 8th ROK Division swinging to the west from Hoengsong for a distance of about 10 miles and thence northwest along Route 24 toward the objective. The Third Regiment of the 8th Division was to attack directly north from Hoengsong along Route 29 to Hongch'on. The eastern jaw of the envelopment was to be provided by the ROK 5th Division, which would attack north on an axis about five miles east of and more or less parallel to Route 29. When it had progressed far enough on its northbound track, the division then would swing east, presumably to meet the units of the 8th Division at the objective.[7]

It was a splendid plan. The double envelopment scheme would have found favor with most tactics instructors at any of the Army's staff colleges. What probably would not have found favor was that the thrust would not originate from a solid defensive line. Instead, the entire X Corps front was but a series of outposts, whose positions, when plotted on a map, resembled a random grouping of bubbles. In the I Corps and IX Corps areas, units were virtually shoulder to shoulder in a line, whether they were in a defense or an offense mode. This posture was largely because Ridgway initially perceived that the greatest threat from overwhelming Chinese numbers lay in his western sector. The central and eastern sectors appeared to be threatened only by recently reconstituted North Korean forces.

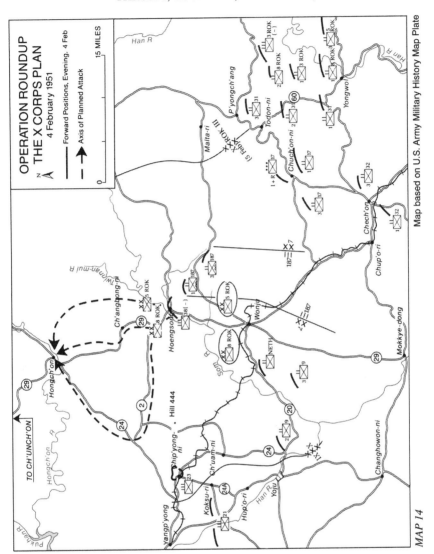

OPERATION ROUNDUP
THE X CORPS PLAN
4 February 1951

Forward Positions, Evening, 4 Feb
Axis of Planned Attack

0   15 MILES

Map based on U.S. Army Military History Map Plate

MAP 14

Another problem with the proposed scheme of maneuver for Roundup in X Corps was that it was to be executed by two ROK divisions. These divisions had been created from scratch in July 1949, and the 8th Division had been mauled thrice, once on the Naktong in North Korea and yet again during the CCF Third Phase Offensive. After each debacle, it had been rebuilt with poorly trained conscripts. Its commander, General Choi, had been only recently promoted from command of a regiment in the ROK 1st Division.

In order to provide support to the ROK formations, Almond directed American units under his command to create some special artillery, infantry, and armor support forces. The 2d Division was to provide a support force consisting of a 105-mm howitzer battalion, a 155-mm howitzer battery, an AAA (antiaircraft artillery) battery, and an infantry battalion. The 2d Division was also tasked to provide the bulk of three armored infantry teams, each composed of a tank company and an infantry company. The 2d Division would provide all of the armor and two of the infantry companies, and the 187th Airborne RCT would provide the third infantry company. All of the 2d Division support team forces were attached to the ROK 8th Division, while the 187th team forces remained under control of X Corps. The U.S. 7th Division created an artillery-infantry support force to work for the ROK 5th Division.[8]

The use of American reinforcing units for ROK forces was not unusual. What made this arrangement novel was that the ROK units were given operational control of these support forces. Given the previous performance record of most South Korean divisions, this action by Almond placed American units in an incredibly risky position.

General Stewart believed, at the time, that Almond was determined to prove to the ROK Army that it could successfully attack the enemy, but he was disturbed about placing 2d Division units under ROK command. "The orders we received were explicit in that these units were removed from the control of the 2nd Division and that our only authority and responsibility was to supply them and evacuate casualties."

Stewart occupied an odd position in the 2d Division. He had been brought in by General McClure after a stint as commander of the 3d Logistical Command. When McClure was relieved, Stewart expected to be fired, but General Ruffner retained him. Ruffner let Stewart know emphatically, however, that he was not in the chain of command nor was he to issue any orders without Ruffner's prior approval. Later, Stewart indicated that when Ruffner declined to let him remain with the 23d RCT at Chip'yong-ni, he occupied himself with two activities. One was to ensure that the air drop of supplies to the 23d was carried out each day, and the other was to visit every unit that had been taken from the division to support the ROK attack.[9]

In his P'yongyang headquarters, General Peng had already set in motion the units that would be in the van of what the Chinese were to designate their Fourth Phase Offensive. While the CCF Fiftieth Army delayed the I Corps advance south of Seoul and the CCF Thirty-Eighth Army virtually stopped IX Corps cold at the boundaries of its salient, General Li began carefully moving units. His Thirty-Ninth and Fortieth Field Armies, hidden north of Seoul, were to move to the east past Chip'yong-ni into concealed positions northwest of Hoengsong. The Sixty-Sixth Field Army, which never had moved south of the Han River, was directed to begin easing its way into positions south of Hongch'on. The Chinese were as scrupulous about concealment as they had been during their movement across the border back in October. A key part of General Li's deception plan was to keep North Korean forces in contact with the ROK units.

On the other hand, portions of the CCF Forty-Second Field Army allowed itself to be located and identified in the Chip'yong-ni area. U.S. Eighth Army intelligence, therefore, assumed the shift of Chinese into the Yangp'yong and Chip'yong-ni area pointed to the Han Valley below Yangp'yong as the likely main axis of an enemy advance.[10]

Author Russell Spurr quoted General Peng as being convinced that Wonju was the key to success in the south. When planning the Third Phase Offensive, he would rather have concentrated his forces in the central sector, outflanked Seoul, and taken it later. But he was overruled by political bosses in Peking and P'yongyang. The North Koreans had seized Wonju, but they were unsuccessful in holding it. According to Spurr, Peng talked at a commanders conference prior to the Third Phase Offensive. "It is there at Wonju," Peng declared, tapping a gnarled finger on the model, "that the battle will be decided. A breakthrough at Wonju will carry us all the way to Taegu."[11]

Spurr's narrative, which told the story of the war from the Chinese point of view, ended with the Third Phase Offensive. This was so because, in his words, "The reason was that by the end of the Third Offensive the Chinese felt (or feared) that they had shot their bolt. They had plenty of fight left but the realisation was dawning that the initiative had passed to the Americans. From here on they knew that their original hopes of seizing the entire peninsula were doomed."[12]

The events that played themselves out in February made it abundantly clear that the Chinese high command still believed that the Fourth Phase Offensive would succeed and could drive the Americans back, possibly as far as Taegu.

1. With only a few buildings remaining, Wonju does not resemble a strategic target. Yet, to retain this vital crossroads town, U.S. troops would fight bitter battles there, first with North Koreans in January 1951 and then with Chinese in February.

U.S. ARMY

2. This photograph of a U.S. Army position near Chech'on illustrates the rough terrain and winter conditions that confronted soldiers of both sides during the battles on the central front. The unit is the heavy mortar platoon of the Seventh Division's Thirty-second Regiment.

3. At the Wonju airstrip prior to the kickoff of Operation Roundup, Maj. Gen. Edmund M. Almond (center), X Corps commander, poses with his pilot, Lt. Robert J. St. Audit (right) and his junior aide, Capt. Alexander Haig (left). Haig went on to gain a measure of fame as a four-star general and secretary of state.

4. Hill 930, known to the Koreans as Oum-San, is where the Chinese destroyed the ROK 21st Regiment on 11 February 1951. Route 29, the main supply route (MSR) from Hoengsong, is in the foreground. The village of Ch'angbong-ni, where the 2d Infantry Division's Support Force Twenty-one was positioned, is just off the picture to the right.

5. Corporal Woodward and Corporal Hofshy of Company D, First Battalion, 187th Airborne Regimental Combat Team (RCT), fire a 75mm recoilless rifle near Pambol-ni, about twenty-five miles northeast of Wonju. They were supporting an attack by the First Battalion against North Korean positions that were holding up the advance of ROK troops moving to a line of departure for the X Corps's Operation Roundup.

6. Cannoneers of the 20th Field Artillery Battalion, ROK 8th Infantry Division, fire their 105mm howitzer in support of the advance by elements of the 8th Division against North Korean positions northwest of Hoengsong. Within days, most of these men were dead or captured after Chinese Communist forces overran their frontline regiments.

7. Men of Company D, First Battalion, 187th Airborne RCT, fire a 75mm recoilless rifle near Pambol-ni, about twenty-three miles northeast of Wonju. They are supporting an attack by the First Battalion against North Korean positions just prior to the kickoff by X Corps of Operation Roundup.

8. Men of Company G, 17th Infantry Regiment, 7th Infantry Division, move forward to support the attack of the 187th Airborne RCT in the prelude to Operation Roundup. Company G later played a key role in the defense of Hoengsong against the Chinese onslaught on the night of 12 February.

9. Troopers of the Heavy Mortar Platoon of Support Company, 187th Airborne RCT, fire a 4.2-inch mortar at North Korean defensive positions in support of an attack by the regiment's First Battalion.

10. Men of Company L, Third Battalion, 187th Airborne RCT, march toward positions to support the attacks by units of the ROK Fifth Division during Operation Roundup.

11. The Second Battalion, 187th Airborne RCT, takes a break en route from Tanyang to Wonju in early February 1951. Fox Company's Lieutenant Baldwin is on the left. Easy Company's Lt. James Nix, who won a Distinguished Service Cross on Hill 255 at Wonju, is on the right.

12. Captains John R. D. Cleland (left) and John D. Miley (right), both still in Company G, 187th Airborne RCT, display their new "railroad tracks" for the camera. Both were promoted just prior to the Wonju campaign. Cleland remained the executive officer of G Company, and Miley, who was the First Platoon leader, was transferred to battalion headquarters. Cleland commanded G Company briefly the night of 19 February. Miley became the fourth commander of the company by the time the battle on Hill 738 concluded.

13. Col. John Coughlin (left), commander of the 38th Infantry Regiment, 2d Infantry Division, greets Ambassador A. A. C. Gieben (right), the Netherlands's representative to the United Nations Temporary Commission on Korea, as he arrives at the 38th Infantry command post near Wonju. In the center is Lt. Col. M. P. A. Den Ouden, commander of the Dutch battalion that was attached to the 38th Infantry. Den Ouden was killed by a Chinese grenade at Hoengsong in the early stages of the Wonju campaign.

14. Elements of the 5th ROK Division advance north of Hoengsong. Note the officer trailed by a civilian bearer toting the officer's gear on an A-frame.

15. A command-and-control helicopter is seen taking off with Maj. Gen. Clark L. Ruffner, 2d Infantry Division commanding general, for a tour of frontline positions. These helicopters often served double duty, the baskets mounted on the skids permitting it to be used as a medical evacuation helicopter.

16. This rare photograph was taken in Hoengsong late on the afternoon of 12 February by Capt. Reginald J. (Jim) Hinton, the 38th Infantry Tank Company commander. The tanks are facing northwest. The bridge across the Twinnan-mul River is visible in front of the tanks. Looming in the background is Hill 303, which was seized and then abandoned by ROK troops during the day. The MSR (Route 29) runs through the steep cut just beyond the bridge. The white slash to the right of the bridge is the trail that the U.S. Seventh Division's Support Force Seven used to escape the CCF trap. Hinton shot this picture with an ancient bellows camera, hence the light leaks visible in the print.

17. Before Wonju, the First Platoon of Company G, 187th Airborne RCT, falls in for an inspection prior to movement of the company to the Hoengsong area. The platoon sergeant, M.Sgt. Othon O. "Jumpy" Valent (front and center), became acting platoon leader when the platoon leader, John D. Miley, was promoted to captain and transferred to a battalion staff position. The platoon had thirty-four men present for duty when the Wonju campaign began.

NINE | **Operation Roundup Unfolds**

The inherent flaws in X Corps' "Operation Plan Roundup" were not long in becoming apparent. The plan envisaged the line of departure for the attacking ROK units as being in the neighborhood of Hoengsong. This might have been okay, except that X Corps didn't own the ground between UN positions in the Wonju area and Hoengsong.

The 187th discovered this almost as soon as the regiment began moving north from Wonju. On 3 February, five light tanks from its support company ran a patrol north and east from Wonju toward what would be the regimental positions east of Hoengsong. The five tanks (M-24 Chaffees mounting 75-mm main guns) encountered road obstacles and heavy small-arms and automatic weapons fire and were forced to withdraw to the west and then to the south. They were hit again with heavy fire from enemy units that surrounded their position. One tank was lost, and the tank platoon leader, Lt. Robert M. Garvin, was killed.

On 4 February, as it was moving to establish a line of departure for the ROK 5th Division to pass through on its attack north, the 1st Battalion, 187th Airborne RCT, also discovered that the North Koreans were not going to leave the territory quietly. As the battalion moved to secure the high ground overlooking the road from Hoengsong to Saemal, it came under heavy fire from the hills that it sought to occupy. Company A assaulted the first peaks (Hills 289 and 300) in the hill mass. The battalion commander, Col. George H. Gerhart, called in air strikes, artillery, and regimental mortars to support the attack. He also directed that a platoon of C Company reinforce Able Company for the assault on the final objective, Hill 312. Eventually all three rifle companies were involved in the attack. Against determined resistance by an estimated North Korean battalion, the paratroopers secured the hill mass by 8:30 P.M. Although the enemy lost one hundred killed on the hills, the cost to the 1st Battalion was also high. Ten men were killed, including two platoon leaders, and thirty-nine were wounded.[1]

All three of the platoons leaders killed in the opening skirmishes were West Pointers, which was not surprising in the 187th. As Blair noted in his chapter about the regiment's combat jump at Sunch'on–Sukch'on, the 187th was a West Point outfit, with U.S. Military Academy (USMA) graduates dominating the officer ranks from commanding general (Frank Bowen, USMA 1924) to platoon leaders.[2] Officers who were not West Point graduates had exceptional experience and leadership skills and had solidified their commissions and grades through tough competitive tours.

Blair, as well as other authors, suggest that the 187th was a second-rate regiment from the 11th Airborne Division, which itself was understrength. MacArthur had wanted a regimental combat team from the 82d Airborne Division, but the 82d had been placed on the "untouchable" list by Army Chief of Staff Joseph Collins.[3]

The pundits were wrong. Just three months before the North Korean invasion, the 11th and 82d Airborne Divisions participated in Operation Swarmer in North Carolina, the largest peacetime Army maneuver to that time. At its conclusion, the 187th Airborne Infantry Regiment had the highest operational readiness test (ORT) scores of the five airborne regiments that participated in the maneuver. Its high scores and the obvious overall combat readiness of the regiment were central to its selection as the regimental combat team earmarked for Korea.[4]

Despite the "untouchable" status of the 82d Airborne Division, a few of its officers and numerous noncommissioned officers (NCOs) of all ranks were shipped to the 187th RCT. That infusion provided a bonanza of combat experience. In G Company, for example, the incoming NCOs were veterans of World War II. When they were added to the NCOs already in the company, the experience factor included probably a dozen World War II combat parachute assaults among them. Fox Company received Medal of Honor winner Jake Lindsay, and so it went throughout the regiment. All the lower-rank enlisted men were double volunteers: they had volunteered for the Army, then had volunteered to jump out of airplanes. Most of them had at least one year of service and many had up to three years of service in an airborne outfit when they were deployed.[5]

When T. R. Fehrenbach, in his 1963 book, *This Kind of War*, wrote derisively about the state of training and readiness of Army units worldwide but praised the Marines, it was clear that he had not been introduced to paratroopers.

The 2d Infantry Division encountered less trouble in occupying Hoengsong, although a tank infantry patrol from the 1st Battalion, 38th Infantry, ran into a defended minefield at a road junction about 4 miles north of the town. In addition, a Netherlands Battalion patrol ran into a North Korean pocket of resistance about halfway between Wonju and Hoengsong and lost two killed and four wounded before routing the enemy.[6] The Netherlands Battalion (also known as the Dutch Battalion) had joined the 2d Division on 11 December and had been attached to the 38th Infantry Regiment at the same time that the French battalion had been attached to the 23d Infantry.

The 38th Infantry needed all the help that it could get. The 38th and the 9th Regiments had suffered devastating casualties during the division's withdrawal through the Chinese gauntlet at Kunu-ri on 28 and 29 November. The 4,950 total battle casualties sustained by the 2d Division represented nearly one third of the division's strength of 15,000 recorded on 15 November. Officer casualties alone totaled 237 and touched on all grades and branches, but most of the losses occurred in infantry battalions. The 9th Infantry was hurt the worst, with 1,474 total casualties of an authorized strength of 3,793. The 38th Infantry sustained 1,178 casualties. When the division finally reached a staging area south of the 38th Parallel, it scarcely had enough troops and equipment to form a regimental combat team.[7]

The Army uses the term *"casualty"* to refer to any individual removed from battle lines for any cause—death, wounds, capture, or injury. A number of the 2d Division casualties, particularly those before Kunu-ri, were wounded and ultimately returned to duty. Once the division entered the deadly gauntlet at Kunu-ri, however, all of the nonambulatory wounded became prisoners, and many of them died in captivity.

The 23d Regiment escaped the horror of the gauntlet because its commander, Paul Freeman, when given the opportunity, chose not to follow blindly down the Kunu-ri–Sunch'on road but rather to accept the invitation of General Milburn, I Corps commander, to bring out his regiment through a western route that had not yet been cut by the Chinese. Freeman's decision was controversial and condemned in some quarters. Fortunately for the UN Command, the 23d Regiment, with only 545 total casualties for November, survived to fight another day.

The 38th Regiment had received a new commander on 29 January. Colonel John Coughlin replaced George Peploe, who was promoted to brigadier general and transferred to IX Corps as its chief of staff. Coughlin was no stranger to the regiment. As a lieutenant colonel, he had been Peploe's executive officer, but, when he was promoted to full colonel, he became the 2d Division's G-3. Coughlin was a 1932 graduate of West Point and considered by his peers and subordinates to be a "damned good soldier."[8]

Coughlin became a regimental commander just in time for Operation Roundup, but by the time that operating instructions from X Corps and the 2d Division had decimated his regiment, he did not have much to command. His 1st Battalion, commanded by Lt. Col. William P. Keleher, was tasked to become the infantry protection for the artillery support force, which was dubbed "Support Force 21." The name was hung on it mostly because the battalion would provide direct-support artillery fire for the ROK 8th Division's 21st Regiment, which would attack straight north up Route 29. The artillery punch for the force was the entire 15th Artillery Battalion, a 105-mm howitzer outfit, and the 155-mm howitzers of Battery

A, 503d Artillery Battalion. Also in the mix, technically an artillery outfit but generally regarded by infantrymen as their direct support, was D Battery, 82d Antiaircraft Artillery Battalion, which fielded the deadly quad-50s and dual-40s. Lt. Col. John W. Keith, Jr., 15th Artillery commander, was named as the support force commander. Support Force 21 was then placed under the direct command of the ROK 8th Division commander.

One of the tank-infantry support teams came from the 38th Infantry Regiment. Support Team B, which also was slated to provide direct support to the ROK 21st Regiment, consisted of L Company, 3d Battalion, 38th Infantry, and the 3d Platoon of the 38th Infantry Tank Company.

Support Team A consisted of K Company, 9th Infantry, and 3d Platoon, 9th Infantry Tank Company. This support team was also assigned to the 8th Division and would provide support to either the 10th or 16th Regiments, with priority to the 16th.

Coughlin's 3d Battalion, minus L Company, originally was placed on a defense line east of Hoengsong, but Almond soon changed that. He personally directed that the battalion follow the advancing South Korean units and, when they cleared a road junction about 4 miles north of Hoengsong, to move in and provide security for that junction. The battalion, commanded by Lt. Col. Harold Maixner, would handle that mission under direction of X Corps, which held the string on when it could be withdrawn from that particular area. The 2d Battalion of the 38th Infantry remained in the Wonju area to provide security for the X Corps and 2d Division forward command posts. This left Coughlin with the Netherlands Battalion and his regimental headquarters at Hoengsong.[9]

The X Corps portion of "Roundup" kicked off on 5 February with both the ROK 5th and 8th Divisions attacking north. The 5th ran into North Korean resistance to the east of Hoengsong, but the 8th made reasonably good progress north and west of Hoengsong. The principal deterrent to the advancing South Koreans was the rugged terrain. During the advance of troops in the I Corps and IX Corps areas in the flatter terrain to the west, Ridgway insisted on each unit maintaining contact with units on its flanks. This proved an impossibility in the wild mountains of central Korea. The dominant terrain feature was Hill 930, about halfway between Hoengsong and Hongch'on just off Route 29. Stretching for 30 or more miles from that mountain, however, were peaks several hundred meters high, separated by smaller peaks, sharply shaped ravines, and narrow valleys. In mid-winter, it was a brutal place to fight a war. With a mechanized army or even the semimechanized army of the South Koreans, it was next to impossible.

Then, too, the ROK 8th Division had a curious scheme of maneuver. The 21st Regiment went straight north on Route 21 and made good progress against sporadic resistance. The 16th Regiment went north on Route 29 to a crossroads near the hamlet of Samael (not to be confused with the larger town of Saemal, which was about 10 miles east and south of Hoengsong) and then headed due west on an unimproved road that Army historian Mossman labeled Route 2. The 10th Regiment started west on a track that was about 2–3 miles south of the path of the 16th Regiment. Despite the rugged terrain, both regiments made good progress without any discernible enemy resistance.

For the first three days of the offensive, General Almond was in his element. Almond's diary extracts filed with X Corps' command reports show a frenetic schedule of flying over the front in his fixed-wing aircraft or in his helicopter or traveling by jeep to other locations. On 6 February, Almond flew to the command post of the ROK 16th Regiment and conferred with the U.S. senior advisor. As Support Team A was starting to move out, Almond did not like the way that the men had packed their individual equipment, so he stopped the team, ordered the team commander, Capt. Sherman D. Jones, to assemble his K Company officers and NCOs. Thereupon, Almond lectured the group about the necessity of proper packing of equipment so that all men could be battle ready. The infantrymen in the rifle company were from the segregated 3d Battalion, 9th Infantry, a fact probably not lost on Almond.

On another occasion, at the command post of the ROK 35th Regiment, Almond personally directed artillery and tank gunfire at enemy positions. He was dissatisfied with the artillery support, provided in this case by the 187th Airborne RCT, and ordered the commander of the support artillery battalion to come forward and personally correct the deficiencies. Then, instead of contacting the RCT commander about the problem, Almond directed his X Corps artillery officer to take action to correct the deficiencies.[10] Whether or not the deficiencies noted in Almond's diary actually existed is not known, but this behavior was typical of the X Corps commander.

Every officer and NCO in the Army is taught to take corrective measures on actions that fall outside the norm, but respect for the chain of command is also taught. Wise leaders judiciously mix the two concepts when developing a leadership style. Almond's leadership style was to bully, to meddle, and to constantly interfere with the normal chain of command. He had an enormous ego and believed that he was a better tactician than anyone in his command. Almond spared no one—officers or soldiers—in his efforts to demonstrate his superiority.

He was also courageous to a fault. Colonel Polk, the X Corps G-2, said of Almond, "I sometimes thought he had a death wish. I thought that he wanted to be killed in battle and he admired me because I had commanded a regiment in World War II. He used to take me with him a lot, visiting headquarters and so forth. As I said, he had this death wish which I didn't have. He used to scare the hell out of me, really scare me."[11]

Almond was the kind of commander for whom there was no middle ground of opinion. Historians, with the notable exception of Roy E. Appleman, have not been kind to the man. Almond's disregard for the well-being of his soldiers and his blatant racism soured his record. Still, even his detractors praised his brilliance. Blair wrote that Almond was a brilliant human dynamo. General of the Army Dwight D. Eisenhower rated him as one of the half-dozen ablest men in the Army. Almond's early career had been very promising. A 1915 graduate of Virginia Military Institute (VMI), he earned a Regular Army commission in 1916. Almond commanded a machine-gun battalion in World War I, and his insistence on pushing his guns as close to supported troops as possible earned

him some close calls, as well as a Silver Star.[12] During the peacetime
years between the world wars, he attended the requisite schools
and was also an instructor at the Infantry School in Fort Benning,
Georgia, where he became acquainted with George C. Marshall,
then assistant commandant of the school and also a VMI graduate.

In 1933, Almond made a trip to China. The interviewer for his
senior officer oral history at the War College asked his impression
of the Chinese fighting capabilities at that time. Almond replied
that his regard for Chinese soldiers and military forces was very poor
in contrast to his very high opinion of Japanese military capabilities.

Almond became a division commander in October 1942, after
serving for six months as assistant division commander of the 93d
Infantry Division, a black division with white officers at Fort
Huachuca, Arizona. When the 92d Infantry Division, also an all
black unit, was to be activated at Fort McClellan, Alabama,
General Marshall nominated Almond to command it. In his oral
history, Almond was asked if he had been selected for this
command partly because he was a southerner. In a roundabout
way, Almond said yes:

"I think that General Marshall felt that General Hall, who was
in command of the 93rd Infantry Division when I was assistant
division commander and was from Mississippi, understood the char-
acteristic of the Negro and his habits and inclinations. The artilleryman at that time was General William Spence from North Carolina
as I recall, who also had that understanding and I, being from Virginia, had an understanding of southern customs and Negro capabilities; the attitudes of Negroes in relationship thereto. I think my
selection for the 93rd and 92nd Divisions was of the same character."[13]

In fairness to Almond, historian Shelby Stanton in *America's Tenth
Legion,* noted some other reasons that General Marshall had for
choosing commanders of black units. Stanton wrote that Almond's
steadfast loyalty to Army policy, his instructional experience, and
uncompromising discipline harmonized with the qualities that Mar-

shall wanted for leaders of black units. In addition, Almond's Reserve Officers' Training Corps (ROTC) duty in Alabama affirmed his ability to win the confidence of civilian leaders in southern communities, where large black units would be placed for training. Marshall believed that Almond's background would defuse any problems arising from that proximity.[14]

Almond took the 92d Division to Italy, where it failed as a combat unit as Army leaders fully expected, a classic case of a self-fulfilling prophesy. Although Almond was not personally blamed for the failure, his wartime service as a commander of black units sidetracked his career. He came out of World War II as a major general with little chance before mandatory retirement of catching up with his contemporaries, some of whom had reached four stars. In 1946, Almond asked to be posted to the Far East and was assigned to MacArthur's headquarters as personnel officer (G-1). Postwar demobilization made this an enormously challenging assignment, and it gave Almond an opportunity to demonstrate to contemporaries in the headquarters both his intellect and responsiveness to direction. He also made a positive impression on MacArthur, and when the Far East Command's chief of staff, Gen. Paul J. Mueller, rotated home in January 1949, Almond was named to replace him.[15]

A good subject for an interesting sociological study would be Almond's interpersonal relationships with his superiors. He appeared to have an instinctive knack of ingratiation. Almond's intellect gave him the ability to anticipate what MacArthur desired, and then his relentless drive produced desired results. Almond thus became the first "outsider" to penetrate MacArthur's inner circle. He quickly became the second most powerful man in the military structure in the Far East. Almond never left his desk while MacArthur was in the headquarters, regardless of the time. One time, MacArthur suggested that his chief of staff need not stay in the office constantly when MacArthur was present and said, "Don't be disturbed by my unusual hours in the office." Almond said that he replied, "General MacArthur, nothing you could do would disturb me emotionally . . . because I once commanded the 92d Infantry Division."[16]

Almond never overcame his bigotry. He tried to isolate the 3d Division's 65th Regiment when the division joined X Corps in North Korea. Almond teamed the 65th, a Puerto Rican outfit, with an all black field artillery battalion and a black tank unit, and relegated these three units to "ash and trash" missions on the southwest flank of X Corps.

Colonel Powell, who became chief of staff of the 7th Division under General Ferenbaugh, remembered that, despite President Truman's order to desegregate the Army, Almond refused to let Ferenbaugh do it. The replacement pipeline had started spewing out black enlisted reservists and draftees. Powell recalled, "So General Almond ordered General Ferenbaugh to put all these Negro replacements somewhere in the rear and not use them at all. We had this bivouac where we had twenty-five hundred of these men just sitting there. We couldn't do anything with them. This wasn't cured until Gen. Almond eventually left."[17]

Almond's bigotry was more than institutional because there were times when he did not hesitate to humiliate and diminish individuals. Lt. Col. Cesidio V. Barberis, who commanded the 2d Battalion, 9th Infantry, had placed a black captain named Forest Walker in command of his E Company. During an attack on Wonju in mid-January, Walker led a bayonet and hand grenade charge up a hill and swept away the North Korean defenders. When General Ridgway visited the scene shortly after the battle, Barberis told him that Walker had led the charge and that he was a "damned good officer." Ridgway ordered that Walker be awarded a Silver Star medal. But, Barberis recalled, "When Almond found out about it, he not only stopped the award, he also ordered that Walker be relieved of command of E Company."[18]

Walker sustained psychic wounds that, although hurtful, would heal. Many wounds of the flesh sustained by men in subfreezing temperatures would not. Almond's generalship unnecessarily cost lives in northeast Korea in November. In February, he began again to move his X Corps to the brink of disaster.

TEN | **Prelude to Disaster**

By noon of 11 February, the frontline trace of the central sector of X Corps resembled a huge bulge, with the uppermost tip along the Hoengsong–Hongch'on road, about 9 miles north of Hoengsong. The base of the salient east and west of Hoengsong was about 25 miles wide. Unlike most salients, which are anchored solidly on a defensive line, however, this one was anchored on nothing. Thus, in reality, the bulge was an indefensible balloon inflated into enemy territory. What was purported to be a defensive line from Chip'-yong-ni through Hoengsong and 20 miles eastward to the X Corps boundary was, in truth, a series of bubbles. The 23d Infantry had a bubble at Chip'yong-ni. East and slightly south, in another bubble a battalion of the 9th Infantry held the top of Hill 444. Hoengsong, 15 miles east of Hill 444, the location of the command posts for the 38th Infantry and the 8th ROK Division, had only the Netherlands Battalion as security for that bubble. Eastward 4,300 yards, two battalions of the 187th ARCT maintained a line extending about 3 miles, but it had no anchors. The 1st Battalion of the 187th had been dispatched by Almond to establish a battalion-sized bubble another 3,000 yards to the east in the ROK 5th Division zone. The 2d Battalion of the U.S. 7th Division's 31st Infantry maintained the last bubble on the X Corps' defensive "line."

The deception plan of the Chinese was working perfectly. The movements of the ROK and American units could not have been more favorable for the Chinese if General Peng had personally been in the X Corps command post and drawn them himself.

When "Operation Roundup" kicked off, the ROK 10th and 16th Regiments of the 8th Division spent two days forging westward from Hoengsong on a parallel track and were impeded as much by terrain as by North Korean delaying actions. Support Team A, made up of U.S. 9th Infantry troops and tanks, provided direct support for assaults of the ROK 16th Regiment. The 76-mm main guns fired on suspected enemy positions on ridgelines while the infantry provided reliable close-in security. Then, on 8 February, the 10th Regiment, which had been on the southernmost track, pivoted 90 degrees and headed north. The X Corps operations journals list the grid locations of all units at the end of each day. The plots recording the positions of the 10th and 16th Regiments make no sense at all. For a period of two days, a reconstruction of the map locations of the two regiments, according to X Corps records, shows the two regiments being intermingled as the 10th crossed through or behind the 16th. By 11 February, the 16th Regiment became the western flank unit for the 8th ROK Division while the 10th ROK Regiment was about 1½ miles to its northeast. Both regiments were facing northwest against now much stiffer North Korean resistance. They had become two separate bubbles within the larger balloon.

The gap between the 10th ROK Regiment and the 21st ROK Regiment, which had been forging ahead and pushing the tip of the salient north against sporadic resistance, was nearly 5 miles. To the right rear of the 21st, another 5 miles distant, was the ROK 3d Division's 22d Regiment.

The ROK 3d Division had been thrust into the line because the original right-flank unit, the ROK 5th Division had run into exceptionally stiff North Korean resistance in the eastern part of the bulge and clearly was not able to move fast enough to complete the double envelopment of Hongch'on that General Almond had envisaged. Moreover, the apparent strength of North Korean forces opposing the ROK 5th Division had the potential of imperiling the entire right flank of the X Corps bulge. So, on 8 February, Almond obtained Ridgway's permission to borrow the 3d ROK division from the adjoining ROK III Corps, and plug it into the line between the 8th and 5th Divisions. Ridgway hesitated to take General Yu's only reserve, but, on the other hand, Yu's two assault divisions were reporting good progress through light to moderate resistance east of X Corps. Because Ridgway had put a restraining string on the 187th Airborne RCT, he knew that Almond did not have any more troops of his own to reinforce his offensive. On 4 February, Ridgway had notified Almond that the 187th was scheduled to be taken off line and that he was not to give them an offensive role in Roundup.[1] Almond, as usual, pushed the envelope of commander discretion and used the 187th to help establish the line of departure for the ROK 5th Division.

The strange maneuvering of the two westernmost regiments of the ROK 8th Division could be explained away simply by considering that this division had been created from scratch in July 1949, just nineteen months before Roundup kicked off. Since that time, it had been badly hurt by the enemy and reconstituted three times. The first time was on the Naktong River line in August 1950; then it was on the Ch'ongch'on River in November when the Chinese rolled up the Eighth Army's right flank through the ROK II Corps. Its final ordeal was during the CCF Third Phase Offensive when it again was shattered and its units scattered throughout the central Korea sector. Considering that most infantry captains in the American Army had more training and experience than ROK division staff officers and even some regimental commanders, the strange meanderings of the 10th and 16th Regiments could be rationalized. It also did not help ROK efficiency that replacement troops were poorly trained. South Korean men were drafted, issued uniforms, and given ten days of basic training that rarely gave the soldier a chance to fire more than one clip of rifle ammunition before being dispatched to line units.[2]

The ROK 8th Division, however, was working for X Corps, which meant that the corps commander would have had to approve all plans. An anecdote related to historian Blair by Lt. Col. Frank T. Mildren is instructive. Mildren had been assistant corps G-3 under Colonel Chiles. When Chiles departed, Mildren inherited the job. "Almond loved to draw arrows on maps," recalled Mildren.

"One time I brought him a map depicting a ROK operation, but I only had two arrows: one for the main effort; one for a secondary effort. Almond got up and drew in a lot more arrows—seven or eight. I thought he was wrong; it was too great a dispersion of the available forces. So I went back to my office and took off most of the arrows. Later, Almond demanded to know, 'Where are my arrows?' Instead of telling him forthrightly that he was overdispersing the forces, I said, 'If you'd presented that solution at Leavenworth [at the Command and General Staff School] they'd have given you a fuzzy U [unsatisfactory].' "

Mildren said that Almond flew into a rage. When he stopped fulminating, Mildren said to him "General Almond, you don't need a G-3." He said, "You're right, I don't." By the following day, Almond had apparently forgotten the affair and Mildren continued as G-3. He escaped X Corps with his reputation intact and eventually rose to four stars.[3] In any event, given Almond's predilection for on-the-spot corrections, it seems clear that the maneuvering of the regiments of the ROK 8th Division was Almond's design. His diary shows that he visited the ROK 8th Division nearly every day of the Roundup offensive.[4]

As the 21st Regiment advanced north on Route 29, it was followed by Support Force 21, whose artillery fired support missions. The tanks of Support Team B (U.S. 38th Infantry elements) provided direct-fire support for ROK troops assaulting hill masses on either side of the road. To their credit, the ROK soldiers did not remain road-bound. On their way north, they scrambled up the steep mountains to push off the North Korean outposts. On 7 February, the 3d Battalion of the ROK 21st Regiment fought a North Korean battalion to a standstill on Hill 773, 2 miles west of Route 29. The ROK unit eventually prevailed and drove the North Koreans off the peak. That the NKPA mission was to delay and then give ground did not diminish the fortitude of the ROK soldiers in advancing against enemy fire in bitterly cold, inhospitable terrain. Each night, the temperature dropped to 10 or 12 degrees above zero and the daytime temperatures always remained below freezing. There was not as much snow in these mountains as there was farther east in the higher Taebaek range, but there was enough on north-facing slopes to make life miserable for infantrymen.

The advance went smoothly enough until the 21st Regiment reached Hill 930, a 3,000-foot–high mountain mass that dominated the terrain in the area. The North Koreans began putting up a stubborn resistance, and the ROKs never conquered the mountain peak.

At the southeastern foot of the mountain was the village of Ch'angbong-ni, about 7 air miles north of Hoengsong. Route 29 turned west at Ch'angbong-ni to work its way around the mountain mass. The road again turned north 2½ miles west of the village and began a series of switchbacks that brought it to a pass some 1,500 feet above the valley floor.

Lt. William M. ("Sam") Mace, tank platoon leader in Support Team B, said that the ROKs never advanced beyond that pass. "They tried for two or three days to take Hill 930. We could get up to the ridgeline where the road went, but we could not get forward of that. There was a light colonel from Tenth Corps who used to harass the hell out of me. During the day, we would make the climb up the hill and it took a while because the road was narrow, twisting, and icy. I would take my platoon up the hill at the request of the ROKs and we would stop just behind the crest and just sit there all day. This lieutenant colonel (Jack F. Wilhm, acting X Corps armor officer) kept asking, 'Why don't you go down that hill?' and I told him that I was never going down that hill until the ROKs took the ridges on both side. Because on that road, once I went down, I could never get back up."

While Support Team B was on the road in the valley, a mortar round directed by an enemy observer on Hill 930 wounded the L Company commander, Capt. Dean A. Gastenbein, and killed his driver, Pfc. Frank S. Sterczek. Lt. Elmer J. Kallmeyer, the executive officer, assumed command of L Company.

Mace had a lot of trouble convincing Wilhm that he needed to return to the base of the mountain at dark. Mace said, "I would go up in the morning, fire a few rounds if the ROKs requested it, spend the day, and then go back down at night. That disturbed the Tenth Corps colonel. He demanded of me, 'What the hell are you doing going back down?' So I asked him, what I was supposed to do at night with my tanks spread out in a column where most of the time the tanks couldn't even see each other because of the bends in the road. We hardly had any place to even turn around."[5]

Mace's stubborn resistance to the demands of the X Corps colonel unquestionably was instrumental in preventing the destruction of Support Team B.

Five miles southwest of the ROK 16th Regiment, the U.S. 9th Infantry Regiment had advanced its 1st Battalion to seize a defensible peak, Hill 444. From there, the battalion ran combat patrols and occasionally linked with patrols from the 23d Infantry at Chip'yong-ni, another 5 miles to the northwest. Attempts by the 9th Infantry to run a contact patrol to the ROK 16th were unsuccessful, due more to the terrain and command limitations than to enemy action. The 9th Infantry battalion commander directed his patrols to return to the perimeter by nightfall, so no one really knew who or what occupied the 5 miles of mountains between the positions.

The 23d Infantry ran patrols to contact the 21st Infantry of the U.S. 24th Division, which was advancing slowly along the west bank of the Han River, as well as to the 9th Infantry position. Attempts to move in strength against CCF positions on the higher peaks surrounding Chip'yong-ni were met by strong enemy resistance. The Chinese made no attempt to conceal their presence in the Yangp'yong–Chip'yong-ni area. Eighth Army, and X Corps intelligence pinpointed a town named Pir'yong-ni, about 5 miles northeast of Chip'yong'ni as the locus of a major CCF buildup.

In the Eighth Army's western sector, I Corps finally occupied Kimpo Peninsula and Inchon. The CCF Fiftieth Army, along with the NKPA 8th Division, successfully delayed without becoming decisively engaged and then crossed the Han River on flimsy foot-bridges into Seoul. In the IX Corps zone, however, the CCF Thirty-Eighth Army resisted fiercely, and progress was measured in yards instead of miles.

Consequently, the consensus of intelligence analysis through the first nine days of February was that a CCF attack, if it came, would be directed south along the Han River valley to and through Yoju. Although Ridgway knew that the intelligence supporting this belief was thin, his command instincts were aroused by Chinese behavior in hanging on to the salient. The salient would be vital to the Chinese to protect the west flank of an offensive south toward Yoju.

As a consequence, Ridgway ordered some repositioning of American units. He directed the 25th Division to pull out of line in the I Corps area and replace the 1st Cavalry Division in the IX Corps zone. The 1st Cavalry Division was placed in Corps reserve near Yoju to provide defensive depth in that area. In X Corps, warning orders were issued to the 9th Infantry, reinforced by the 38th Artillery Battalion, and to the 32d Infantry Regiment of the U.S. 7th Division to be prepared to move to Yoju when ordered.

All during February, while elements of the CCF Forty-Second and Thirty-Ninth Field Armies demonstrated in and around Pir'-yong-ni to deceive Allied intelligence about the real intentions of the Chinese, seven more divisions of General Li's CCF Thirteenth Army Group covertly moved farther east. These movements occurred mostly at night, with units remaining motionless and camouflaged during the day. Because Ridgway's offensive thrusts had surprised the CCF high command and preempted some of the Chinese moves, Peng and Li had accelerated the planning for their Fourth Phase Offensive. In an address on 4 February, Peng discussed the Chinese plan for resuming the offensive. His talk is preserved on a document that was captured later in February. Peng considered the thrust of the 23d Infantry into the twin tunnels area as an inauspicious event that forced his armies to hasten their preparations for the Fourth Phase Offensive.[6] The Chinese had counted on the UN forces remaining relatively quiet on a defensive line. The reconnaissance in force sorties initially sent out by Ridgway were anticipated, but the Chinese were caught off guard by the aggressive offensive that Thunderbolt had become.

The acceleration process meant that the Chinese could not maintain the degree of secrecy they had kept during their movements across the border and into North Korea the previous November. In order to get the troops and supplies into position, it was sometimes necessary for them to move in daylight, which permitted aerial observation. Moreover, the mixing of North Korean and Chinese forces in South Korean territory left the Chinese more vulnerable to detection from line-crossing agents.

Of course, line crossing was a two-way street. Colonel Polk, X Corps' G-2, said that the communists used a kind of massive agent attack by mixing agents with all of the refugees pouring into Allied lines. So Polk organized a line-crosser unit that he called the "Blue Boys" and sent these Koreans back north. He noted, however, that the reliability of agent reports often was suspect. "We were raised in America to believe that spies get shot. But orientals wouldn't think of shooting a spy over there in that area; they would double them. Some of the agents were tripled, even quadrupled. They worked for the British, the Americans, the Chinese and the North Koreans. They'd go around and tell the same story and get paid all the more."[7]

Despite the stories of line-crossers, intelligence summaries by X Corps, as well as by the Eighth Army, continued to list the enemy in the central and eastern zones of X Corps as being North Korean. Colonel Polk, in his senior officer debrief in 1972, boasted that he had predicted the Fourth Phase Offensive: "The February attack I called—laid it out in pretty close terms, very close to even the day it was going to hit us because our intelligence was pretty darn good."[8]

Well, not exactly.

The X Corps Periodic Intelligence Report (PIR) No. 138, issued on 10 February, is a study in contradictions. Under the heading of "units in contact," Polk listed, for units in contact with the 2d

Infantry Division, the following: "Unidentified enemy forces, possibly elements of the 12th NK Div and the 125th CCF Div." The 125th Division was subordinate to the Forty-Second Field Army, and it had purposefully remained visible around Chip'yong-ni. For the information of the ROK 8th Division, the report listed elements of the NKPA 6th and 12th Divisions and the CCF 198th Division. For the ROK 3d Division, it listed the NKPA 6th and 7th Divisions and the CCF 198th Division. The identification of the 198th Division was highly speculative; it was based on a single Chinese soldier killed north of Hoengsong on 8 February. The map that accompanied the intelligence report displayed the Sixty-Sixth Field Army, the parent unit of the 198th Division, as being more than 30 miles north of the X Corps' forwardmost positions.

In the discussion paragraph of the report, Polk wrote, "The enemy concentration northeast of Chip'yong-ni received further strengthening during the period and appears to be ready to start a drive southward. Groups of varying sizes were noted moving east and south of Piryong-ni. This may be the first indication of a general move southeastward by the main body. It has become increasingly apparent that the enemy has noted the gap between the 23d Inf Regt and elements of the 8th ROK Division and has decided to take advantage of this situation before the gap is closed."[9]

As far as it went, this was a fairly good summary, but it did not sound a cautionary warning to subordinate commanders that every step their units took was a possible step into jeopardy. Certainly, the X Corps commander did not heed the information. Polk, in recalling his "calling the attack correctly," said, "He (Almond) didn't quite believe me."

Polk also ruefully recalled an intelligence coup that he disbelieved: "We had a doctor captain, a Chinese defector, come over before the attack. He was attached to a field hospital that was supposed to follow a regiment, and he was a nationalist Chinese but the Commies didn't punish him because they were short of doctors. So he told us the total, grand plan of attack and we wouldn't believe him because why would a captain in the medical corps, who was captured by the Communists, know all this? He said, 'because the hospital political commissar told us, told the whole hospital, the grand final attack plan and then told us what the hospital was supposed to do as part of the grand attack.' " Polk said that they checked the story later, and it turned out to be "the absolute gospel truth."[10]

While X Corps officers were disbelieving, intelligence analysts in Eighth Army G-2 were not. Responding to Ridgway's relentless quest for superior combat intelligence, the G-2 section, under Col. Robert G. Fergusson, the acting G-2, sifted through prisoner and defector interrogation reports and ordered intensified aerial reconnaissance. On 11 February, Fergusson handed Ridgway the best intelligence estimate that he had received since assuming command.

Fergusson told Ridgway that the long lull between the New Year's Day offensive and the present was purely the consequence of Chinese resupply, transportation, and reinforcement difficulties. The slogan repeatedly given in statements by Chinese government officials never varied from the theme of driving the United Nations forces out of Korea. Fergusson predicted that once the logistical problems were sufficently relieved, and the G-2 believed that time was imminent, another campaign to push the UN forces into the sea would commence.

The Eighth Army G-2's enemy order of battle holdings placed the CCF Forty-Second, Thirty-Ninth, Fortieth, and Sixty-Sixth Field Armies in an arc above UN lines from Yangp'yong to just east of Hongch'on. He predicted that the next enemy advance would be down the Han Valley toward Yoju. This was nothing new.

Fergusson's more significant revelation was an expectation of a major Chinese attack down the Route 29 axis through Hoengsong and Wonju. The twin thrusts would have the same deep objective of Ch'ungju, 25 miles south of Wonju. His estimate indicated that the advance might include deep sweeps to the southwest to envelope units of the I and IX Corps. Fergusson believed that the Chinese would not open an offensive until major units of the Ninth Army

Group, which had been reconstituted, were moved from northeast Korea into reinforcing range. Based on this, he predicted the date for attack as 15 February.[11]

After Ridgway had studied and absorbed the implications of the intelligence estimate, he sent a radio message to X Corps to hold up any further advances by the U.S. 2d Division or the ROK 8th Division toward the Chip'yong-ni–Hongch'on road (Route 24). Almond's scheme of maneuver had been to have the ROK 8th Division use Route 24 as an axis of advance to attack Hongch'on.

In another radio message to the X Corps commander, Ridgway expressed concern over Almond's complex organization for battle in Operation Roundup, which referred to the intertwined command and control arrangements among Corps headquarters, the ROK assault units, the American support forces, and the parent units of these support forces. Ridgway had expressed mild concern earlier when he approved the X Corps Roundup plan, but the command relationships were workable under close supervison during an offensive. Now, Ridgway was not sure that these measures would provide the tight control needed to prevent a confused intermingling of units during an enemy attack.[12]

If Ridgway's concerns had an impact on Almond, it was not immediately discernible in message traffic to subordinate units. The first instance of the order to hold up advances to the northwest was logged into the 2d Division G-3 shop at 0034—thirty-four minutes after midnight—on 11 February. By then, the Chinese Fourth Phase Offensive had been under way for two hours. The message from X Corps stated that there would be no more movement to the north and west by the ROK 10th and 16th Regiments until further orders. The same message included a postscript that X Corps had received a report that infiltration had cut the road behind the ROK 10th and 16th Regiments. Infiltration, indeed. Those two units had already been cut off and mostly destroyed. There was absolutely no warning to subordinate units about the massive Chinese buildup. Of course, by midnight on the eleventh, a "heads up" message would have been moot for many of the units in X corps.[13]

When Colonel Fergusson made his estimate, he erred in considering the arrival of Ninth Army Group units as a precondition for the Chinese attack. When Ridgway sent out his warning, he believed that he had perhaps four days in which to make adjustments and prepare for the Chinese attack. Unfortunately for the soldiers in X Corps, General Peng didn't need any reinforcements.

ELEVEN | **Peng's Plan for the Fourth Phase Offensive**

As the sun dropped below the horizon, the men of the CCF 349th Regiment, 117th Division, began stirring from their camouflaged positions. For the past eight nights, the regiment's troops had carefully plodded from their rest areas north of Seoul to take up their present positions just east of the road that connected Chip'yong-ni with Hongch'on.

The men of the 349th, who had participated in the assault across the Imjin River on 1 January that routed the ROK 6th Division, had been given the special mission of closing the jaws of a trap, which promised the annihilation of thousands of puppet troops and many Americans, too. The commanders and commissars had told the men of this "honor" when they revealed the plan of an all-night forced march to reach the ambush positions. The distance to be covered was about 15 air miles, but the route did not follow any roads because there were none. After detouring through valleys and going over a couple of 2,000-foot mountains, they probably would cover a distance closer to 25 miles. A document captured later in the war said that the night march covered 70 li. (1 li equals 1,890 feet, or a little over ⅓ mile).[1] The reaction of the troops to being honored with this 25-mile forced march was not revealed in the document. Many Chinese soldiers had suffered frozen feet during the brutal below-zero weather in January. The high-top tennis shoe that was standard issue in the Chinese Army did a miserable job of protecting feet from wet snow and freezing temperatures. Some Chinese soldiers' feet were so swollen that they no longer could fit them into the shoes, and they had to wrap their feet in rags.

The regiment's destination was a pair of 900-foot–high hills that crowded in close to Route 29, just 2½ miles northwest of Hoeng-song. The captured document listed the destination as Hak Kok-ni, but that was the Chinese translation of a Korean place name. A hamlet named Hakkong-ni was located exactly where the 349th Regiment was to establish roadblocks and fire blocks.

After making the march, there would be no immediate rest for the tired men of the regiment. Positions had to be prepared and occupied. Mortars would be sited but not fired. Of the preparations, the captured document said: "Comrade Hsueh Fu-li, assistant regimental commander of the 349th Regiment, personally inspected positions, made troop adjustments, and by commanding the strategic position and intercepting enemy reinforcements coming from Hoeng Song, the fleeing enemy was intercepted."[2] Everyone who later had to run the gauntlet established by the 349th agreed that they took fire from 120-mm mortars, as well as the usual 82-mm battalion mortars.

The M-43 Soviet-manufactured 120-mm mortar was a brute that weighed in the neighborhood of 600 pounds. It fired a 34-pound shell to a maximum range of 6,500 yards. In flat terrain, it could be moved on a two-wheel transporter cart, but there was no flat terrain on the central front. When moved by men or animals, the mortar could be broken down into transportable components. If carried by men, the components—barrel, bipod with its recoil buffer, and baseplate—were slung under two poles, in parallel per module so that at least four men could carry each load.[3] The record does not reveal what mode of transport was used by the 349th Regiment. The Chinese made extensive use of horses for all facets of their operations. All that matters is that the big mortars were in position to interdict by fire the main supply route north of Hoengsong.

The weather was suitable for the Chinese plan. The forecast for 11 and 12 February called for scattered low and broken middle clouds, no precipitation, and temperatures ranging a minimum of 10° to a maximum of 26°F. There would be no visible moon.[4]

The area from Chip'yong-ni east to the X Corps boundary and from Wonju north to Chongch'on totaled nearly 2,500 square miles.

A comparable piece of terrain in the United States might be a large chunk of the Adirondacks or the Catskills in New York. One can visualize this country in January or February with sparse timber cover and without roads or lakes, walking 25 miles across it in inky darkness, and then living in it without shelter or proper clothing while being the hunted as well as the hunter. The mountains in this part of Korea were not quite as high as some of those in New York but, nevertheless, still formidable. The dominant peak was 3,000 feet high. Dozens of other peaks were 2,000 feet or more in altitude. These were mountains, although the U.S. Army term was "Hill such and such." The very cold weather was an advantage to the Chinese. While it was physically tough on the peasant soldiers of the communist army, it tended to drive their enemy's undisciplined soldiers deeper into sleeping bags and encourage soldiers in rear areas to light warming fires, which made them easy targets.

The commanders of the CCF divisions had excellent intelligence concerning the disposition of South Korean and American units. Compared to the job of obtaining intelligence about positions and unit boundaries when the defense is in a shoulder-to-shoulder posture (as was done prior to the New Year's Day offensive), scouting inside the X Corps lines was child's play. Although members of various South Korean and American units had reported spotting enemy formations that they surmised might have been Chinese, they never had any proof. There also had been numerous civilian and North Korean prisoner reports of a strong Chinese presence north and west of Hoengsong but, again, no real proof. Finally, on 8 February, in a skirmish with an Allied patrol north of Hoengsong, a Chinese soldier was killed. Documents on his body identified him as a member of the 594th Regiment, 198th Division of the Sixty-Sixth Field Army. This was the first and only positive identification of any Chinese in the battle area.[5]

Chinese battle planners also had another advantage. The North Koreans had occupied this territory since early January and were intimately familiar with every terrain feature in the operational area.

Therefore, the Chinese, by 9 February, knew with some precision where every Allied unit was located in this vast area and had plans to annihilate all of them. General Li planned to commit five CCF divisions in the initial thrust. The Sixty-Sixth Field Army was the most fresh, and its 198th Division would strike directly south from Hongch'on. Two regiments were to smash into the ROK 21st Regiment and scatter its forces, while a third regiment would bypass the target on the east and race along ridgelines on both sides of Route 29 to establish roadblocks some 3 miles south of the positions of the American artillery support force.

About 5 miles east, the CCF plan called for the 197th Division of the Sixty-Sixth Army to attack the 22d and 23d Regiments of the ROK 3d Division. A battalion of the 197th Division would detach itself and cross a pair of 2,000-foot ridgelines to attack the American artillery support force. This blow was timed to occur after the comrades of the 198th Division had established their roadblocks and fire blocks.

To the west, General Li planned to hurl the 120th Division of the Fortieth Field Army against the ROK 10th Regiment, which was just barely getting itself sorted out after confused marching and countermarching with the 16th Regiment.[6] One of the regiments of the 120th Division was to start early and slip easily through the 4-mile gap between the 10th and 21st Regiments to its northeast. The mission of this force was to establish two battalion-sized roadblocks on Route 2 and bar the retreat of the ROK units to the east. According to the plan, the remainder of the regiment would proceed to positions north of and overlooking the perimeter of the U.S. 3d Battalion, 38th Infantry, which was providing security for the junction of Routes 2 and 29.

The ROK 16th Regiment was targeted by the 117th Division of the CCF Thirty-Ninth Army. The key to success of the attack on the western portion of the X Corps salient would be the movement of the ambush units into position before the quarry was flushed. The two ambush regiments commenced their movements as soon as dusk and cloud cover forced aerial observers to hurry back to their landing strips. The timing for the frontal assaults was set for 8 P.M. against the ROK 21st Regiment, 11 P.M. against the ROK regiments farther east, and midnight against the ROK 10th and 16th Regiments.

The Chinese Thirteenth Army Group had no intention of neglecting Chip'yong-ni. At the same time that the assaults on the ROK regiments commenced, General Li planned to send two divisions on a sweep to the south and west. The 116th Division of the Thirty-Ninth Field Army headed for the 9th Infantry enclave on Hill 444. After that position was reduced, the CCF plan was to interdict the two roads from the south that were the lifelines for Chip'yong-ni. The plan then called for an assault by regiments from the other Chinese divisions in the area to overrun the defenses of the U.S. 23d Infantry RCT and force the troops to flee on one or both of the two roads to the south.

Generals Peng and Li planned to make the Fourth Phase Offensive a replay of the Chinese triumph on the Ch'ongch'on River in November, where CCF fire blocks on mountain roads had resulted in hideous American and South Korean casualties. To the east, the NKPA V and II Corps were to hammer the east flank of U.S. X Corps and ROK III Corps. Deep penetrations by the North Koreans toward Chech'on would flank ROK I Corps positions on the east coast and force a withdrawal of ROK units there.

Given the limited mobility of the Chinese armies, Peng realistically hoped for no more than getting his units as far south as Ch'ungju. With flanks exposed by the deep communist penetrations, the Chinese and North Koreans believed that the UN forces would have no choice but to make a serious withdrawal, perhaps as far as the old Naktong River line, where the only really defensible terrain features remained. Even though the Chinese might not penetrate south of Ch'ungju on this offensive, the Americans in the past had always retreated a great deal farther than the actual situation warranted. Thus far, Peng and Li had been given no reason to doubt that the American tiger was still made of paper.[7]

TWELVE | **The Agony of Another Gauntlet**

The Chinese Fourth Phase offensive began right on schedule and developed just as its planners had anticipated. At 8:30 P.M. on 11 February 1951, the CCF 198th Division assaulted the ROK 21st Regiment. It is unclear whether or not the 21st Regiment attacked up Hill 930. Accounts of the events differ depending on who reported the action. The reality was that it did not much matter. Within one hour, ROK soldiers began fleeing to the rear, and, by 10:30 P.M., communications with the 21st Regiment had ceased. One regiment of the 198th Division had begun its silent trek over and around Hill 930, the peak of which had always remained in enemy hands. Its mission was to establish a fire block at a bridge 2½ miles south of the hamlet of Ch'angbong-ni, the position of Support Force 21 and across which the American and ROK elements would have to pass in a withdrawal south. The regiment, on its way south with about eight hundred men, scattered a battalion along the road and concentrated the remainder of its forces near the bridge with the bulk of its firepower on the east side of Route 29. Grenadiers and bazooka teams prepared positions close to the road. The Chinese didn't bother trying physically to block the road. Experience had taught them that American vehicles, when knocked out, performed that task for them.

Earlier that day, anticipating that the struggling ROK 21st Regiment would take heart at the proximity of Support Force 21, Lt. Col. Keith, its commander, ordered the artillery-infantry formation to move forward. During the early morning, the unit vacated its positions at the hamlet of Haktam-ni and moved about 2½ miles

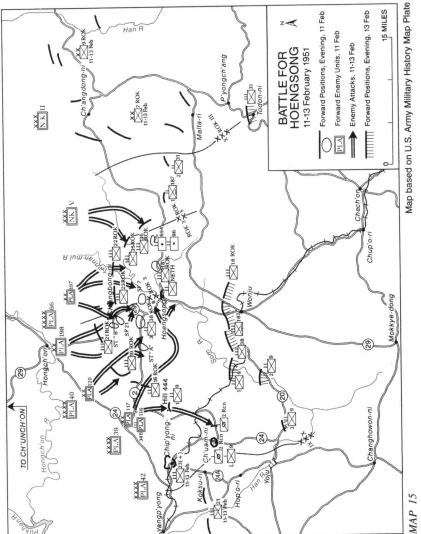

MAP 15

Map based on U.S. Army Military History Map Plate

to Ch'angbong-ni. The movement was completed by 11 A.M. The change in positions, made with the best of intentions, inadvertently placed the unit in great peril. The Chinese ambush force, instead of having to fight for possession of a key concrete bridge across a stream, now gained key terrain that could be used to bottle up a retreating force.

To the southeast, along what the Army history, *Ebb and Flow*, labeled Route 2 but what was known that night only as the "East-West MSR," Chinese troops of the 120th Division had established two major fire blocks. The first American contact with the Chinese occurred along that road when Support Team A, consisting of K Company, 9th Infantry, and a platoon of tanks from the 9th's regimental tank company, began receiving machine-gun fire from supposedly friendly territory. Captain Jones, commander of Support Team A, which had been in support of the ROK 16th Regiment, knew that his command was in big trouble when elements of the ROK regiment—troops, vehicles, and artillery pieces—began streaming east on the road. Jones didn't seek anybody's permission to withdraw—the 16th Regiment had ceased to exist. He turned his force to the east and began to fight his way back toward the road junction being secured by the 3d Battalion, 38th Infantry, a distance of about 4 miles, but the fight was against uneven odds. The Chinese had established two battalion-sized fire blocks, and it would take more than an understrength rifle company, even one reinforced by five tanks, to eliminate the firepower mustered by the CCF units.[1]

Without knowing exactly what was happening, the commanders and staff of Support Force 21 became alarmed when they saw ROK soldiers straggling through their positions. Maj. John Blackwell, S-3 of the 1st Battalion, contacted the infantry element that was part of Support Team B. About 2½ miles west of the Support Force 21 positions, at the curve in the MSR where it again turned north, Support Team B was maintaining its night positions. Lieutenant Mace said that his platoon and a platoon from L Company were camped in a little flat area at the point where the road began its climb into the pass. Mace remembered that night vividly:

It must have been about 9:30 that night when the platoon leader got a message—I didn't get one—that they were to immediately move back and the tanks were to come with them. Nobody knew what was going on. From our position, we couldn't hear a thing.

The infantry had a squad tent they used as a warming tent at night. I asked Barbey [Lt. John C. Barbey, the platoon leader], "Are you going to take that tent down?"

He said, "Hell, no. They told us to get out of here as fast as we can, so we're going."

I loaded them up on my tanks, and we moved back to the artillery.[2]

When Support Team B pulled into the Support Force 21 perimeter, surviving ROK soldiers from the 21st Regiment, who were moving rapidly to the rear, made it clear that there was no cohesive organization in front of the support force. At 10:30 P.M., Colonel Keith was notified by U.S. 2d Division Artillery headquarters that the ROK 21st Regiment had received orders to withdraw. Immediately, Major Blackwell made radio contact with the senior American advisor with the 21st Regiment—the regimental headquarters had not yet been overrun—and asked him to have the regiment attempt to hold until the Support Force could displace to the location where they had been the previous day. Concurrently, Keith contacted Brig. Gen. Loyal M. Haynes, the 2d Division Artillery commander, and requested that Haynes contact General Choi, commanding general of the ROK 8th Division, and ask him to hold his troops until the support force could move back to Haktam-ni. At the same time, he asked General Haynes for permission to make the withdrawal. Nothing was done on the request for help from the 21st Regiment. General Choi was no longer in communication with his regiments.

On the request for permission to withdraw, Haynes lobbed the request into the court of General Ruffner, division commander. Ruffner, who had been General Almond's chief of staff before taking over the 2d Division, was keenly aware that his boss did not like retrograde movements. Moreover, authority over the support force was vested in X Corps Headquarters, so he was reluctant to approve Keith's withdrawal. He told Haynes to check with the X Corps artillery officer. Army historian Mossman made the point that Ruffner's deference to X Corps emphasized the command and control arrangement about which General Ridgway had expressed concern the day before.

Mossman wrote:

> As a matter of orders, and as an eventual matter of practice in controlling the artillery support forces, unity of command in Operation Roundup was vested in corps headquarters, no lower. The arrangement worked well enough during the advance. But after the Chinese engineered the collapse of the ROK 8th Division, corps control inhibited the American commanders of support forces and of units on the line of departure in reacting rapidly.[3]

Keith waited one-and-one-half hours to receive clearance to withdraw. The Divarty report on the Hoengsong debacle indicated that Keith tried to use the time wisely by placing his artillery units in march order. After Ruffner tossed the ball back to Haynes, the Divarty commander contacted Col. William P. Ennis, Jr., X Corps artillery officer. He had no authority to approve the displacement, so he bucked it up to Col. William J. McCaffrey, X Corps chief of staff, who asked Almond himself. Almond approved the withdrawal, and his approval message passed back from McCaffrey, to Ennis, to Haynes, and finally to Keith. Because the message to Almond was apparently garbled in passing through so many messengers, Almond believed that he had approved withdrawal of Support Force 21 all the way back to Hoengsong, rather than just to Haktam-ni.[4]

Neither Almond nor any other commander or staff officer in X Corps or the 2d Division had any inkling of the magnitude of the Chinese offensive at that time. Indeed, the terms *Chinese*, *CCF*, or *PLA* did not appear in any of the unit operations journals for the first twenty-four hours of the offensive.

During the four days that the 3d Battalion occupied the ground at the junction of Routes 29 and 2, there had been no hint of trouble. With only two rifle companies, reinforced by the heavy weapons company, available to him, Colonel Maixner, the battalion commander, did not have the luxury of an elbow-to-elbow perimeter. The road junction was surrounded by hills, 1000-feet high, all within machine-gun range of the road junction. Maixner established a horseshoe-shaped outpost line perimeter with the open end on the south. The outposts were established on as much of the high ground as possible, with the battalion automatic weapons and recoilless rifles in positions facing both west and north along the roads. Maixner's command post was in the open end of the horseshoe near the hamlet of Saemal. Headquarters personnel provided security for the open south end.

Maixner was aware of the problems faced by Support Force 21, some 5 miles to the north on Route 29, but midnight came and there was no enemy yet in the 3d Battalion area. At 12:30 A.M., K Company outposts reported small-arms and mortar fire about 2 miles west on the east-west MSR. The fire appeared to be near the village of Ch'owon-ni; however, K Company was not receiving any fire at that time.

At approximately 1:30 A.M., men from Support Team A began arriving at the 3d Battalion positions. The wounded men were taken to the battalion aid station, while able-bodied men were integrated into the K Company line. Within a few minutes, the K Company command post reported that Captain Jones had arrived in the perimeter. He had been wounded and was sent to the battalion aid station. While he was being treated for his wounds, which were not serious, Maixner questioned him about the status of the ROK 16th Regiment. Jones told him that the ROKs had been overrun and that his company had been badly mauled in trying to get back to the Saemal crossroads. Two tanks had been lost, but two managed to get back to Saemal. The wounded were loaded on the tanks, which then made it safely to Hoengsong, where they were incorporated into the 38th Infantry's tank company. Men who had been scattered during the running firefight spent the night dodging Chinese units, and those who made it out reached the 3d Battalion perimeter around dawn.[5] The cost to K Company, 9th Infantry, was steep.

Twenty-five men perished, either killed outright or dying later as prisoners. Seventy-five men and three officers were wounded.[6]

In Ch'angbong-ni, at about 2:30 A.M., while Keith was still waiting for authority to withdraw, the assault force from the CCF 197th Division had completed its march across the ridgelines of Hill 930 and began attacking the east and north defenses of the support force. Those positions were manned by Company A, commanded by 1st Lt. George W. Gardner. As the executive officer of Company A in November, Gardner had soldiered well and survived the Kuni-ri debacle. When the 1st Battalion had moved into Ch'angbong-ni around noon on 11 February, Gardner had organized platoon perimeter outposts on three small hills overlooking the support force assembly area from the east. On orders of Lt. Col. Keleher, Gardner established a combat outpost on Hill 639, a peak on a ridge leading south from Hill 930. On this outpost, he posted three forward observers, one for artillery, one for the battalion's 81-mm mortars, and one for the company's 60-mm mortars. The outpost was about 1,600 yards from the support force perimeter. The battalion's B Company had the west portion of the perimeter, and C Company covered the southern part.[7]

Also, while waiting for official orders to withdraw, Keleher had dispatched two tanks and a platoon of infantry from Support Team B to secure the bridge just north of Haktam-ni, the proposed destination of the support force. Lieutenant Mace left his other three tanks in position to help defend the perimeter and started south. Chinese machine gunners on the heights overlooking the MSR from the east began firing on the tank force almost from the moment that it started south. The infantry hugged the tanks for protection, as did a group of South Korean soldiers trying to stay with the American force. About a mile down the road, an explosion under the second tank brought Mace out of the turret, while the tank was still moving, to check for damage. A concussion grenade, thrown from the ditch on the east side of the road, blew Mace off his tank and into the ditch on the west side of the road. He was stunned but unwounded. The tankers, unaware that Mace was gone, continued down the road and gradually outdistanced the infantry. Mace joined the walking soldiers. He recalled, "There were three GIs and five or six ROK soldiers. One of the ROKs was carrying a 81-mm mortar base plate and he carried that thing until we ran into a Chinese patrol and we all split up to evade the enemy and that's the last I saw of them."[8]

Mace's tanks ran into trouble just north of the bridge. The leading tank was hit by a bazooka round, ran off the steep edge of the road, and overturned. The second tank attempted to pass but was hit in the engine compartment and slowed to a stop on the left side of the road. The crews fled into the hills on the west and eventually made their way to the 3d Battalion perimeter at Saemal. The Chinese now had their anticipated physical roadblock to go with their fire block.[9]

Keith's march order for the movement south had A Battery of the 503d Artillery leading, followed by the three batteries of the 15th Artillery Battalion. The 1st Battalion, 38th Infantry, was to follow in a column of companies, starting with B Company. C Company, Headquarters, D Company, and A Company brought up the rear. This was a perfect administrative march formation, well suited for Fort Benning or Fort Sill, Oklahoma. It was not the formation for a combined arms group preparing to make a retrograde movement while under attack. This formation was the result of another of the command and control glitches that doomed so many Americans in this valley.

Keith was an artillery commander, and, by all accounts, he knew his business as an artilleryman. He was not, however, a combined arms commander, and Support Force 21 did not have a combined force command post. The artillery units maintained their own command posts, as did the 1st Battalion. In an attack mode, where there was no immediate danger to the force, this arrangement worked reasonably well. In time of crisis, however, it resulted in a total lack of coordination, and the cohesiveness necessary to survive desperate battles was missing. The statements of officers from all units had a commonality—they could not find or communicate with their commander or another unit's commander. Keleher could not locate Keith at times, and vice versa. Keleher's S-3, Major Blackwell, could not locate Keleher at critical points. Fortunately, there were some warriors present—men who could take charge when the ostensible commanders could not be located. Blackwell was one of those. M.Sgt. Jack M. Anderson, operations sergeant for the 1st Battalion, in *Warrior . . . by Choice . . . by Chance,* a book about his life in the Army: "Blackwell was in three places at once, as he tried to keep an attack going to the south, a rear guard action intact, and coordinate some kind of relief for us from troops south of us."[10]

Among the first victims of the Chinese attacks were the forward observers on the Hill 639 outpost. When the situation began to deteriorate, Gardner, himself a warrior and proven commander, radioed the forward observers and told them to withdraw to the company perimeter. They replied that they were surrounded and could not. None of these men was seen again, and the record is silent as to their fate. Two of Gardner's platoon positions were surrounded and had to fight their way back to the road where A Company had the mission of being rear guard.

Some other early victims of the Chinese were men of the 155-mm howitzer battery, a segregated unit. A Chinese raiding party dashed into the 503d's assembly area as Capt. Luther C. Jones was trying to get his howitzers hitched to their tractor prime movers and moved out on the road. The raiders seized Jones, his first sergeant, and several men, many of them key people, and took them back into the hills. Leaderless, the men of the battery went into a bugout mode and abandoned four of the howitzers. Jones would spend the remainder of the war in a Chinese prison camp.[11]

There were still enough of the battery's vehicles—mess, supply, and ammunition trucks—and even one howitzer that were able to get onto the road and form the head of a column. Between 3 and 4 A.M., the column lurched ahead for a few hundred meters, and no one spotted the abandoned howitzers in the predawn darkness. At 4 A.M., Chinese fire stopped the front of the column before the rear had organized to get under way.

2d Lt. Wilbur Webster was a platoon leader with D Battery, 82d Antiaircraft Battalion. He was directed (he can't remember by whom) to take an M-16 (the quad-50 half-track) down the road and see if he could break up the Chinese fire blocks. An earlier mortar round that hit the half-track had damaged the turret, but no one as yet knew that. Webster said that the M-16 came upon two tanks that were blocking the road. "When we got to the tanks, we had to stop, of course. The Chinese had a force upon the side of the hill and were shooting down at us. That's when we found out the turret wouldn't rotate." With the guns fixed in a straight ahead mode, Webster said that the crew had no choice but to abandon the vehicle after they drove it off the road. "We got down in the creek bed and I told the crew to follow me. There was a lot of firing and I don't know if they heard me or didn't hear me. But anyway I crossed the creek bed and started toward the hill on the west side of the road. I looked around and the crew wasn't with me. About that time, there were a number of Chinese moving on my side of the road, and I hit the ground and lay there a couple of minutes until I could detect no further movement. I got up and started moving again, and a Chinese soldier raised up right in front of me and fired his rife, hitting me in the right knee. It didn't break the bone, fortunately—people ask me how that can happen, I don't know but it just didn't. It knocked me down, though. When I tried to get up, I was surrounded by Chinese and I was caught. I kinda' played up my wound because I didn't want to get taken too far from the lines. I was one of thirty-two men left behind when the Chinese began moving prisoners to a POW camp up north."[12]

With the dawn came a sense of relief to the members of the trapped column. Daylight meant an opportunity to bring inherent American fire superiority into play. Keith, Keleher, or someone else ordered some of the 105-mm howitzers into action to place direct fire on the ridgelines to the east. Keleher's after action report claims that he ordered the howitzers to fire. Divarty's report said that Keith did.

A statement by Capt. Robert G. Conrad, operations officer for the 15th Artillery Battalion and also a warrior, however, gives a different picture:

I went forward to see what was causing the delay and learned that the enemy had cut the road between the 503rd battery and Battery C, 15th FA Bn. At this time, bugles began to blow up and down the ridge and in the absence of the battery officers, I ordered the men to take up defensive positions alongside the road where there was good defilade.

I then ordered two howitzers uncoupled and ordered that direct fire methods be employed against the ridge using white phosphorus shell. At this time, more officers came up and I assigned them various duties to assist me. About an hour later, an infantry major (This could have been either Blackwell or Major Leonard Lowry, who, despite being a major, was commanding Charlie Company) came up to me and requested that I place fire directly on top of the ridge as a company of his men was going to attack. I asked him if he had any way of notifying me as to when to lift my fires so that his men could gain the top of the ridge. He said they were not going to the top of the ridge, but would sweep along the side, in the direction of the head of the column.[13]

With daylight, Keleher moved his battalion out of a column formation and into a convoy protection formation. C Company advanced to clear the slopes on the east side of the road. B Company took the west side and A Company, reinforced by two tanks, brought up the rear. As the infantry units started their sweep of the high ground, Keleher started looking for drivers for vehicles. Conrad wrote:

"Lt. Col. Keleher asked if we could round up some M-5 tractor driver and some truck drivers as the drivers of a number of vehicles up forward had become casualties. Drivers were rounded up and I went forward with them as did two other officers to see if we could get the column rolling. In a short time, the column commenced to move out. The wounded and some dead were carried out."[14]

Conrad's matter-of-fact commentary fails to convey the utter terror and despair of those early morning hours. The Chinese, firing at point-blank range, aimed specifically at the driver compartments of vehicles. Because there was no flank security at first, Chinese soldiers could press close to the vehicles, and they took as prisoners those unfortunates who were not shot or bayoneted. Some of the prisoners were released after being searched and relieved of their valuables, but most remained in captivity.

It was a hard job for officers and NCOs to recruit drivers for the stalled vehicles. The soldiers could see the tracers of Chinese machine guns lancing through the cabs of the trucks, so it took an abundance of raw courage for men to pick themselves out of the perceived security of a ditch and clamber over dead or wounded drivers and make themselves targets behind a steering wheel. On the plus side, there were enough brave soldiers to keep the vehicles in the column moving. Unfortunately, others did nothing but blindly attempt to flee the enemy.

As Gardner's company fought its rear-guard action, daylight brought the revelation that, first, the rear of the column had hardly moved and, second, the 503d had abandoned three 155-mm howitzers, a full ammunition truck, and several jeeps and trailers. Gardner had no men who could drive the M-5 tractors, nor did he have the time or the explosives to destroy the guns. Company A fought briefly from the artillery position. Gardner's men used the .50-caliber machine guns mounted on the artillery vehicles until they exhausted the ammunition and then left everything for the Chinese.[15]

Blackwell said that he came upon abandoned cannons in the dark. Lacking thermite grenades, he experimented with a destruction method. He shoved a 155-mm projectile into the breech backward, pulled the pin on a fragmentation grenade, slammed the breech, and ran. The grenade detonated, but the shell did not. Because he had too many other responsibilities, Blackwell, with his radio operator in tow, reluctantly left the artillery pieces.[16]

Maj. Lowry was another warrior in the 1st Battalion. He had commanded Charlie Company as a captain and had volunteered to stay in command until the support mission was completed. His company had the toughest assignment because the bulk of the blocking Chinese forces were on the east side of the road. In order to clear the high ground, Lowry again and again organized his dwindling number of fighters and charged Chinese machine-gun positions, eliminated them, and pushed the Chinese back. The heroic efforts of C Company gave enough respite to permit the column to keep moving.

It was clear to Keith and Keleher that the former location at Haktam-ni was solidly in enemy hands. They had no choice but to continue the column south for another 1½ miles to the 3d Battalion perimeter. Keleher notified Maixner by radio that Support Force 21 was moving to join the 3d Battalion. Sgt. Neil Aiken, the 1st Battalion communications chief, was operating the longer range radios that could communicate with other battalions and with regimental headquarters. Aiken had set up his radios in a ¾-ton truck. He lined the truck bed with SCR-300 radio batteries and made making a nest for himself and the radios. At 10 inches long and 5 inches wide, the high-density batteries served as bulletproofing for the radios and their operator. Aiken said that he was more secure in his truck than "the guys in the ditches," who were a lot more vulnerable.[17]

As the support force pushed through each fire block, the Chinese closed in on the road behind it and pressed hard against Gardner's embattled rear guard company. ROK soldiers from the 21st Regiment were scattered throughout the column, but efforts to organize them were fruitless. The language barrier and the sheer terror of the moment transformed them into disorganized rabble.

At Saemal, the situation remained quiet until 3:30 A.M., although members of the ROK 10th and 16th Regiments were fleeing past the 3d Battalion positions. Maixner established a checkpoint at the crossroads and began collecting members of all friendly units that were retreating. He intended to use as many bodies as he could collect and legally use to bolster his defensive positions. Because Maixner had no command control over the ROK soldiers, he had them held in one area until contact could be made with KMAG advisors to the Korean units or with Korean commanders if any had escaped the Chinese traps.

At 2:30 A.M., K Company, manning the west leg of the horseshoe perimeter, reported observing a concentration of enemy in the vicinity of Ch'owon-ni, a little more than a mile in front of the company positions. Maixner immediately ordered his artillery liaison officer to request fire on this area. Because of the command and control situation, the request had to be relayed to the ROK 8th Division commander, who refused to give clearance on the grounds that his formations were somewhere in the vicinity of the proposed impact area.

Maixner argued in vain that no organized friendly units were west of his position. So he did the next best thing—he directed K Company and the heavy weapons of M Company to fire mortars, machine guns, and recoilless rifles at the enemy positions, a remarkable act of defiance given the sensitivity of relationships between American and ROK elements. The 3d Battalion renewed the request for artillery fire, and Divarty again replied that it could not obtain clearance from the ROK 8th Division, which, at that time, was a division in name only.

At 3:30 A.M., I Company began receiving fire from Hill 333, which was located just outside the east leg of the horseshoe. Stragglers continued to arrive in the 3d Battalion perimeter. Included among arrivals in the early morning hours were members of the ROK 16th Regiment KMAG team, who promptly gave Maixner permission to use the retreating ROK soldiers as he saw fit. Maixner wasted no time in directing that the ROK soldiers be used to help hold the line and to beef up some thin portions of the perimeter. As the ROK soldiers were being assembled, K Company informed the command post that an ROK engineer unit had taken up defensive positions with K Company's right-flank platoon. General Choi had sent this unit to attack west in order to relieve the pressure on the 16th Regiment.

When Divarty radioed at 4:00 A.M. that it still was unable to obtain clearance to fire forward of the 3d Battalion's position,

Maixner hastened to inform the artillery headquarters of the status of the ROK engineer unit. Because it was safely within his perimeter, he argued, there was no reason why artillery fire could not be placed forward of the 3d Battalion perimeter. His argument apparently cut no ice at ROK Division Headquarters in Hoengsong. The maddening answer came back—no clearance.

By daylight, both Item and King Companies were receiving heavy small-arms fire. At 6:30 A.M., K Company was assaulted. Some Chinese soldiers were successful in getting inside the perimeter by integrating themselves in with retreating ROK soldiers. At 7:00 A.M., the command posts of both rifle companies were overrun and men on the perimeter positions were fighting desperate battles for survival. Mortar fire fell unceasingly inside the perimeter even as measures were taken to wipe out the pockets of enemy soldiers that had occupied the rifle company command posts. Maixner marshaled all available forces to fill in the gaps on the south side of his position that previously had been open. The fire coming from the south made it clear that the battalion now was surrounded by a force vastly superior in numbers.

Fighting and dying continued unabated for the next three hours as the support force inched its way south on the MSR and the 3d Battalion fought to maintain a semblance of a defensive perimeter. Maixner called his boss, Colonel Coughlin, at the 38th Regimental command post on Hoengsong and obtained permission to integrate Support Force 21 into his defenses. Coughlin did this even though he had no direct authority over either of his battalions or the artillery units.

At 10 A.M., the last of Gardner's rear guard company closed into the 3d Battalion perimeter. Running the gauntlet from Ch'angbong-ni to Saemal had been costly. Because the perimeter was under fire, commanders could not take careful musters; however, total casualties appeared to be in excess of four hundred. Company A had suffered the highest casualty rate, with the loss of two officers and about 110 men. When Keith learned that the 155-mm howitzers had been left behind intact, he relayed a request to 2d Division Headquarters for air strikes on the weapons.[18]

Getting into a friendly perimeter in daylight where supporting arms could be brought to bear seemed like salvation to the surviving support force troops. For the beleaguered defenders at Saemal, the arrival of the support force with its troops and weapons instantly improved morale. No one had any inkling that the worst was yet to come.

THIRTEEN | **Failed Rescue**

By early morning of 12 February, the CCF 349th Regiment of the 117th Division was in position and well prepared to interdict any movement on Route 29 between Saemal and Hoengsong and to blunt any reinforcement moves north out of Hoengsong. At the 3d Battalion perimeter at Saemal, there was general knowledge that the battalion's positions were surrounded by Chinese, but no one knew about the regiment lurking just to the south. Certainly, no one in Hoengsong knew, nor did anyone in the headquarters of the 2d Division and X Corps.

Entries in the operations logs for the two headquarters indicated that desk officers were unaware of the gravity of the situation north of Hoengsong. The message traffic between the 2d Division and X Corps concerned a large enemy buildup north of Chip'yong-ni and the threat to that outpost and to Yoju to its south. Despite a communication from 38th Infantry headquarters at 2:45 A.M. that both its battalions north of Hoengsong were engaged with the enemy, 2d Division headquarters relayed a X Corps warning order for the 38th to be prepared to move to counter the Chinese threat to the west. X Corps wanted the 38th Infantry either to support the 23d RCT at Chip'yong-ni or to establish a defensive blocking position in the Som River valley about 9 miles southwest of Wonju. This warning order was sent out at 3:52 A.M. At 5:10 A.M., the 38th Infantry sent a message to the 2d Division telling the G-3 that said two of their battalions were heavily engaged with the enemy and one was out of its control as the X Corps reserve at Wonju. The message concluded: "We have nothing left here in Hoengsong except the Neths. Therefore we don't believe we can move on that warning order."[1]

The situation continued to be murky for Colonel Coughlin in Hoengsong. He was still operating on some very old information that the Support Force 21 column was halted mostly because of a road blockage caused by two knocked-out tanks. His message to division at 6:33 A.M. indicated that he was sending a platoon of tanks to clear the road blockage.

The murkiness at higher headquarters was not entirely the fault of desk officers and higher commanders. They were entirely dependent on spot reports from engaged units. In some cases, small-unit commanders were too beleaguered to make timely and accurate spot reports to higher headquarters. The other aspect was that commanders habitually tended to give low-ball estimates of enemy engaged. This underreporting started at platoon level and extended up to battalions and even regiments. It is a psychological phenomenon in all modern wars. No commander wants to be accused of "the sky is falling in" estimates of enemy strength. The result is lack of solid information at higher headquarters upon which commanders can make appropriate and timely decisions.

The failure to communicate was not entirely a one-way street. Too often, command levels failed to inform subordinate units of important intelligence. Even experienced company commanders, in times of great stress, sometimes failed to provide subordinates with detailed operations orders. Platoon leaders too often forgot what they had learned in their officer basic course about a five-paragraph field order.

The human element in the failure to communicate was aided and abetted by the lack of good signal communications equipment. Infantry companies were authorized two SCR-300 backpack radios. These sets, first fielded in World War II, were frequency modulated (FM) battery-powered sets. With a short antenna, the range was supposed to be 1–3 miles. Because FM transmission was line of sight, only men carrying an exceptional pair of FM radios could have communicated over a 3-mile separation in the Korean mountains.

By sitting the radio down and mounting the long antenna, it was sometimes possible to reach 3 miles. The company commander used a handheld radio, the SCR-536, to communicate with his platoons. Its maximum range was supposed to be 1 mile. Most of the time, the radios did not work; the antenna system had a lamentable tendency to short out in the presence of any moisture. At a battalion headquarters, a mast-mounted antenna, the RC-292, enabled radio transmission to company radios, but it was often a short one-way conversation because the company's responding transmission could not be heard. The battalions maintained radio contact with regiments and other battalions by using the ANGR-9, a combination voice radio and Morse code–capable set. The only way that the infantry could communicate with the artillery or the Air Force was through the use of vehicular-mounted BC-608 and BC-610 radios.[2]

At 7:30 A.M. on 12 February, the 1st Platoon of the 38th Infantry Tank Company, along with two tanks from the 9th Infantry, joined the 38th Infantry's Security Platoon under 2d Lt. Francis Uzzo. The entire little task force was under the command of 2d Lt. James Howden, the tank company platoon leader. After crossing the Twinnan-mul River just west of Hoengsong, the task force spotted a lone Chinese soldier walking toward the head of the column. They did not fire on him because Uzzo assumed that he wanted to surrender. When he reached the head of the column, the man put up his hands in the fashion of a boxer and went through motions indicating that he wanted to fight Uzzo. He then began unslinging his weapon from his shoulder, but Uzzo was quicker on the draw and killed the man with one shot from his pistol.

The task force continued on and spotted five enemy soldiers to its right front, fired at them, and killed all five. When the column moved forward another 150 yards, the Americans saw about two hundred men coming down the road. (Witness statements also have the number as high as four hundred.) As soon as these men saw the task force, they began waving their hands to indicate that they were friendly. Uzzo thought they were ROK soldiers—ROK stragglers had been passing through Hoengsong all night—consequently, they were permitted to approach the lead tank and Uzzo. When the group was within 6 yards of them, one of the group said in English, "We are friends." This brought on an exchange of handshakes all around, for now Uzzo and his men on the ground thought these were ROK allies.

Lieutenant Howden, in the second tank, was not so sure. He radioed his company commander, Capt. Reginald J. Hinton, for guidance. Hinton told him not to take any chances, but if these were really enemy and wanted to surrender, then give them that opportunity.

In fact, what the Chinese wanted was for the Americans to surrender. One of the men in the group threw a piece of paper to Uzzo. It read: "Surrender. Give up your arms and cartridge belts and we will allow you to keep your personal effects and lead you back to your lines unharmed."

This was the first indication to Uzzo and his platoon sergeant that they were face to face with an enemy and not friendly ROKs. Uzzo took immediate action. He directed his platoon sergeant to have his men withdraw and take up firing positions. Simultaneously, the lead tank, commanded by Sgt. 1/C Jack Rogers, opened fire with both the bow and turret machine guns. As soon as the tank guns opened up, a bugle was heard and the Chinese blazed away at the column. A swarm of Chinese appeared as if by magic on both sides of the road and covered the depth of the column. All of the tanks opened fire and kept most of the enemy pinned down. A few Chinese soldiers managed to climb onto some of the tanks and attempted to drop grenades down the hatches. Security Platoon soldiers on the ground swept them off the tanks with rifle fire.

Uzzo was hit by a burst of machine-gun fire. Sergeant Rogers tried to get Uzzo to lie still so that he could drive the tank over him and pull him into the tank though the belly hatch, but Uzzo waved him away. Finally, Rogers got out of the tank and headed for Uzzo. "He gave me an order a couple of times to back off and leave him be. I told him, 'I'm not going to do that,' and I didn't. He was just shot to pieces. I rolled him up in a shelter half (the canvas half of a two-man shelter, perhaps better known as a "pup tent") and finally got him on the tank deck that way. Just as I was getting back on my tank, a machine-gun slug went through my left hip and up through my bladder." Rogers was awarded the Silver Star for his heroism.

The tanks could not turn around on the narrow road, so the tankers had to back up the tanks and fire as they drove backward. The tank in which Howden was riding was hit by a charge from a high-explosive weapon, and the stunned driver backed off the road. The tank slid down the embankment and rolled over. Howden was pinned under the gun, but Sgt. Freddie Clark and Cpl. Arthur Lockrem, while being subjected to intense fire, succeeded in extracting the lieutenant and evacuating him to the relative safety of another tank.

The Chinese continued to move to the southeast in an attempt to outflank the task force, but, as they approached the river, the Netherlands Battalion in positions along the banks of the river provided covering fire for the task force to return to Hoengsong.[3]

Colonel Coughlin now knew that his two battalions and the 15th Artillery were trapped by a much larger force than had been anticipated. Even as his tanks were fighting their way to Hoengsong, he informed the division G-3 that the tanks were surrounded and that the enemy was on the southwest slopes of Hill 303, the high ground just across the river from Hoengsong. Air observers also spotted a regimental-sized column 5 miles west of Hoengsong. Coughlin placed mortar and artillery fire on enemy positions and called in air strikes. He also asked for return of his 2d Battalion from the palace guard mission at Wonju, but General Ruffner chose not to ask for its release from X Corps. The 2d Division commander, however, told Coughlin to be ready to assume control of Support Force 21 and to get it back to Hoengsong. Coughlin immediately recommended that his 3d Battalion be relieved from guarding a useless road junction and return with the support force. Ruffner denied this request and told Coughlin that the corps commander wanted the junction held until that afternoon.[4]

The X Corps commander flew in to Hoengsong at 10:00 A.M. to confer with General Choi and Lt. Col. Donavin, the senior KMAG advisor to the ROK 8th Division. The content of the discussions was not divulged in Almond's diary extracts for 12 February except that Almond left Choi's headquarters with the order for Choi to regain control of his division.[5]

At 11 A.M., Almond ordered that the 38th Infantry be reconstituted as a regimental combat team with the 2d and 3d Battalions remaining in place until further orders. Being constituted as a regimental combat team gives an infantry regiment a representative slice of division combat assets—armor, artillery, and engineers, in particular. In the case of the 38th Infantry, its artillery was the 15th Artillery Battalion, which, at that moment, was simply trying to survive the Chinese onslaught at the Saemal road junction. (At forty-eight years' remove, this order at that particular time appears to create an unnecessary burden on the regiment's commander and staff. Research in X Corps files fails to unearth a written rationale for the action. In context with the tactical doctrine of 1951, it might have been a reasonable and logical direction. What was unusual, however, was the order coming from Almond and not from Ruffner, the division commander, who should have been responsible for the tactical structure of his division.)

Support Force 21 was not the only artillery support force stuck out on a limb. Support Force 7, composed of the U.S. 7th Infantry Division's 49th Field Artillery Battalion and the 2d Battalion, 17th Infantry Regiment, was located about 2 air miles due north of Hoengsong. Support Force 7, commanded by Lt. Col. Barney D. White, the artillery commander, had been supporting the ROK 3d Division. This division's two regiments, the 22d and 23d, both staged counterattacks in early morning after being hit and driven back by Chinese assaults during the night. The intent was noble, but the ROK was not capable of staging a successful counterattack against two CCF Divisions. By noon, both regiments were trying to fight their way south through encirclements. They had not broken and run, as did the regiments of the ROK 8th Division, but their withdrawal could quickly imperil White's artillery. Seven miles east of the ROK 3d Division, the NKPA V Corps violently assaulted the positions of the ROK 5th Division and forced its regiments west and south. The entire area, both east and west of Hoengsong, was becoming extremely hazardous to American units working in close support of the ROK Army units.

At noon, with Colonel Ennis, his artillery officer, as the conduit, Almond ordered Support Forces 21 and 7 to withdraw immediately to Hoengsong. If necessary, they were to fight their way out. Ennis relayed the order through artillery channels. The curious aspect of Almond's desire to extricate the artillery is that he left the 3d Battalion, 38th Infantry, in place at the road junction. Nothing in the record supports his decision to keep the battalion in that exposed position unless the commander of the ROK 8th Division convinced him there still was active ROK resistance either west or north of Saemal. Almond's failure to recognize the gravity of the situation north of Hoengsong and his stubborn insistence on keeping Maixner's battalion at that road junction for several more hours resulted in the virtual destruction of the 3d Battalion, as well as Support Force 21.

When he deployed in support of the ROK 3rd Division, Colonel White had brought Support Force 7 up Route 29 near to Haktamni and then turned east along the north bank of the Kumgye Ch'on River, which was not really a river but a small frozen stream. His firing positions were about two miles east of Haktam-ni. When he received the order to withdraw, he sent a reconnaissance party west to investigate, but Chinese troops pounced on it well before it reached the MSR. White, now confronted with the knowledge that many Chinese troops were located to his west and, thus far, none to his south and east, looked in the latter direction for a withdrawal route. What White termed a *goat trail* followed the Kumgye Ch'on River for about 300 yards to where it merged with the Kye Ch'on to form the Twinnan-mul River. At that point, the trail became a primitive road through the Twinnan-mul Valley to where it met the MSR at Hoengsong. The little-used road was ice coated and in poor shape, but White had a small engineer unit that made hasty repairs. At 3 P.M., White's column started pulling out of the area, and his rear guard was clear about two hours later. The initial part of the withdrawal was made without a shot being fired.[6]

The 7th Infantry Division had another support unit endangered by the rapidly withdrawing ROK units, but it withdrew safely during the day. The 187th Airborne RCT, whose 674th Field Artillery Battalion and its reinforcing 96th Field Artillery Battalion had been in direct support of the ROK 5th Division, extracted from a dicey position and established new firing positions east of Hoengsong. The 187th's 1st Battalion also escaped unscathed and established a defense around the artillery positions.

Support Force 21 was not so lucky. The 3d Battalion perimeter was under fire all morning. Infantrymen could seek some degree of cover in a perimeter, even when returning enemy fire, but artillerymen could not. As soon as the 15th Artillery tubes were inside the perimeter that morning, Colonel Maixner ordered the artillerymen to place their guns in firing position in the vicinity of the road junction and to fire on the hill masses surrounding the perimeter. This was done so hastily that the gun trails were not properly dug in, and the recoils shoved the tubes out of firing position. An A Battery gun crewman, Oscar Cortez, remembers part of the ordeal. "I stood on the trail, pulled the lanyard, after which I would push the gun back into firing position. I would look through the barrel for aiming, put another round in place, jump back on the trail and pull the lanyard and did it again and again." Cortez said that he continued firing the howitzer until his ammunition was exhausted.[7]

Without protective revetments, the artillery tubes were vulnerable to small-arms and mortar fire, and a number of crew members were killed or wounded while manning their guns. It was a throwback to Civil War times when artillerymen and their tubes were cheek by jowl with the infantry.

During the morning, the fire support by the artillery, along with air strikes, had relieved the pressure on both the K and I Company portions of the perimeter. Artillery support was provided not only by the howitzers but by the quad-50s and twin-40s. Men from D Battery, 82d Antiaircraft Battalion, blazed away at targets beyond the range of infantry weapons. As it had been while moving the column from Changbong-ni, this fire support by D Battery often made the difference.

As the threat on the flanks was suppressed by firepower, the Chinese shifted their pressure to the southern portion of the perimeter. The high ground, a 700-foot ridgeline to the south and west of Maixner's command post, was twice taken by the Chinese, but, on both occasions, direct artillery fire and determined counterattacks by a composite unit regained the hill. This unit consisted of men from K Company, 9th Infantry; some overhead people from the artillery; Headquarters Company of the 3d Battalion; and even some ROK soldiers.[8]

The 3d Battalion aid station was overflowing with wounded. Maixner, Keleher, and Keith jointly decided to load as many of the wounded as possible on the vehicles of Support Force 21, which was under orders to start fighting its way back to Hoengsong. About that time, a helicopter piloted by a Lieutenant Strawn (only his last name appears in the X Corps G-3 log) made one last trip into the firestorm that was the Saemal perimeter. Lieutenant Mace, on the ground, was trying to keep out of the line of fire. He remembered, "One of the bravest things I ever saw was that helicopter coming in there. He came right down into that fire, picked this guy up, and took off. And the Chinese never shot him down."[9] Sadly, two men helping to load the seriously wounded man were killed by small-arms fire.

Just before noon, Keith and Keleher began complying with Almond's order for the support force to fight its way to Hoengsong. Keleher placed C Company on the west side of the road, where most of the Chinese forces were now located; B Company on the left; and A Company in reserve. When the attack started, C Company fixed bayonets and charged the first ridge. The Chinese wanted no part of cold steel and fled. Corporal Wall of C Company charged a machine gun and threw a hand grenade, but he forgot to pull the pin. The throw was accurate, striking the enemy gunner on the head and stunning him. While the Chinese soldier struggled to regain his wits, Wall was on him and killed him as he ran past the gunner. Major Lowry led the C Company assaults despite being wounded, which he ignored as he continued to lead his men. Lowry survived the forthcoming night in Massacre Valley and later received the Distinguished Service Cross for his actions.

Company B advanced about 1,500 yards before it met stiff resistance and could advance no more. Keleher ordered A Company to pass through B Company and to continue the attack. The Chinese had flowed in behind B Company, and Gardner's company had to fight every inch of the way even to reach B Company. By this time, the two companies were so depleted that, between the two units, only forty able-bodied men remained. The two companies merged into a composite unit and tried to fight on, but the Chinese stopped them cold, as it had C Company by this time.

In this fight, Gardner again had tried to get ROK troops to help. He spotted the commanding officer of the ROK 21st Regiment and told him to "get his cowardly troops into the fight." The ROK officer had no subordinate officers or NCOs and, as a result, did nothing. With the help of his first sergeant, Gardner clubbed and kicked ROK soldiers as he tried to force them into a line. He finally resorted to moving the terrified Koreans at gunpoint and forced them across ground that Gardner described as "littered with dead Americans, ROKs and Chinese."

Gardner then sent a runner, one of the fourteen men remaining in his company, to the road at the rear to bring up any reinforcements that he could find. The man returned without any help. He reported to Gardner that there were many artillerymen sitting in their vehicles along the road. Some were securing their flanks, but many more were cowering in the ditches. Gardner went to the rear, rousted out the slackers, formed them into groups, and sent them to his skirmish line and also to the west of the road where a fight was going on for some high ground. Gardner said that some of these men gave a good account of themselves, but all too many found secluded spots and cowered in the hope that angry officers, such as Gardner, would not find them. Also, Gardner said that five artillerymen from the 503d Artillery told him that they were not fighting men and could not fight as infantrymen.

Keleher's report said that at 3:30 P.M., a strong Chinese counterattack forced back his A and B Companies nearly 500 yards. At that time, he said that more than 200 ROK soldiers were in the road column: "All efforts to get these people organized and to help us were in vain. They would hide in trucks, ditches and some were observed throwing away their belts and ammunition and posing as wounded to avoid combat. One ROK soldier was caught breaking his rifle."[10]

Major Blackwell, according to his practice, was everywhere as he tried to keep the attack moving. He spotted a Chinese machine gun on a ridge to the left of the road that had stopped the vehicles in the column. Blackwell called back to the field command post manned by Sergeant Anderson, the operations sergeant, and M. Sgt. Guenther A. Burrer, the intelligence sergeant. Burrer, from Gillespie, Texas, was, by preference, known to his close associates as "Gunner Burr." In 1997, Anderson, who had fought in World War II with the 163d Infantry Regiment of the Montana National Guard, wrote and published a book about his wartime experiences. In the book, Anderson used Burrer's favorite nickname as a tribute to the man whom he termed "the best soldier he ever knew." Anderson wrote about what happened next on that Korean road:

Major Blackwell wanted us to get some troops to knock it [the machine gun] out. We told him we could hear the gun on the next little ridge but there just were no troops to do anything about it. He said the gun had to go, so Burr and I looked at each other, shrugged our shoulders and said we would go do it. The major didn't object, so we closed the CP. Our SCR-300 radio we set out in the open, stuffed our reports, orders and maps under some brush and organized the CP group as an assault team.

Without much planning we made the attack with Burr and I leading. We got the gun without much trouble as they were not expecting us, but what we didn't know was that there was a second gun, just above it. The rest of the assault team watched as this gun crew took Burr and me on. There was some wild grenade and rifle fire going on until I took a machine gun slug through the head and was knocked down the hill and lost my rifle. Burr rolled down with me. This gun position was now out of grenade range, but it didn't keep them from rolling them down on us.

As Burr raised up to see what my wound looked like, a burst of fire hit him three places, breaking the skin on his forearm, nicking his shin and wrecking his carbine. In Burr's words, "You are bleeding like a stuck hog," so we rolled down the hill a bit farther and he started stopping the flow of blood with a battle dressing. By the time the wound was dressed there were six CCF soldiers standing around us and motioning us to come along with them. We had no choice but to obey. They took us right out across the road on to an open field, and as we went we could hear our little assault force silence the enemy gun crew to allow the column to get going again.

In a note following the passage, Anderson reported that the after action report covering his action simply said: "The Bn. CO had to commit his Hq Co here, which silenced the fire."[11]

Despite the heroics of Anderson, Burrer, and scores of other soldiers in the First Battalion and D Battery, 82d Antiaircraft Artillery Battalion, the attack was absolutely stalled. Support Force 21 was going nowhere.

About the time that the support force was stopped cold, Colonel Coughlin received word that General Almond had directed the ROK 3d Division to send a battalion of its 18th Regiment to Hoengsong to attack north on Route 29. The attack would be reinforced by Support Team E, which consisted of a platoon from the 72d Tank Battalion and Company G, 187th Airborne RCT. Almond assigned the 3d Division's assistant commander to head this force and, in typical style, also directed his acting armor officer, Colonel Wilhm, to coordinate the armor-infantry advance. Coughlin, in whose area of operations all of this was to occur, had no part in it at all.

1st Lt. Jones Epps, platoon leader of G Company's Weapons Platoon, wrote a "Lessons Learned" document for the company on 13 March when memories still were fresh. He wrote that the ROK battalion, which was to attack at 1 P.M., was late getting started and did not jump off until 2:15 P.M. By 4:50 P.M., the ROK forces advanced to the top of the first hills across the river. Support Team E, operating in a senior leadership vacuum, advanced to positions about 600 yards up the valley when it ran into heavy small-arms and automatic weapons fire. Epps noted that the company's mortars set up in battery but had to displace three times because of accurate sniper fire from just across the river. From their positions, the support team members could see that the ROK soldiers had stopped their advance.[12]

Colonel Coughlin had sent his S-3, Maj. Warren D. Hodges, to observe the action. When Hodges saw the ROK battalion halt its attack, he sought out the South Korean commander and pleaded for continuing the advance. The ROK colonel refused. His orders, he insisted, were to take the hills and hold them only until dark. He said that he would remain in position until the forces withdrawing from the north passed through.

Coughlin was a frustrated regimental commander. He did not have the authority to order the ROK force to continue. After slapping a small bandage on a hemorrhage, Almond flew to Wonju for a conference with Ridgway and left Wilhm to represent X Corps interests. The only bright spot in a dismal afternoon occurred at 2:30 P.M. when Almond released the 3d Battalion back to Coughlin's control and gave permission for it to withdraw from the road junction.[13]

The ROK battalion never waited for night. In the fading light, troopers in Support Team E could see the troops running off the hills. With the ROK withdrawal, and seemingly without any mission, the armor-infantry support team turned around and headed back into Hoengsong.

Another rescue mission had failed.

FOURTEEN | Into the Valley of Death

General Almond released the 3d Battalion from its blocking assignment at the road junction at 2:30 P.M. By the time that the directive filtered through Corps G-3 to Division G-3 to Colonel Coughlin, another half hour had elapsed. Coughlin immediately relayed the message to Maixner and Keleher, but he left each battalion on its own. Coughlin was hampered by fuzzy command relationships. The order establishing X Corps control on the support forces never had been rescinded. Moreover, division and corps headquarters apparently continued to believe the fiction that Support Force 21 was still a viable combat force. The new direction was for Maixner's battalion to assist the support force withdrawal to Hoengsong. No one was placed in overall command, and, by default, it became a triumvirate command arrangement—certainly not the best for the situation at hand. Keleher and Maixner conferred and formulated the plan for the attack south. Keith's role was to keep the vehicle column moving inside the sleeve of infantry on the high ground on both sides of the road.

The tactical plan called for Maixner's battalion to break contact and disengage from its perimeter and then form an attack formation on the west side of the MSR. The road would be the axis of attack and boundary between the two battalions. Maixner designated his King Company to lead, followed by Item Company. As each hill was taken, one platoon would remain on the hill to keep it secured until all friendly elements had cleared. 3d Battalion Headquarters troops, along with remnants of Love Company, formed the rear guard. Keleher directed his C Company, which had attacked to gain

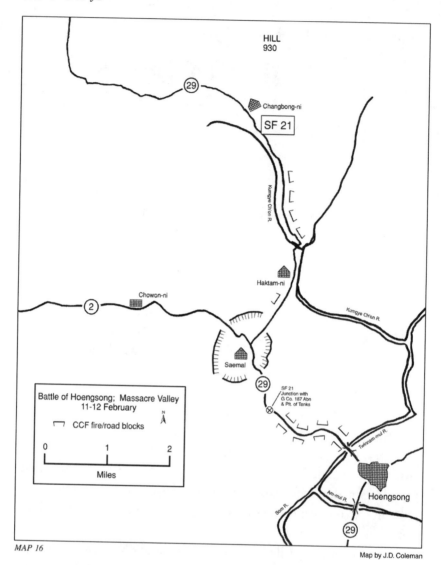

HILL
930

Changbong-ni

SF 21

Kumgye Ch'on R.

Haktam-ni

Kumgye Ch'on R.

Chowon-ni

Saemal

SF 21
Junction with
G Co. 187 Abn
& Plt. of Tanks

Twiramn-mul R.

Battle of Hoengsong; Massacre Valley
11-12 February

N

CCF fire/road blocks

0   1   2

Miles

Am-mul R.

Hoengsong

Som R.

MAP 16

Map by J.D. Coleman

the high ground west of the road during the early afternoon, to hold its ground until K Company attacked through it. At that point, Charlie Company was to move to the east side of the road.[1]

By the time that the 3d Battalion extracted from its positions and moved abreast of the 1st Battalion, it was 4:30 P.M. and light was rapidly fading. The combined force began moving south, but it was at a crawl, and the cost was high. Chinese mortar, machine-gun, and small-arms fire continued to sweep across the infantry and punish the motor column.[2]

At Hoengsong, Coughlin was frantic. He had two battalions of infantry and a battalion of artillery trapped by a vastly superior enemy force, and there was not a thing he could do about it. Coughlin and Hodges spent the afternoon in coordinating fire support and air strikes for the beleaguered force. Coughlin fervently hoped that relief promised by Almond would amount to more than the battalion of reluctant ROKs. At 6 P.M., Colonel Wilhm, the acting Corps armor officer, went to the 38th Infantry's CP to notify Coughlin to take charge of all American troops in the Hoengsong area. Wilhm had received these instructions when he radioed Corps headquarters to notify his bosses of the ROK battalion's failure to advance more than a few hundred yards from the Twinnan-mul River. Oddly, there is nothing in either the X Corps or 2d Division G-3 journals about this order. It only came to light during an interview with Wilhm by the Eighth Army Inspector General.[3]

Although Coughlin could not use the ROK battalion, which was still in the Hoengsong area, he had no doubts about getting some value out of Support Team E. He summoned Captain Hinton, a trusted officer and long-time regimental tank company commander. Hinton had been working as regimental assistant operations officer before a command failure in the tank company pressured Coughlin to send him back to the tanks.

Hinton remembers the occasion well. "I had been called to the regimental CP just before dark by Coughlin, and met a warrant officer named Merton standing just outside the CP. He said, pointing at a hill just north of the town, 'Well, it looks like we got some help coming down the hill over there.' I said, 'Hell no, Mert, those are gooks.' " Hinton said that every time Coughlin had a tough mission for him, he had a habit of saying, "Jim, you are a very senior captain." Hinton said this time it was no different. "Coughlin told me I was to take command of G Company, 187th, and a platoon of tanks from the 72d." [The 2d Division's organic tank battalion.] Hinton was a man Coughlin could trust to carry out a mission, and he handed the captain a tough one. Forthwith, Hinton was to move up the MSR to relieve the pressure on the southbound battalions. There would be no flank security except that which the rifle company platoons could provide, and, because of the darkness, there would be no artillery fire support and, obviously, no air strikes.[4]

Hinton hastened to round up Support Team E from where it had stopped after withdrawing across the river. At the same time, he ordered two of his tanks to join the task force. Hinton pretty much knew what he was getting with the 72d's tank platoon. He didn't know, however, who or what G Company was. He said that he wasn't even aware that the 187th was in the area. What he was getting was a well-trained, disciplined fighting outfit. Since arriving in Korea in September, G Company had seen limited action on the Kimpo Peninsula, had experienced some spirited fights after the combat jump at Sunchon, and then had chased North Korean guerillas in North Korea, where it sustained its first battle death thus far in the war. Most recently, it had been pursuing North Korean guerrillas in the frigid mountains between P'unggi and Tanyang southeast of Wonju, where it had another man killed and several wounded. In effect, this experienced crew had engaged in what amounted to live-fire maneuvers for several months and had solidly learned the infantryman's trade without getting seriously hurt. Capt. James D. Cook, G Company commander, was a seasoned leader. Cook had fought as a noncommissioned officer with the 517th Airborne Infantry Regiment in Europe during World War II until he won a commission. After the war, when the Army did not need as many officers on active duty, he reverted to NCO status but maintained his Reserve commission. In December 1950, the Army desperately needed seasoned officers. Cook, who had been a platoon sergeant in E Company, took off his stripes, pinned on captain's bars, and assumed command of G Company.[5]

Hinton said that it was dark before the task force started its mission, and he and Cook immediately had a problem with the tank platoon leader from the 72d. "He seemed to think that he was a free agent and did not need to take orders from me or anybody else. Both Cook and I argued with him for a few minutes, and I finally told him there wasn't time to mess with him any longer and we moved out," Hinton recalled. Hinton said that he respected Cook because he had accepted the new command arrangement with a smile and handshake. The two 38th Infantry tanks were in the lead, and the five tanks from the 72d followed behind the lead tanks.[6]

All the tanks were Shermans (M-4A-3E-8), known by tankers as "Easy Eights." They mounted a 76-mm main gun and were further armed with a .50-caliber machine gun mounted on the turret and two .30-caliber machine guns, one coaxially mounted in the turret with the main gun and a bow gun in the driver's compartment. The 76-mm shells carried by the tanks included high explosive (HE), high explosive armor-piercing (HEAP), and white phosphorus (WP). When a tank fired an antitank round, with its muzzle velocity of 3,300 feet per second, infantrymen standing close to the blast deflector on the muzzle were momentarily stunned and deafened by the blast.

Hinton remembers, as do other members of the task force, that it was pitch black when the force crossed the river and started toward Saemal. In his after action report, Lieutenant Epps wrote that the attack formation adopted was for the 2d and 3d Platoons to be abreast of the lead tanks and on both sides of the road. The weapons platoon was to follow immediately behind the last tank, with the 57-mm recoilless rifle (RR) section on one side of the road and the 60-mm mortar section on the other. The 1st Platoon formed the rear security. Epps wrote that the disposition of the 57-mm RR squads proved not to be the best, but to have attached them to the rifle platoons would have delayed the start of the task force up the valley.[7]

The task force was barely 600 yards into the valley when it was met by a hail of small arms and automatic weapons fire from the same positions that had confronted the force earlier in the afternoon. The lead tanks laid down heavy suppressive fire on the positions and silenced the enemy guns sufficiently for the infantry platoons to establish some degree of flank security.

Pfc John Hare, a rifleman in the 2d Platoon, remembered that the Chinese had the high ground on both sides. He recalled:

> Our flank guards had themselves some job of staying put. One of our Rakkasans was up there on one of those hills when he got shot in the thigh. Three of us went up to get him and it looked like there were a lot more enemy up there than we could handle. We had to run them off before we could get close. When I finally got to him, he had a big smile on his face and told me how happy he was after getting his "million dollar wound."

Hare said that the man was a pretty heavy deadweight, like a big bag of chicken feed that had gotten wet, but they got him back to the road and hoisted him onto a tank.

"The enemy holding both sides of the valley had a field day shooting at us," Hare added. "It was like a firing range and you were the target. A bullet makes a 'pop' sound as it passes close to you. The whole trip up and back was full of those pops."[8]

The task force pressed on for another 400 yards and then was subjected to intense mortar fire. The tankers could do nothing to suppress indirect-fire weapons, and the mortars began to cause casualties.

Cpl. Johnny Bramblett, a 60-mm mortar section leader in the weapons platoon, said that someone was moaning out in a rice paddy and M.Sgt. Phillip J. Wilkes, the weapons platoon sergeant, told Bramblett to go over and check it out. Just as Bramblett reached the moaning man, who turned out to be an ROK soldier, a 120-mm mortar barrage struck the trailing part of the task force where G Company's mortar section was walking. "That barrage seemed like it wounded nearly everybody in the mortar section. When I got back to the road I started loading wounded on the tanks," Bramblett said.[9]

Some of the Chinese had taken up positions close to the road, and the lead rifle platoons and the weapons platoon had to fight desperate little battles to provide close-in protection for the tanks.

As the task force moved forward, the CCF tried to flow back to the road at the end of the procession of tanks. G Company's first platoon, led by a legendary character in the airborne community, M.Sgt. Sergeant Othon O. ("Jumpy") Valent, waged running gun battles to protect the end of the column.

There was a time, about a mile and a quarter into the valley, that the fires grew so intense that the task force stalled and Hinton radioed Coughlin for permission to withdraw. Coughlin told him to give it another try. Hinton recalls conferring with Cook and G Company 1st Sgt. Paul Kellam when Kellam was dropped with a serious wound. He was wrestled on board a tank, and the column lurched forward. Kellam later was blown off the tank by a mortar round, but he was reloaded onto another vehicle and survived the night.[10]

At the rear of the column, Sergeant Wilkes was waging a one-man war against the enemy. Despite a shrapnel wound from a mortar round, Wilkes carried four wounded men to the roadside, where they could be picked up by vehicles when the column started back toward Hoengsong. With only his M-1 and pockets full of hand grenades, Wilkes stood off about twenty Chinese who were trying to wedge their way back to the road and establish a new fire block. His fight resulted in six Chinese dead and a number of others wounded before the Chinese gave up on establishing a fire block in the area Wilkes guarded.[11] Unfortunately, there was no opposition to the Chinese moving back to the road in the areas well to the rear of the relief column.

At about 9:30 P.M., contact was made between the task force and the two battalions of the 38th Infantry. The report, written by Epps, said that the initial contact was with a small patrol from the 3d Battalion, 38th Infantry. The patrol gave Captain Cook and the radio operators the call signs and frequencies on which the 38th Infantry operated.[12]

The commanders of the two battalions had been informed by the regimental headquarters that a relief task force was fighting its way north to meet them. Tragically, the regimental source neglected to inform them of the size and composition of this task force. None of the men in command of units in the Saemal area, who had been in constant contact with overwhelming Chinese strength for eighteen hours, thought to ask. It was but one of several command failures during the period, beginning the day before, that would doom hundreds of men.

Although it was excruciatingly painful, the head of the trapped force had made progress on the route south before meeting Hinton's task force. With the arrangement of the 1st Battalion on the left side of the road and the 3d Battalion on the right, the infantry units working the high ground on both sides of the road kept most of the Chinese forces away from the vehicle column. In some cases, CCF elements filtered in toward the vehicles and brought small-arms fire to bear on vehicle drivers. The stopping and starting began to have an effect on the integrity of the convoy. Vehicles were bunched together, with large gaps between the groups, and the rear of the convoy fell farther and farther behind the lead elements.

The most devastating blow came when a heavy mortar round struck a 2½-ton truck towing a 105-mm howitzer just as it was entering a narrow defile. The truck jackknifed and formed an impassable roadblock. A Chinese machine gunner, firing directly on the cab of the truck, prevented anybody from trying to restart the truck and drive it away. After unsuccessful attempts to bulldoze the wrecked truck, the two 38th Infantry tanks that had been working with the rear guard were able to bypass it by sweeping out across paddy dikes. The wheeled vehicles did not have that kind of cross-county mobility. With no means of moving the truck and howitzer, all vehicles behind them, including the trucks, jeeps and their trailers, and ¾-ton trucks carrying the nonambulatory wounded, had to be abandoned. The walking wounded started shuffling down the road toward Hoengsong. They were followed by those few members of L Company and 3d Battalion Headquarters Company who remained in a cohesive formation to furnish a rear guard.[13]

Just ahead of the stalled truck, Captain Conrad of the 15th Artillery was working to keep vehicles moving at the rear of the column.

Conrad was in radio contact with Colonel Keith and checked in with him from time to time when the column stopped to determine if it was also halted at Keith's location. At about 8 P.M., with the motor column stopped again, Conrad noticed men streaming past him from the rear of the column. He halted one of them and asked what was happening behind him. The man told Conrad that the enemy was rolling up the rear of the column. Conrad later reported:

> I called Col. Keith again and gave him this information and he asked me if I could stop them. I told him that I would try, but I didn't think I could, especially since the tanks had pulled out. Up to this point from the time that we moved out from Ch'angbong-ni, I thought that the morale had been extremely high and that the men had done a fine job, even though our casualties were heavy. I tried to stop the men and get them to hold, but was not successful. I called Col. Keith again and he told me to do every thing I could and then to walk out. I destroyed our radio and my driver fired a couple rounds into the motor of the vehicle and we started to walk out. I tried to locate men from my battalion, but in all the noise and confusion, I met with no success. I did what I could to keep the men ahead of me moving and to keep them from bunching up. As I passed along the column, I saw that many vehicles had been knocked out and that others had been pushed into the ditch.[14]

Meanwhile, behind the stalled truck, the rear of the formation had deteriorated into an "every man for himself" mode. Although the infantry units still on flank security maintained good order and discipline, that, too, would soon end. All of the commanders believed that the road to Hoengsong was now clear of the enemy, and, according to both battalion after action reports, the flank security was called in. The infantry then fell in on the road in front of and around Hinton's tanks, which had turned around on the narrow road and started back toward Hoengsong.

While the tank column was stopped during the linkup and turning of the tanks, Sergeant Bramblett decided to fire his 60-mm mortar at some flashes on the distant hillside. With Lee, the weapons platoon interpreter, handing him ammunition that another platoon member was carrying to him, Bramblett sent a couple rounds toward the hill. When he heard no explosions, he discovered that Lee was not pulling the pins. He remembers, "When I discovered it and started pulling the pins, we got a barrage of counterfire. The tanks were ready to head back, so we had to leave the mortars because I didn't have any way to destroy them."

Bramblett was present when Sergeant Wilkes was shot. "He was standing there on the road with wounded men waving his arms," Bramblett later told the author, "and a gunner on the lead tank, thinking Wilkes was a gook, shot him with a .50 caliber gun. Delmer Manual and I put Wilkes on the tank along with some of our seriously wounded."[15]

Wilkes died on the trip out of the valley and was posthumously awarded the Distinguished Service Cross.

This is probably an appropriate time to debunk a pervasive war story circulating among G Company veterans. The legend has it that one hard-bitten member of the weapons platoon shot the tank gunner as an "eye-for-an-eye" revenge gesture. If he did take a shot, he missed. An examination of Department of the Army casualty records for the 72d Tank Battalion reveals no gunshot deaths or wounds on any of the dates in question.[16]

Before the tanks started, foot elements of the infantry battalions, artillery units, and ROKs began moving south on the MSR. The regiment's report reads:

> As leading elements started down the road, they encountered heavy mortar fire, small arms and machine gun fire from points that previously had been physically secured. It became necessary for the column to run a gauntlet of fire the remaining distance to Hoengsong. The fire was being delivered at point blank range. In numerous instances, friendly forces would hold one side of the road and the enemy the other. Hand grenade duels were fought all along the route.[17]

The report fails to discuss how it was expected that a single rifle company and seven tanks could secure 2 miles of roadway.

INTO THE VALLEY OF DEATH | 151

Among the unsung heroes of the disorganized stages of the withdrawal were soldiers manning the quad-50s and twin-40s. When gunners were wounded, other soldiers stepped up to take their places, and they were not all members of D Battery, 82d Artillery. The volume of fire that these weapons could place on enemy positions kept the CCF from totally dominating the battlefield. The automatic weapons, however, quickly became targets, both from enemy automatic weapons and indirect-fire weapons. The half-tracks also served as ambulances for the wounded.

On the way in, trooper Frank Scalzo had a 5-inch chunk of his left buttock blown away by a mortar round. He crawled to the road where medic Cpl. Carlos Sanchez slapped a field dressing on the wound and gave Scalzo shot of morphine. On the way out, someone picked up Scalzo and sat him on the running board of a half-track, where he held on for dear life to the handle of an axe fastened on the side. A mortar shell hit the side of the half-track and turned it over. Scalzo said that as the vehicle started to tip, he let go and crawled as fast as he could: "The half-track missed me by inches. The half-track was full of dead and wounded. I don't remember what happened to them, but I was picked up again and put on the hood of a jeep near the windshield, with another G Company trooper, Cpl. Jack Crowley. As we moved out, a machine gun opened up and killed the man riding shotgun, missed my head, but stitched me down the side where I had already been hit."[18]

The trek out of the valley was a horrific experience for the soldiers. Trooper Hare remembers walking in front of and to the side of a tank in the darkness. As it started to pass him, he was struck in the back and knocked to the side. When Hare recovered, he saw that the blow had been delivered by a man's arm and upper torso that had been caught in the drive sprocket of the tank.[19] No one knows to whom the grisly remains belonged, but more than likely it was that of an ROK soldier. The terror-stricken South Koreans tried again and again to clamber onto any vehicle they could reach, only to be clubbed mercilessly by GIs. There was barely enough room for the seriously wounded, and, with vehicles being destroyed by enemy fire, the carrying capacity of the motor convoy continued to diminish.

As command jeeps and radios were turned into scrap metal along the road, the command and control of units deteriorated rapidly. Major Blackwell, who had been one those most responsible for keeping tactical integrity in the 1st Battalion out of Ch'angbong-ni, took a bullet in the head, which temporarily blinded him, shortly after the linkup. He was placed on a jeep, where, like Scalzo, he was struck by machine-gun slugs on the trip out.

Captain Hinton lost his command jeep and radio and, thus, contact with his tanks. When he started to walk out, a mortar round detonated close by and blew him off the road. He was stunned but not wounded. "When I came to," he remembered, "Charlie Heath was prodding me with his carbine."

Captain Heath, assistant S-2 of the 38th Infantry, who accompanied the task force into the valley, had been wounded in the thigh. He and Hinton limped and stumbled the remaining distance to Hoengsong.

Somewhere in the melee, Colonel Keith's jeep was lost. Keith, who had been lightly wounded before the support force started south from Saemal, was wounded again and captured. He died in captivity on 30 March 1951.

Colonel Coughlin was standing on the road at the bridge across the Twinnan-mul at Hoengsong to meet his troops moving out of the valley. He intended to have the battalion commanders continue on through Hoengsong and reorganize in an assembly area some 3 miles south of town. From there, the units were to move to a new defense line being established at Wonju. Colonel White's Support Force 7 was to do the same when it came in along the Twinnan-mul from the northeast. Coughlin's plan came unglued when the Chinese began attacking the Netherlands Battalion's defensive positions.

At about 9:00 P.M., as the first elements from Saemal were arriving in Hoengsong, a column of men were detected moving on a road from the northeast through the center of town toward the Netherlands Battalion's command post. The CP guard opened fire on the column, and from the group came shouts of "OK, ROKs! OK,

ROKs!" Lt. Col. M. P. A. den Ouden, the battalion commander, was not so sure. The firing had stopped, as had the movement toward the CP. Colonel den Ouden directed Sgt. Pakker, the battalion S-2 sergeant, and his interpreter to identify these troops. As Pakker and his interpreter drew near to the column of troops, the interpreter heard them talking and shouted, "Sergeant, they are Chinese." Immediately the column of men began firing, and Pakkar shouted back to the CP, "Men, something is wrong." Alerted by the firing and Pakkar's shout, den Ouden ordered his troops to fall back about 20 yards to positions by his headquarters company. As he was issuing orders, a hand grenade detonated at his feet and mortally wounded him. Four of his men tried to drag the colonel over an embankment but could not. Several others were wounded, including the S-3, Captain Tack, who still managed to send for reinforcements from B Company. Eventually, the Headquarters Company situation stabilized and fought the Chinese to a standoff. Along the river, the Dutch line companies held firm against Chinese assaults.[20]

Support Force 7 received heavy small-arms, machine-gun, and mortar fire as it neared the end of its icy trek down the Twinnanmul Valley. One 155-mm howitzer had been lost when it slipped off a narrow, ice-covered ledge that the support force was using for a road. Engineers had to do some hasty repair work to make the ledge passable for the remainder of the artillery column. The 2d Battalion, 17th Infantry, commanded by Lt. Col. Denzil Baker and assigned to protect White's artillery, escorted the lead elements of White's convoy through Hoengsong without trouble. Colonel Coughlin learned of this movement and summoned Baker to his CP. He informed Baker of the command arrangement directed by X Corps and told Baker to get the rest of White's artillery out and then report back to the 38th CP for further orders.

When the Chinese struck the Netherlands Battalion's position, they created mass confusion. Baker's troops fought to keep the route open for White's artillery, which finally was able to withdraw south of Hoengsong. There, the artillery column struck a major Chinese fire block. Baker's battalion, led by its Company G, assaulted and destroyed the Chinese position. With the exception of a few scattered snipers, Chinese attempts to cut the MSR south of Hoengsong then ceased.

The Dutch fought a determined fight long enough for the last of the vehicle column from Saemal to clear through Hoengsong. Many of the individuals who were moving on their own veered to the west to avoid the firefights between the Dutch on the south side of the river and the Chinese on the north. These men later got back on the MSR south of Hoengsong and were scooped up by 38th Infantry officers trying to gather troops and reorganize their force.

The Dutch fought until all forces had withdrawn behind them, and then they broke contact and began withdrawal to Wonju at 1 A.M. George Company had maintained tactical integrity throughout the ordeal and was trudging south on the MSR when Captain Cook finally located Colonel Coughlin and asked for further orders. A radio exchange between the 38th Infantry and 2d Division Headquarters indicated that G Company was still under operational control of the 2d Division and was to return to Wonju. With no transportation available, the company had to walk. Despite its casualties of six men killed and more than fifty wounded, George Company had survived the valley of death in remarkably good condition. For it and the remnants of the 38th Infantry, however, even tougher times loomed ahead.

FIFTEEN | **Revelations and Recriminations**

At 8 P.M. on 12 February, X Corps issued an operational order (Number 104) that, in effect, ratified what General Peng's offensive had already accomplished—the dissolution of the artillery, armor, and infantry support forces that were attached to ROK units. The elements in the support teams were returned to the command and control of their parent units.

General Almond directed that the new X Corps defense line would extend from Chip'yong-ni southeast to Wonju and from there east and northeast to the coast. Almond had discussed the establishment of this line during a meeting with General Ridgway on the afternoon of 12 February. The linchpins for the defense would be Chip'yong-ni on the west and Wonju in the center. ROK units were expected to be able to hold their own against the North Korean forces that were advancing to the east of Hoengsong. In order to improve command and control of the ROK efforts, Ridgway had approved Almond's request to have the ROK I Corps headquarters attached to X Corps and given control of the ROK 3d and 5th Divisions to the east of Wonju. Almond reasoned that the ROK I Corps would be a good fit with X Corps because they had worked together in northeast Korea. The ROK III Corps assumed control of the ROK Capital Division on the east coast.[1]

At daylight on 13 February, X Corps began to count the horrendous losses sustained by the 2d Division units north of Hoengsong. Support Force 7 escaped the Chinese dragon's jaws with the lightest casualties. In actions above and below Hoengsong, the 7th Division units sustained 12 killed, 125 wounded, and 53 missing. The major equipment losses were thirty-five vehicles, the single 155-mm howitzer that had slipped off the road, and a quad-50 half-track that had thrown a track just above Hoengsong and was abandoned.

Given the confusion that pertained to the entire X Corps area, a breakdown of casualties into categories of killed, wounded, and missing was not possible for some units, especially the ROK 8th Division. X Corps had placed the remnants of the ROK 8th in corps reserve at Chup'o-ri, 18 miles southeast of Wonju. In an interesting footnote to the ROK 8th Division's debacle, its commanding officer, General Choi, left Hoengsong sometime on 12 February and headed south for the division's assembly area. Apparently he became lost en route. 1st Lt. Joseph P. ("Joe") Kingston, an assistant S-3 of the 3d Battalion, 32d Regiment, at Chech'on, was on duty that night when one of his companies reported that its men had almost shot an ROK general who seemed to be wandering around lost. When he was brought to the CP, Kingston learned that he was General Choi. The battalion fed the general and the two aides with him and arranged to get them connected with KMAG people. Kingston said that Choi appeared to be totally despondent and disoriented.[2]

The first head counts revealed mind-numbing casualty figures. Of course, the term *casualty* includes wounded, injured, and missing in action, as well as killed in action, and many of the men listed as missing from two South Korean divisions eventually found their way back to friendly lines. For most of the ROK 8th Division, however, there had been no escape from the encircling Chinese, and the bulk of that division's posted losses would not be mitigated later by rounding up stragglers. Exactly how many of the 8th Division's losses were killed or captured was never known.

The special report by the 38th Infantry on the Hoengsong action listed its casualties for the three days at 25 killed in action (KIA), 185 wounded (WIA), and 724 missing in action (MIA). The assumption that most of the MIAs became prisoners of war was dispelled in early March when the U.S. Marines reoccupied the area above Hoengsong. The carnage that they saw led them to dub the road north of Hoengsong "Massacre Valley." The 2d Division formed

Table 1   Casualties by Major Units, 11–13 February 1951

Unit	Total
ROK	
3d Division	1,238
5th Division	1,141
8th Division	7,465
Total ROK casualties	9,844
U.S. and UN	
2d Infantry Division	1,769
7th Infantry Division	190
187th Airborne RCT	59
Total U.S. and UN casualties	2,018
Total Allied Casualties	11,862

Source: Mossman, *Ebb and Flow*, 279.

a salvage and recovery team that accompanied the Marines to recover bodies and equipment. During the period 3–12 March, this team recovered more than 250 bodies. All had frozen and were in good condition for identification except for a few that had been burned or crushed by tanks. Mortar fragments had killed a number of the men, but most bodies had multiple bullet wounds.[3] After the war was over and an accounting for most missing men was made, the 38th Infantry's death toll for those three days stood at 468 men— 255 who were killed outright and 213 who died in captivity. The artillery units suffered equally. The 15th Artillery battalion had 83 killed outright and 128 more who died as communist prisoners. The single battery of the 503d Artillery had a total of 56 dead, and the gallant D Battery of the 82d Artillery lost 34 dead.[4]

The tally of equipment losses was correspondingly heavy. ROK units lost 27 105-mm howitzers, 901 other crew-served weapons, and 88 vehicles. They lost 390 radios, ranging from platoon hand-held radios to the big vehicle-mounted sets.

American equipment losses, almost as high, included 6 tanks and 280 other vehicles, many of them with mounted radios. There were 195 radios left behind, as well as two small items almost unnoticed in the tabulation of lost equipment. These were M-209 converters, a field encoding machine that permitted transmission of classified messages between units. Also lost were 14 105-mm howitzers and 6 155-mm howitzers.[5]

The abandonment of the big howitzers enraged Ridgway. He initially considered the high equipment losses to be evidence of weak leadership. In a message to Almond on 13 February, Ridgway wrote, "While there is nothing sacrosanct about a piece of artillery, compared to the loss of the lives of men, I don't expect to hear again of such loss as reported to me this morning of five 155 Hows of Battery A, 503rd. It is prima facie indication of faulty leadership of serious import in some echelon." In addition to sending the message, Ridgway instructed his inspector general to investigate "all the circumstances attending the loss by X Corps artillery pieces and other major items of equipment on or about 12 February 1951."[6]

Alarmed by the Ridgway rebuke and hastening to ensure that his echelon of command remained blameless for the debacle, Almond ordered General Ruffner, 2d Division commander, to conduct an immediate investigation. His message to Ruffner revealed Almond's belief that most of the casualties and losses occurred because Support Force 21 had paused at the Saemal perimeter after running the gauntlet from Ch'angbong-ni during the night. Almond concluded his directive to Ruffner by declaring that until he received Ruffner's report, the Corps commander presumed that "aggressive leadership on the part of commanders concerned was lacking." In a preliminary response to Ridgway, Almond expressed similar sentiments, stating that "in only one instance, now under investigation, have I found loss of U.S. equipment due to faulty leadership, and all the facts on this are not evident yet." Almond also wanted to dispel any suspicions that Ridgway might still harbor about his command and control arrangements. He also wrote, "The operation, as conceived and coordinated, included the protection of the U.S. Artillery units involved and was, in my opinion, all that could be desired. It worked out as planned except for two battalions of infantry and one of artillery which became enmeshed in the onslaught of Chinese who poured through the ROK formations. There has never been any loss of control of the major units."[7]

X Corps eventually produced an after action report on Hoengsong, with the staff officers who authored it being careful not to imply that command and control problems might have resulted in the loss of men and equipment. Indeed, General Almond wrote a foreword for the special report, part of which read:

> It is my desire that each tactical unit commander in X Corps study this account with the purpose of avoiding the errors and profiting from the successes revealed.
>
> The fundamental principles highlighted by this incident are self-evident yet I wish to reiterate them:
>
> a. We must hold the commanding ground before passing vehicles and equipment through a defile.
>
> b. Our losses in combat against the enemy are less when we form a tight, integrated perimeter than when we attempt to march over routes covered by his fire.
>
> c. The senior combat commander present when emergency conditions arise must aggressively assume command of all troops in his vicinity and vigorously employ all means—air, artillery, armor as well as infantry to annihilate the enemy surrounding our forces. He must report to his higher commander what he has done and what he requires to accomplish his objective.
>
> d. Each commander must retain or be assured there is available a force sufficient to extricate any element of his command that becomes surrounded."[8]

This document must have infuriated everyone in the 38th Infantry from Colonel Coughlin on down. Coughlin told historian Appleman in an interview in December 1951 that Almond blamed him for not taking command of the troops in the Hoengsong area, when it became apparent there was an impending disaster, because he was the senior American officer there. Appleman commented that in the command structure that had been set up, which bypassed Colonel

Coughlin completely, this was an odd charge to make and one which Coughlin resented at the time.[9]

General Stewart, as assistant commander of the 2d Division, was tagged by Ruffner to conduct the investigation. Stewart protested the assignment: "I was amazed, angry and dumbfounded. I was being ordered to investigate the actions of my corps commander. I protested to no avail. I assembled all the orders we had received taking units from our control. I took testimony from officers who had been in the thick of things, but I absolutely refused to place these brave and exhausted men under oath."[10]

If Ruffner and Almond thought that Stewart would merely rubber-stamp a condemnation of Colonel Keith's leadership, they were mistaken. Stewart, a gutsy officer, was not afraid to rock the boat if it became necessary. He was handicapped in the initial stages of the investigation in that he was also charged by X Corps to conduct the defense of Wonju. Lt. Col. Herman C. Duvall, the division inspector general, assisted Stewart with his inquiry and probably carried the heaviest investigative load. A member of the Eighth Army Inspector General section also sat in as a member of the investigating panel. Stewart and his surrogates conducted a thorough investigation. They interviewed all surviving principals, as well as men who were not principals but who could shed light on what transpired.

Five days after receiving his charge, Stewart signed off on a report to Almond and immediately laid to rest any suggestion that Keith was somehow to blame for the debacle. The Eighth Army Inspector General concurred in Stewart's conclusions and recommendations.

In his report, Stewart declared that "there had been only strong, courageous and aggressive leadership at all levels." He pointed out that Keith had withdrawn from Ch'angbong-ni as soon as he was cleared to do so. He wrote that Keith had not yet received orders to proceed to Hoengsong when he stopped and joined the 3d Battalion, 38th Infantry, and had made every effort to reach Hoengsong as soon as such orders reached him. The cause of the losses in equipment and personnel among 2d Division units, General Stewart continued in his letter, was "the sudden and complete defeat of the ROK 8th Division with little or no warning to the 2d Division forces." Stewart was emphatic in his recommendation that there never be a similar intermingling of U.S. and South Korean units in the future. All of the 2d Division personnel were particularly critical of a command and control arrangement that put American units under South Korean command.[11] Placing this recommendation in his report was, in effect, a slap in the face to Almond because Operation Roundup had been his brainchild.

The true magnitude of the Hoengsong disaster was never fully reported in the media. At first, the news was deliberately suppressed by the Eighth Army's newly arrived public information officer, Lt. Col. James T. Quirk, who had been a PIO for Generals Omar N. Bradley and George S. Patton in the European theater during World War II. With his consent, Quirk was recalled to active duty from a position with the *Philadelphia Inquirer*. When the Marines found the bodies north of Hoengsong and dubbed the area "Massacre Valley," an abundance of reporters covering the Marine advance north of Hoengsong witnessed the discovery of the American bodies strewn along the roadway for several miles. The news stories about the debacle that had occurred three weeks previously made headlines in the United States, including a full-page story in *Time* magazine. The only thing that mitigated the revelations was that the Eighth Army was advancing; the bad news was old news, and the fresh news was good news. Moreover, in those days, reporters tended not to salivate over the hint of a cover-up. In a statement to Ridgway, Quirk wrote: "In my original anxiety to protect the reputation of the 2d Division, I made the mistake of giving out no information."[12]

Owing to the speed with which the unfavorable news moved off the front pages, Quirk was able to take sole blame for the cover-up. Anyone familiar with Army public information procedures, however, would seriously doubt that a lieutenant colonel in a field army headquarters would take it upon himself to suppress information of that magnitude, or, if he did and his actions caused embarrassment to a three-star commander, that he would be around the headquarters long enough to write a letter of regret. Moreover, because reporters present in X Corps covered Operation Roundup, a finger of suspicion also could be pointed at the Eighth Army censor.

The entire concept of Operation Roundup was fundamentally flawed. Ridgway understood this and commented on it years later during an oral history debrief at the U.S. Army Military History Institute: "The Roundup offensive showed good initiative, good originality, boldness and all that." Ridgway, however, cited the operation as one example of how Almond was apt to undertake "a very risky operation that might jeopardize his command."[13]

Gen. Paik Sun Yup was even more critical of Almond. He wrote:

> On the negative side, the severe losses suffered by Almond's ROK Army divisions in the Chinese Fourth Offensive raised a question about his ability to command. Why did he position Korean units at the vanguard of the attack when this was not done elsewhere?
>
> One cannot help but wonder whether Almond implemented his otherwise inexplicable strategy solely to allow the Korean units to absorb the initial force of the expected Chinese attack. I cannot rule out this possibility.[14]

In his book, Paik also pointed out that the statistics compiled by the Americans on South Korean losses invariably were inflated because the Americans failed to allow for the fact that many Korean officers and men "missing in action" were merely scattered in battle and would eventually find their way back to their units.[15]

This was also true for some Americans who were carried on morning reports as missing in action. Chinese practices in handling prisoners varied. In some cases, the Chinese shot prisoners, but they were in the minority compared with the North Koreans' treatment of American prisoners. At other times, the Chinese stripped their prisoners of valuables, gave them safe conduct passes, and sent them on their way south.

In addition, some Americans who realized that they were not going to be released became determined not to spend the war in captivity. Two such men were M.Sgt Jack Anderson and 2d Lt. Wilbur Webster. Although their experiences were different, there were similarities.

When Webster was captured near the bridge at Haktam-ni, he was taken to an assembly area containing a number of American prisoners. The Chinese separated the wounded and the nonwounded and marched the able-bodied prisoners north to a prison camp. Webster remained behind in a group of twenty-nine enlisted men and two other officers. Capt. Carroll D. Harrod, who had been wounded in the left shoulder by shrapnel, was an artillery forward observer team leader from the 7th Division's 49th Field Artillery Battalion who had been working with the ROK 21st Regiment. The other officer was 2d Lt. Roy T. Byrd of B Company, 38th Infantry. Byrd was further separated from the group and spent the war in captivity.

Webster said that the Chinese intended to release the enlisted men and handed out safe conduct passes. "I got in line and so did Harrod and got a pass and we were going to try to slip out with the men. But the Chinese made sure there were three officers standing in a group away from the men. But I kept my safe conduct pass."

The Chinese did not waste able-bodied men to guard wounded prisoners. Webster said that the wounded Chinese evacuated themselves. If they could survive the trek to Manchuria, their war was over.

"We were put in with this group of Chinese wounded," Webster said, "who told us they were headed for Manchuria and were taking us with them. On the 6th or 7th of March, we were in Hongch'ong. When we got there about 2 or 3 o'clock in the morning, it showed very little war damage. By 4 that afternoon, it was completely leveled. The target, we learned later, was a major communist base underground in a park near the center of town. And that park was about 200 yards from where we were."

Webster said that his Chinese captors were anxious to get away from a place that drew such attention. Harrod, who wore glasses but was "blind as a bat without them, especially at night," had to walk at night by holding on to Webster's coat or arm. All along, they both had talked about escaping. When the Chinese escorts moved out that night, Webster told Harrod that if they were ever to get away, this was the night to do it.

"We got away by just walking slower than them and, they just went off and left us. We took our insignia off, buried them, and hid our identification cards in our boots. Both of us had been enlisted at one time and both of us had pictures in our wallets with our stripes on. So we went back down the road, posing as wounded enlisted men that had been in a Chinese hospital farther north and given a safe conduct pass and told to go to an American hospital. We didn't evade or hide or anything," Webster said.

For a scary thirty-six hours, he and Harrod underwent an interrogation at a North Korean headquarters, but, at the end, they were permitted to keep moving south. In fact, they were heading southwest down Route 24 toward Chip'yong-ni. Webster remembered that they walked down the road at night and were stopped quite often, but he could speak a passable Japanese and both he and Harrod had picked up enough Chinese words so that they could communicate. On the morning of the day that they were to be liberated, they knew they were close to the Allied lines. Until 4 A.M., Chinese had been moving north in a column of fours.

"Then, all at once, we ran out of them," Webster said. "And at about 7:30 an artillery observer plane flew over and we tried to attract his attention. We sure did because the next thing we got was a registration round. My favorite hidey hole was a culvert under the road and I found one and dove in and the next thing that happened was a fire for effect. Every time we moved in the daytime, we got bombed or strafed and now we got hit with artillery."

They found a village a little way down the road and went in there. A Korean brought them some food and watched over them while they slept. Their rescue was a dicey affair. Four tanks came up the road, and an enemy delaying force fired at them. The tanks retaliated by firing at the buildings in the village.

"A .50-caliber machine gun stitched the wall about three feet above us," Webster said. "Then the tanks started turning around, one by one. While the third one was turning, I told Harrod, 'If we're going to make it, now's the time.' I didn't know if I was going to get shot or not, but I ran out of the building and was waving my trigger-finger mitten and hollering at them. The tank commander yelled at me to come on. I went back and got Harrod and we got in the tanks."

The American unit was from the 7th Cavalry Regiment of the 1st Cavalry Division. Webster continued a career in the Army. Later, he was instrumental in efforts to have a monument placed and dedicated near Ch'angbong-ni that memorializes the dead of those terrible two nights in February 1951.[16]

When Anderson was captured, he had just been shot in the jaw while he and the S-2 sergeant, M.Sgt. Guenther A. ("Gunner Burr") Burrer, had been assaulting a Chinese machine gun and the machine gun had temporarily won. The remainder of the headquarters force eliminated the gun but not before Anderson and Burrer were taken prisoners. In his memoirs, Anderson indicates that they were moved away from the battle area by line soldiers who were pretty happy to get out of the attacking and being attacked business: "They did not hurry us much and, at one point, let us stop so Burr could work on my neck to try to stop the bleeding. This was unsuccessful, but it was much better than before. The problem was that, to stop the blood flow, he had to put so much pressure on my neck that I couldn't breath."

As the group moved north from the battle area, the guards picked up more prisoners and then joined a larger group until there were about seventy or eighty Americans, many of whom were not wounded. Just south of Ch'angbong-ni, the prisoners were herded off the road and merged with another group of men. Anderson said that their original six guards had shaken down the first prisoners for anything of value. They called this an "involuntary donation to the Chinese People's Liberation Army." Anderson had made a point of concealing his wedding ring, and it escaped becoming a contribution.

The Chinese segregated the NCOs, about thirty in all, and began an interrogation process. Anderson said that, obviously, the lower one's position, the less he would be expected to know. So he demoted himself to a platoon sergeant who had just come in as a replacement and did not even know where he was. If the Chinese knew that he was an operations sergeant and had had access to secret materials, they "would have singled me out to work on and I did not want that." He remembered that he learned more from them than they did from him. Because of his head wound, Anderson did a lot of mumbling and thus escaped any kind of serious questioning.

"That evening was the first real opportunity we had to really take a look at my wound," Anderson wrote in his memoirs. "It was still bleeding too much so we got a piece of rag from an old Korean blanket and Burr packed it in the hole at the back of my neck and that stopped it." Anderson said that he looked terrible, but there was no pain; if he had hurt as bad as he must have looked, he was not sure that he could have survived. It was bitterly cold at night but warmed to just about freezing during the day. The advantages of the cold weather were no flies and a low infection potential.

While the group was holed up in a camp, an air attack provided enough distraction for Anderson, Burr, and three more men to get up and start walking south. When they encountered CCF troops, they tried to explain they had been released to go back to UN lines and attempt to persuade UN forces to stop fighting. Anderson recalled that the language barrier was too great, and they were soon back in custody but greatly relieved that they were not shot for making an escape attempt. They resolved to plan better for the next attempt.

They did not have a chance to plan one because a couple of Navy jets came over the next day and dropped napalm on a copse of trees sheltering the Chinese guards. Burr had recruited a South Korean who wore a 2d Division patch on his uniform and had been smart enough to speak only English to his captors. Anderson and his group took advantage of the confusion of the Navy jet attack and headed south again. They decided to capitalize on Chinese propaganda which postulated that ordinary American soldiers were peace loving at heart and more than willing to try to persuade their comrades that the war was unjust. They hastily hatched a story that they had been released to carry a message of peace to other American soldiers. This time, with the Korean explaining their mission of peace, they made pretty good progress.

"We were being congratulated, patted on the back, smiled at and encouraged along the way," Anderson wrote. "We were at a point where we could hear distant firing when some dumb squad leader wouldn't believe us and detailed a couple of his men to return us. They were so happy with their new assignment that we had no chance to do anything but obey. We were returned to the same group we left and no one acted as if we had ever been gone."

The Chinese moved the group to another compound. On 20 February, the prisoners were informed that all able-bodied men would be moved north by foot and those that could not walk would remain where they were and be moved by vehicle later. Anderson recalled that the guards and interrogator spent the day sorting and resorting the prisoners. William E. ("Bill") Mashburn, another master sergeant whom Anderson had known, had been wounded in the foot. Mashburn had made a big deal of his injury by limping and carrying on, and he was tabbed to remain with Anderson and the other wounded.

Burrer was selected to march north. He managed to slip over to the infirm group to tell Anderson and Mashburn good-bye. Burrer, whom Anderson considered "one of the finest soldiers I ever knew," died in captivity on 15 May 1951.

Anderson said that the walking group had hardly left camp before his group's four guards started a fire to cook their daily rice ration. The fire was barely started before the prisoners began planning to escape.

"Escape never left our minds," Anderson wrote. "Bill Mashburn was ready to leave, but in talking about it there were others that wanted to go too. Both of us knew that the larger the group the harder it would be to manage and succeed, but at the same time there was a shortage of leadership, so the two of us did owe something to the group."

Anderson and Mashburn set some stern rules of behavior for the group that had to be obeyed if the men were to survive. The primary rule was that each man had to be able to travel without help and not ask for help. Everyone was wounded and could barely help themselves. The group would travel only at night. Mashburn, who had fought over this ground a couple of times, knew the terrain firsthand, and Anderson, as operations sergeant, knew the area from maps that he had studied. The group would remain holed up during daylight hours. There would be no waiting for stragglers. Each man had to pledge that, if he were to be recaptured, he was not to reveal any information about the other escapees. Both Mashburn and Anderson knew that a total of twenty-eight men was too large a group and the endeavor probably would fail because of it, but they were helpless to change the situation.

It had snowed the day that the groups were split, but the snow changed to rain when the escapees began their trek south. One man had walked only about 1,000 yards when he started yelling for help. The group left him there standing in the snow and screaming curses at them. The men traveled during the nights of 20 and 21 February. During the second night, they saw gangs of coolies pulling American 105-mm howitzers north by hand. They tied several lines to the trails and, chanting as they moved, humped the guns along the road. The group kept going and avoided enemy contact through the next two nights.

On the night of the 24th, Mashburn suggested that the group leave the road and take a trail that cut over a ridgeline and dropped down into the valley of Twinnan-mul, about a mile south of Hoengsong. There, they holed up in an abandoned village. Early the next morning, four or five of the men woke up Anderson and said that the group had talked it over and had decided all of them were going to pull out and make a run for the bridge into Hoengsong. Anderson protested in vain, but they left.

By this time, after days of no food, combined with loss of blood, Anderson was sick and weak, and he went back to sleep. He drifted in and out for some time before he heard footsteps approach and stop beside him. He was sure that it was the Chinese. When he opened his eyes, he saw a pair of dirty combat boots. Pfc Joseph Dorshefski of L Company, 38th Infantry, was standing there.

"We just didn't think bugging out to the bridge was the thing to do so we stayed here with you," Dorshefski said. The "we" included Mashburn.

When Mashburn came into the room, he said that he thought it was a beautiful day to cross the river. Anderson explained that he didn't have the strength to even get to his feet, much less walk the couple of hundred yards to the river and then try to cross. He told them to leave him and save themselves. Neither man heeded Anderson's plea and informed him that the original agreement about not helping each other was off because the other men had bugged out on them.

Anderson recalled, "It must have been just before noon when I decided they were not leaving and I could jeopardize their lives no longer, and we started the trip. Mashburn led out, and I followed at about thirty yards with Joe in the rear. I went down about fifty yards from the river and Bill and Joe rushed to me and hustled me on to the cover of the river bank."

Mashburn and Dorshefski started to make a reconnaissance up and down the bank for a more favorable place to cross when the Chinese took the little group under fire from the ridgelines on their side of the river. Anderson wrote:

> It was a now or never situation. Bill and Joe got under each of my arms and we hit the water. The river was swift and a little less than waist deep. It had pieces of ice swirling in it and I was of no help to either of my supporters. Just as in Exodus 17:11&12 as Aaron and Hur held up Moses' arms to win the battle, so, with Bill under one arm and Joe under the other I would win. If they had dropped me, I would have lost.
>
> In the shape we three were in, the swift freezing water was bad and the gooks shooting their rifles at us from long range made it worse. Then a Marine Corps outpost started shooting at us. With

bullets popping in the water all around, we made the shore and just kept slugging through the mud toward our lines. The Marines decided that if the gooks were shooting at us, then perhaps they shouldn't be and sent a patrol out to pick us up. They helped us into their lines. We were in safe haven on February 24, 1951.[17]

Their timing was fortuitous. The Marines had occupied and secured the south bank of the Twinnan-mul only the day before. Anderson was later to learn that, during his ordeal, a lot of hard fighting had gone on to the south and west of Hoengsong. Altogether too many of his friends and associates were dead or badly wounded.

By dawn on Tuesday, 13 February, General Li's Thirteenth Army Group had pretty much accomplished the missions planned for the first impulse of General Peng's offensive. Although Peng weighted that offensive impulse on the Hongch'on–Hoengsong–Wonju–Ch'ungju axis, he was not planning to neglect the Chip'yong-ni area or the zone to the east of Hoengsong.

Even as the American forces were fighting for survival in Massacre Valley, two other battalions of the 2d Division were unwittingly moving into harm's way. The admonition from Eighth Army to X Corps concerning the Chinese buildup was relayed by X Corps in an extraordinarily casual fashion. There was no tocsin cry in the messages from X Corps, simply a dry statement that there would "be no further movement N & W by the 10th and 16th ROK Regiments until further orders. This message is also for the 2d Div." Twenty minutes later, the 2d Division G-3 sent a message to X Corps with information that the 3d Battalion, 23d Infantry, was maneuvering to take Hill 583. (Actually, the hill number was 539.) The corps G-3 came back immediately with a message that the division would have to cancel that attack. At 2:14 A.M., the division sent a message to the 23d Infantry to explain that the attack was canceled because of a directive from higher headquarters.[1]

The same kind of message was never relayed to the 9th Infantry Regiment, whose 1st Battalion was holding on to Hill 444, about 3,000 yards northwest of Hill 539, where X Corps had canceled the attack. According to plan, the 1st Battalion, 9th Infantry, kicked off an attack on Hill 414 but did not get far in the face of heavy

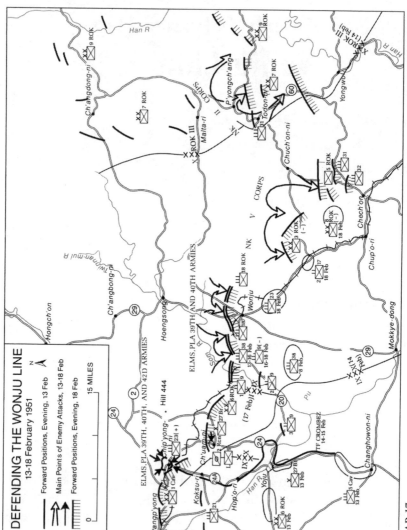

DEFENDING THE WONJU LINE
13–18 February 1951

▬▬ Forward Positions, Evening, 13 Feb
🠉🠉🠉 Main Points of Enemy Attacks, 13–18 Feb
🠉🠉🠉 Forward Positions, Evening, 18 Feb

0 ⊨⊨⊨⊨⊨ 15 MILES

MAP 17

Map based on U.S. Army Military History Map Plate

Chinese fire. The 9th Infantry's commander did not know it, but its 1st Battalion was right in the path of the CCF 116th Division, which intended to move southwest to cut the MSR to Chip'yong-ni. The stalemate existed for most of the day until General Ruffner perhaps realized that he had an infantry battalion hung out like a ripe plum for the Chinese to pluck. At 3:10 P.M., he ordered the battalion to disengage and withdraw to positions west of Wonju along the Wonju–Chip'yong-ni railroad. The record is not clear whether Ruffner, even then, was alarmed by the battalion's exposed position or simply wanted it to move posthaste to become part of the defense at Wonju. At any rate, the battalion was able to break contact and get out within an hour of receiving the order. The 3d Battalion, 23d Infantry, was already back inside the perimeter at Chip'yong-ni. For U.S. forces in the western X Corps zone, that was the extent of Monday's action.

When the 9th Infantry pulled out—its 2d and 3d Battalions already had been ordered into blocking positions near Yoju—Colonel Freeman became distinctly uneasy at Chip'yong-ni. He was now the plum on the tree, and he desperately wanted to get his regiment out of Chip'yong-ni and back to Yoju. Everybody in X Corps agreed with him. Freeman's first inkling that he might not be going anyplace soon came as early as 4 P.M. on 12 February, when the 2d Division G-3 telephoned him with the news: "EUSAK [Eighth United States Army Korea] CG has decided that you stay where you are for now. The other two regiments are pulling back to the south somewhat. I am trying to get this changed as soon as the CG comes back." Freeman's response was that he did not want to pull back that night, but he warned G-3 that, if he got hit, he would need help. "I will have two choices if I am badly pushed; one toward the 24th Div. and the other back to where I was. And if I move it will have to be under an air umbrella if I am hard pushed."[2]

East of Hoengsong, the North Korean Fifth Corps was providing a potent left hook to complement the powerful Chinese thrust down Route 29. Although the NKPA units were understrength, they were still formidable foes. On 11 and 12 February, elements of five NKPA divisions struck at the regiments of the ROK 5th Division and sent them reeling. Left holding the lines to enable the ROK units, along with supporting American artillery, to withdraw to safety were two battalions of the 187th Airborne RCT. The last paratrooper battalion out, the 2d, was briefly surrounded by NKPA forces and had to fight its way out. It lost three killed and forty-five wounded, with most casualties occurring in Fox Company.[3]

The communist offensive stopped briefly in the Hoengsong area to regroup and prepare for the next stage. Here was the great weakness of the Chinese army in Korea. Its lack of transport for tactical moves, as well as logistical support, killed momentum. For UN forces in the central front, which badly needed the respite, the Chinese halt was welcomed.

The town of Wonju became the center of attention in X Corps when Almond, prodded by Ridgway, decided to make its defense the key to the overall defense of the X Corps sector. By mid-February 1951, Wonju was a town in name only. Nearly every building had been leveled during the seesaw battles that had raged through the town since the war began, but buildings were not the prize at Wonju. The following terrain sketch written by the 2d Division historian gives a better picture of why this town was important:

The Korean city of WONJU is a typical communications center for a mountainous country. It lies almost in the east-west geographical center of Korea and in the south end of a valley basin which is approximately eight miles in width. The city itself is comparable to a wheel, it being the hub and the roads being the spokes. Five important roads pass through this city. The WONJU–HOENGSONG ROAD and the WONJU–SAEMAL ROAD (this Saemal is larger than the hamlet by the same name in Massacre Valley and lies about dozen miles east of Hoengsong) run north and northeast respectively, thus forming the avenues of approach from the north. These avenues were dominated by large hill masses to the north and by steep, rocky mountains directly east which ranged in elevation from five hundred ninety seven to one thousand two hundred eighty meters (1,958 to 4,198 feet). Small trees, brush, and undergrowth covered the lower terrain features. To the southeast runs the road to CHECHON. The road to MOKKYE-DONG (and on to Ch'ungju) runs south from Wonju. The mountains east of Wonju also dominated these roads. To the west lay the YOJU-WONJU corridor with its accompanying road. All five roads were primary routes, eighteen to twenty-four feet wide, hard packed earth and gravel and capable of supporting divisional loads.[4]

A critical transportation feature not mentioned in the 2d Division history was the railroad. One of the Seoul–Taegu–Pusan railroad lines ran through Wonju.

A line of low hills, ranging in height from 600 to 700 feet in elevation, were located about 4,000 yards north of the town center and to both west and east of the Hoengsong road and Wonju River. The problem for defenders was that immediately in front of these hills were still higher ridges, particularly on the west side of the river. Defenders at Wonju were confronted with the same dilemma that Freeman faced when he was organizing a defense at Chip'yong-ni. The higher hills around that town were better suited for defense, but he did not have the troops to man them. The most defensible terrain in the Wonju area consisted of the higher ridges south of the town, but defending them would have conceded the railroad and the crossroads to the Chinese. Almond had relieved General McClure for conceding the town in January. Nobody in X Corps was about to concede Wonju in February.

General Stewart, who was ramroding the defense of Wonju by order of General Almond, was not informed of his assignment by his boss, General Ruffner, but by Colonel Chiles, X Corps G-3. In his memoirs, Stewart remembered that he received a lot of advice along with the assignment. Chiles told Stewart: "General Almond directs that you take command of all the troops in the vicinity of Wonju [and] defend and hold that important road junction at all costs. [This violated Ridgway's dictum that "hold at all costs" defenses were discouraged.] The general believes that the Chinese will attack on your right, BUT THE DECISION IS YOURS. The general believes you should place the one intact battalion of the 38th on the line, BUT THE DECISION IS YOURS."[5]

The troops that Stewart had available for the defense of Wonju were the three battalions of the 187th Airborne RCT; the 38th Infantry Regiment with its attached Netherlands Battalion; the 7th Division's 2d Battalion 17th Infantry; 1st Battalion, 9th Infantry; and ROK 18th Regiment. He also had several quad-50s and twin-40s to reinforce his positions, along with a company of tanks from the division's 72d Tank Battalion.

While Stewart, after the fact, might have remembered Almond's advice as worthless, it is instructive to note that he heeded some of it. Most of the commanders from X Corps on down believed that the Chinese would attack the town by following Route 29 south from Hoengsong. Accordingly, Stewart placed two battalions of the 187th astride the road and the Wonju River, which flowed north some 6 miles to merge with the Som River. The 3d Battalion (3/187) had about 3,000 yards of frontage on the line of low hills, roughly 4,000 yards north of the town center and to the west of the road and river. The 1st Battalion (1/187) was assigned about 3,000 yards of frontage on similar-sized hills on the east side of the road. The ROK 18th Regiment, which was attached to the 187th Regiment, occupied good defensive positions for another 3,000 yards to the right of the 1st Battalion.

These were solid positions. Both of the 187th battalions had the late afternoon and the night of 13 February to prepare positions and coordinate final protective fires. Tanks and gun carriages of the 82d Antiaircraft Battalion were situated to cover the road and the river.

Earlier in his career, Stewart had served a tour with the Artillery School at Fort Sill and understood as well as artillery officers the value to a defense of massed artillery. He wrote that, on 13 February, he put heavy pressure on General Haynes, 2d Divarty commander, to prepare data to enable every tube to fire promptly at specific areas on call. Stewart directed that concentrations be registered and identified by numbers on map overlays accompanying defense plans. Haynes complied, albeit reluctantly, but he did provide most of what Stewart demanded.[6]

Haynes had a lot of artillery at his disposal. With the 187th under operational control of the 2d Division, Haynes controlled the airborne 674th Field Artillery Battalion plus the X Corps' 155-mm battalion, the 96th Field Artillery, that had been attached to the 674th. Battery A of the division's organic 155-mm battalion, the 503d, took up positions south of Wonju. Because the 15th Artillery Battalion had been decimated north of Hoengsong, the surviving three tubes from its Charlie Battery were attached to C Battery of the 38th Artillery Battalion, which dropped its trails fairly close to the 503d. The other two batteries of the 38th Artillery were sent about 6 miles to the west in order to provide direct support to the two battalions of the 9th Infantry that were deployed about 8 miles east of Yoju. These two batteries of the 38th could also reinforce the fires of the remainder of the division artillery at Wonju. Altogether, Stewart, through Haynes, could summon the fires of thirty-nine tubes of 105-mm howitzers and twenty tubes of 155-mm howitzers.[7]

The lineup of forces available to defend Wonju on the face of it appeared formidable. However, they were much less than met the eye. The 1st and 3d Battalions of the 38th Infantry Regiment had been decimated during the ordeal north of Hoengsong. At nightfall on the 13th, a muster in the 3d Battalion (3/38) registered only 200 men or roughly 20 percent of its authorized strength. The 1st Battalion had even fewer men, and it was placed in a position near the artillery well to the rear. The 38th's 2d Battalion, commanded by Lt. Col. James H. Skeldon, had taken some heavy casualties during the battles for Wonju in January. It was nowhere near full strength, with critical shortages of both officers and noncommissioned officers, but it had escaped the carnage of Massacre Valley and represented the only intact battalion in the 38th Infantry. The Netherlands Battalion had pulled together about 400 men by nightfall. Despite the weaknesses of the 3/38 and the Dutch, Stewart directed that they establish positions on the higher ridge in front of the 187th's positions.

Hill 342 was the dominant terrain in the second row of hills north of Wonju. The peak was a little more than 1,000 yards due north of the positions of K Company, 187th, which was holding down the left side of the 3d Battalion line. From that peak, a long ridgeline, running about 2,000 yards from northeast to southwest, descended to another prominent terrain feature, Hill 255. On those 2,000 yards of rugged terrain, plus another 1,000 yards to the southwest of Hill 255, either Stewart or Coughlin placed the 3d Battalion, 38th Infantry—all two hundred men who had survived Massacre Valley. The pitifully understrength outpost on Hill 342 had absolutely no one to its immediate right. To the left of the 3d Battalion, the Netherlands Battalion covered another 2,000 yards of frontage. To the left of the Dutch, after a gap of about 1,000 yards, the 1st Battalion, 9th Infantry, was arrayed in blocking positions for another 3,000 yards.

There is nothing written in either the 2d Division G-3 journal, operating instructions, or the 38th Infantry S-3 journal that indicates the rationale for this bizarre placement of men. When the author was researching this book, all of the principals were dead. There were a couple of small written clues. One was noted in an entry in the 13 February X Corps G-3 journal at 6:45 P.M. It stated that the 2d Battalion, 187th Regiment (2/187), would replace the 3/38 on the ridgeline on 14 February. This begs the question: Why was the 2/187 not placed on the ridgeline immediately? This is where the second clue might be useful. In his memoirs, Stewart wrote: "A study of the map convinced me that the attack would come on our left, and I kept the one intact battalion of the 38th in reserve."[8]

Stewart did, in fact, disregard Almond's advice about placing the 2/38 on line and kept it coiled in reserve so that it could react to pressure on the left flank. Because commanders and staff at Division and Corps Headquarters believed that the Chinese attack would come down Route 29 from Hoengsong, the strength of the defense was in that sector, and the positions of the 3/38 and the Dutch appear to have been more of an outpost line than a solid defensive line. Stewart kept the 2/187 in reserve positions where the battalion could react quickly to any penetrations of the main line of defense on the right. Stewart also had Colonel Baker's 2/17 Infantry in a reserve posture south of the ROK 18th Regiment.

The defense posture of Wonju was as good as it could get against what commanders believed would be a conventional attack. Unfortunately, Americans had not yet fully comprehended that the tactics of the Chinese People's Liberation Army were far from conventional. Ever since the Chinese had entered the war, the number of times that they had attacked down a road into an established position could be counted on one hand. The CCF consistently had shown it preferred ridgelines and hilltops to roads and valleys. The Chinese high command did not believe it necessary to make a bloody assault on Wonju when, with a repetition of its "fix and flank" tactics, the town soon would be abandoned by Americans seeking to escape the jaws of yet another encirclement. To this end, once darkness had fallen, six CCF regiments started south from Hoengsong along the valley of the Som River. The Som paralleled Route 29 from Hoengsong to a point about four miles north of Wonju, where it doubled back on itself, flowed north for about 1½ miles, and then began a twisting, turning path to the west and then southwest to where it eventually flowed into the Han River south of Yoju.

At about midnight, the 360th Regiment of the CCF 120th Division split off from the main body at the point where the Som doubled back on itself, crossed the river, and headed overland toward Hill 342, which was manned by only a handful of bone-weary and badly shaken 38th Infantry soldiers. The other five CCF regiments continued along the twisting Som Valley.

West of Wonju, most of the CCF 116th Division had already reached Route 24, the MSR from Yoju to Chip'yong-ni. Two battalions had been diverted to deal with the positions of the U.S. 2d Division's Reconnaissance Company and its reinforcing L Company, 9th Infantry. These two units occupied a small crossroads at

Ch'uam-ni, about 6 air miles south of Chip'yong-ni. The CCF 115th Division, also of the Thirty-Ninth Field Army, slipped around to the south of the Chip'yong-ni perimeter and dropped off a regiment on Mangmi-san, Hill 397, which was due south of G Company, 23d Infantry, positions on the perimeter. The other two regiments continued on to Koksu-ri, a 24th Infantry Division outpost on Route 24-A, the alternate route into Chip'yong-ni. The Chinese, almost as casually as swatting a fly, pushed the American outpost away from the road.

Their thinking still rooted in conventional tactics, the American leaders were oblivious to the real threat. On the afternoon of 13 February, Almond visited Freeman in the perimeter. In a subsequent telephone message to the 2d Division G-3, Freeman said, "The CG of X Corps was here and asked for my recommendation on when I could move back to Yoju. I told him in the morning. I have changed my recommendation to as early as possible this evening, due to conditions of 2d Recon and around my area." The G-3 acknowledged the message and told Freeman that the CG of X Corps would have to get the answer from the CG of Eighth Army.[9]

Ridgway had, in effect, already given his answer. On 13 February, he issued a commander's concept that directed Eighth Army units to take the following steps:

a. X Corps to hold the shoulders of the Chinese penetration. This includes making the strongest possible stand at Wonju and for Freeman's 23d RCT to stay put at Chip'yong-ni. If Wonju could not be held, the Wonju defenders would be withdrawn southeast to Chech'on, joining the 7th Division. The combined forces there would then be in a position to attack the left flank of the CCF salient.

b. The British Commonwealth Brigade would pass from IX Corps to X Corps control and advance north on the Yoju–Chip'yong-ni road. The ROK 6th Division would replace the Commonwealth Brigade for the security of Yoju. Col. Ed Messinger's two battalions of the 9th Infantry would also advance toward Chip'yong-ni. Should Wonju fall, the 9th Infantry would fall back to Munmang-ni, east of Yoju.

c. The 1st Marine Division, in the process of moving from Andong to replace the 24th Division in IX Corps, in accordance with an earlier plan, would be diverted to prepare strong defensive positions at Ch'ungju.

d. The 1st Cavalry Division, on the left flank of IX Corps, would be replaced by the 25th Division from I Corps and repositioned near Yoju where it could join with the 24th Division in an attack on the Chinese salient.[10]

Despite all of the enemy activity in and around Chip'yong-ni, the infantrymen of the 23d RCT had not dug in that well, according to historian Roy Appleman, who walked the perimeter when he visited the battle site in August 1951. He said that he saw very few real foxholes, although the artillery had done a much better job of getting their guns dug in.[11]

What seemed like a conflicting report was published by Army historian Russell A. Gugeler quoting Capt. Edward C. Williamson, who visited Chip'yong-ni immediately after the battle. Gugeler wrote that "Col. Edwards (2/23 commander) supervised the siting of all weapons, and the digging of the holes which he insisted be of the standing type and deep enough for good cover."[12]

A report corroborating Appleman came from Sherman W. Pratt, in his 1992 book, *Decisive Battles of the Korean War*. Pratt, then a captain commanding Company B, the reserve company, walked the entire perimeter accompanied by his platoon leaders on 13 February. He said that he and his lieutenants made notes at each company's position in the event that they might be called on to occupy them. At the conclusion of his inspection, Pratt was debriefed by a regimental staff officer. He reported that he did not like the depth of the troops' dugouts. "Many are barely below the surface," Pratt said, adding that "many of the individual positions are too far forward and exposed."[13]

Nevertheless, aside from personal protection positions, where different commanders established different standards, the defenses at Chip'yong-ni were as good as any regimental-sized perimeter had ever been in the Korean War. Still, there was a strong desire on the part of Freeman, the 2d Division, and X Corps to get the 23d RCT back to safer ground.

Commanders and staff officers at the 2d Division and X Corps were still unaware of the true nature of the Chinese threat. The 2d Division G-3 journal had a final comment in its summary of Tuesday's (13 February) activities: It appears that the enemy was determined to drive RCT 23 from their defensive positions, as this regiment presented a constant threat to the right flank of that enemy force attacking in the Wonju sector.

The X Corps G-2 Periodic Intelligence Report for the same day expressed similar opinions: "The Chip'yong-ni salient is a thorn in the side of the enemy, and it is expected that he will soon attempt to remove this irritation with the forces available to him in that immediate area."

By nightfall on Tuesday, Chinese fire blocks were established on both roads leading from the 23d Infantry's perimeter. The traps were set; all that was needed was the prey.

At 10:00 P.M., the Chinese began to goad the defenders of the perimeter to abandon their positions and flee to the south. Heavy and extremely accurate mortar fire began falling on the Chip'yong-ni perimeter, along with fire from 75-mm pack howitzers and Soviet-built 76-mm field guns. Probing attacks on the perimeter began just before midnight. These attacks intensified during the night.

Since October, the Chinese Army, the so-called People's Volunteer Army, had had everything go its way. After the rout of UN forces north and east of Hoengsong, the CCF leadership had every reason to believe that the Americans would continue to run. The Chinese anticipated that the next day, Wednesday, 14 February—Valentine's Day in America—would be a day of decision for the CCF. What Generals Peng and Li and all of the commanders in the Thirteenth Army Group could not know was that the next two days would be to the Chinese what day three at Gettysburg had been to the Confederate Army.

SEVENTEEN | First Fight at Chip'yong-ni

At the beginning of the CCF Third Offensive on 31 December, General Peng was convinced that the Americans would need a miracle to avoid another crushing defeat.[1] The Americans received their miracle when Matthew Ridgway assumed command of the Eighth Army and managed a controlled withdrawal instead of the pell-mell retreat envisioned by the Chinese. Nevertheless, well into the Fourth Offensive, with the unbroken streak of CCF successes, Peng and his generals still likely believed that the Americans would need more miracles to avert another crushing defeat. But, being practicing atheists and communists, they could not admit belief in miracles or other unexplainable inauspicious events.

Peng certainly would not have believed that Ridgway's arrival in Korea was the first piece of Chinese bad luck. Although Ridgway had been forced to relinquish Seoul again, he rallied his troops and began inculcating a fighting spirit in his Eighth Army. Ridgway would have been the first to scoff at any kind of miracle talk, but the fact remained that the Eighth Army, in an astonishingly short time, had been turned around from a defeated rabble to a formidable fighting force.

Ridgway was also a smart general who, while conducting a retreat at the outset of the CCF Fourth Phase Offensive, was concurrently planning to retake the offensive. He needed Chip'yong-ni as a springboard for future attacks north, and the Chinese experienced their next piece of bad luck at this vital crossroads town. The Chip'-yong-ni garrison was going to stand and fight and would not be running any Chinese gauntlets.

Starting on the afternoon of 13 February and continuing into the evening, troops manning the perimeter at Chip'yong-ni could see signal flares in the distance. There was no doubt in any soldier's mind that the Chinese attack would come that night.

The town of Chip'yong-ni was, like Wonju, a road hub and a railroad town. It was elongated along the axis of the railroad. The roads through the town from the east were the road from Hoengsong and Route 24, which ran northeast from the twin tunnels. These two roads joined just east of the town. Route 24-A, which ran from the south from Yoju through Koksu-ri, entered the western third of the village and terminated at its juncture with Route 24 in town. The combined routes then continued north. The road to Yang-p'yong exited the town on the west. The town also straddled a stream in the lower end of the small valley overlooked by mountain masses. On the northeast was Pongmi-san, Hill 348, and on the south was Mangmi-san, Hill 397, the latter to play a critical role in the fights at Chip'yong-ni.

Freeman had deployed his 1st Battalion on the northern arc of the perimeter, the 3d Battalion on the east, the 2d Battalion on the south, and the French Battalion on the west. The inevitable gaps in the perimeter were mined, blocked by wire entanglements, and covered with fire. The tanks and the gun carriages bearing the quad-50s and twin-40s were carefully sited to add their direct fire to the defense. Indirect fire was provided by the 37th Field Artillery Battalion, the organic 105-mm howitzer outfit, and a battery of 155-mm howitzers provided by B Battery, 503d Artillery, the segregated unit assigned to the 2d Division. These weapons supplemented the organic fires of the regiment, the regimental 4.2-inch mortars, the 81-mm mortars of the battalions, and the 60-mm mortars in each rifle company. As a regimental reserve, Freeman earmarked B Company and the division Ranger Company.[2]

Also, Freeman established daylight positions in front of his main defenses. In remembering the preparations of the perimeter, he said, "We thinly held these outlying hills in the daytime and then would fall back into our main defensive positions under cover of

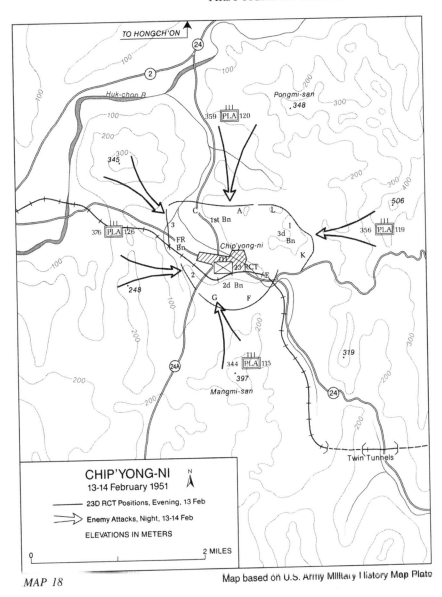

TO HONGCH'ON

Huk-chon R

Pongmi-san
.348

359 PLA 120

345

376 PLA 126

506

C   A   L
1st Bn   I
3   3d
FR   Bn   Bn
Bn
Chip'yong-ni   K
23 RCT
2   E
248   2d Bn

G   F

356 PLA 119

319

344 PLA 115
.397
Mangmi-san

Twin Tunnels

CHIP'YONG-NI
13-14 February 1951

——— 23D RCT Positions, Evening, 13 Feb

⟹ Enemy Attacks, Night, 13-14 Feb

ELEVATIONS IN METERS

0   2 MILES

MAP 18   Map based on U.S. Army Military History Map Plate

darkness, which we did very well, I thought. We patrolled extensively and we tried to give the impression that we were a much stronger force than just a regimental combat team." Freeman used his time in Chip'yong-ni to bring in supplies. "In fact," he said, "we had more ammunition on position than we ever had in Korea and I was apprehensive that if we had ever left there without a fight I might have gotten myself into trouble for hoarding all this ammunition. But it had seemed in the past that we never had enough and, as it turned out in this case, we didn't have enough."[3]

All day on the 13th, Freeman kept enemy formations approaching his position under artillery fire and air attacks. Since it seemed apparent that his MSR had been cut, Freeman asked division headquarters to schedule an airdrop of food, ammunition, signal, and medical items on the following day. After dark and after the daytime positions had been booby-trapped and abandoned, the defenders saw signal flares in the distance all around Chip'yong-ni. Freeman said that the Chinese first attacked the daylight positions and, in the confusion of exploding booby traps, ended up fighting among themselves. Besides being booby-trapped, the positions were targeted for part of the defensive fires of the indirect fire weapons on the perimeter.

The first infantry contact was made just after 10 P.M., when mortar and automatic weapons fire struck at the C Company positions on the north side of the perimeter. Charlie Company's positions were astride the valley containing Route 24 and the lower elevations of Hill 348. Accurate enemy artillery and mortar fire struck key locations within the perimeter, the artillery, and mortar positions and the regimental command post, as well as the defenses along the outer perimeter.

The men, fully alert, waited for the inevitable cacophony of whistles, horns, and bugles. The sounds came at 11:30 P.M. at the C Company positions. Minutes later, on the south, an attack was aimed at the George Company positions. They were followed by attacks at two locations in the French sector on the west and at the juncture between I and K Companies in the 3d Battalion area on the west. The extremely tight perimeter thwarted the Chinese "fix and flow to the flanks" tactics, and the attacks subsided within an hour. The only major damage at that point was the burning 1st Battalion command post and a damaged M-16 (quad-50) half-track on the southeast part of the perimeter.

The lull lasted until an hour past midnight. Then, the Chinese launched more attacks, this time from the north and northwest. At 2 A.M., a platoon-sized unit of Chinese formed up about 100 yards in front of the French 2d Company's position. With bugles, whistles, horns, and fixed bayonets, they started running hard toward the French position. The French began cranking a hand siren, and a squad, screaming battle cries and throwing hand grenades to the front and side, jumped and ran toward the Chinese. When the two forces were within 20 yards of each other, the Chinese suddenly turned and and ran even harder in the opposite direction. The French counterattack brought calm to this sector.[4]

The CCF continued hammering the Chip'yong-ni perimeter in other sectors. It launched an assault against the French 3d Company on the northwest sector of the perimeter but had great difficulty penetrating the protective wire in front of the defensive positions that the French covered with grazing machine-gun fire. Soldiers in K Company beat away another determined attack in the early morning darkness. The heaviest assault fell again on G Company's position on the south perimeter. From Hill 397, just 1,200 yards from G Company, a long ridgeline nosed right into the heart of the company's positions. It provided the best approach route for the attacking Chinese and they tried hard to capitalize on it during the early morning hours of 14 February. The ridge terminated close to where G Company's 3d Platoon was dug in. Platoon leader Lt. Paul J. McGee, in order to conserve ammunition, cautioned his men to fire only when there was a target.

When one of his squad leaders was wounded by a grenade, he cried out the name of his platoon leader: "Lieutenant McGee, I'm hit."

Not long afterward, McGee was closely watching some dark forms down the slope. He heard his name being called.

"Who is that?" he asked a BAR man beside him.

"It's a Chink," the BAR gunner responded.

McGee tossed a grenade down the hill and wounded the enemy soldier, who rolled down the slope. McGee borrowed the BAR and killed him. The Chinese troops made four unsuccessful runs at

McGee's position before breaking contact and moving back onto the hill.

The boundary between G Company and the French Battalion was the road that entered the perimeter from the south (Route 24-A), cutting through a low hill in the process. Responsibility for the security of the road cut itself was that of the 503d Artillery, which placed two .50-caliber machine guns there. Once the firing started, one of the artillery officers, Lt. John E. Travis, and his machine-gun section leader, Cpl. William H. Pope, grabbed several boxes of ammunition and headed for the road cut. The rice paddies in front of the position were covered with snow. On previous nights when Travis had checked the position, the area had been smooth and white, but now, when illuminating flares lit the area, he could see lines of dark forms crossing the frozen rice paddies. The Chinese had pinpointed the heavy machine guns firing at them for counter-fire. Shortly after Travis and Pope arrived at the outpost, a mortar round crashed into the road cut. It killed two men next to Travis and wounded six, including Travis and Pope. Travis hastened back to the battery's fire direction tent and yelled for some men to help. Capt. John Elledge, the Divarty liaison officer, gathered up ten men and told them to follow him. Mortars were now falling in the battery area, and five men dropped out and scooted back to their holes.

When Elledge and the five remaining men reached the cut, they discovered that one of the machine guns was jamming, so Elledge and Pfc. Leslie Alston returned for another gun and carried one of the wounded men back with them. Then, they made several more trips between the road cut and the battery's positions to carry out ammunition and to bring wounded men back.[5]

Because the battery was in the Second Battalion area, they were evacuated to the battalion aid station where Dr. (Lt.) Roland J. Kohen performed field medicine. All battalion surgeons did this, of course, but Dr. Kohen was unique in that he was a Navy doctor. He said that he had been in training for his specialty when he suddenly received orders that the Navy Department was loaning him to the Army. This was right after the debacle in November when aid stations throughout the 2d Division had been overrun and doctors and medics had been wounded, killed, or captured. Kohen said that, within three weeks of receiving his orders and without any field training, he was at the aid station of the 2/23 Infantry. He remembers:

> When we arrived at Chip'yong-ni, we knew we were going to be in for it. I took over an old house for an aid station, and then had our men dig a deep hole and reinforce it, so our team would have a shelter. When darkness fell, so did incoming mortar rounds. The house got shattered. But we had to concentrate on taking care of the wounded. I would treat them and then send them to the regimental collection station for evacuation. But, of course, there was no way out. It was a night of terror. I had received a little wound, it wasn't much. But we were losing so many men and my own men as well. When the dawn came, we were able to take care of more men, but the shelling didn't stop.[6]

With the dawn came one more try by the Chinese on the east side of the perimeter, but the attacks were beaten back by K and I Companies. The enemy made another stab at the French lines in the northwest. Finally, just before 8 A.M., the Chinese broke contact all around the perimeter and retired into the hills surrounding the Chip'yong-ni bastion.

Sometime before midnight, a 120-mm mortar round crashed into the regimental CP area. It mortally wounded Maj. Harold W. Shoemaker, the regimental S-2, and wounded the assistant S-3. The blast blew Lt. Col. Frank Meszar, the regimental executive officer, across the tent that he shared with Colonel Freeman but otherwise did not harm him. A thumb-sized fragment struck Freeman in the left calf. A medic bandaged the wound and opined that a leg bone might be cracked, but Freeman, walking with a limp, continued with his duties.

It did not take long for word of Freeman's wound to reach division headquarters and, from there, X Corps headquarters. The record gets a bit murky at this point. The X Corps Command Report for 14 February states that, during a commander's conference at X Corps Headquarters in the afternoon, General Ruffner asked General Almond to assign his G-3, Lt. Col. John Chiles, to replace the wounded Freeman. Almond agreed, and instructions were given to Chiles to fly into Chip'yong-ni and replace Freeman, who was to be evacuated.[7]

Clay Blair has another version. He wrote that Almond ordered Chiles to fly into Chip'yong-ni without consulting Ruffner. Blair wrote that "many believed that Almond acted too hastily, that it was another instance of placing an X Corps 'teacher's pet' in a job that would lead to a promotion."[8]

Regardless of which version is closest to the truth, there was no mistaking Freeman's reaction. He was incensed and refused to leave when Chiles arrived by light plane on 14 February. General Stewart wrote later that, when Freeman adamantly refused to relinquish his command, Ruffner turned the matter over to Stewart: "I had a long talk with Paul Freeman by radio. Paul said he was being relieved from command while his regiment was in combat, and that was the worst disgrace an officer could suffer; he said he was not going to come out. I finally convinced him that no one questioned his performance and that he would undoubtedly be decorated and promoted. He finally agreed to be evacuated."[9]

But what Freeman said he would do and what he did were two different things. He simply was not going to turn over his command until reinforcements had arrived and his regiment was out of danger. Freeman said that he told Chiles to find a shelter and stay out of the way until his departure.[10]

At X Corps Headquarters, Almond fumed. He had never liked Freeman because the crusty colonel had been vocal in his loyalty to General McClure and not reticent in his criticism of Almond's relief of McClure.[11]

It had been tough going inside the perimeter, but, elsewhere, other 2d Division units were undergoing a nightmare. At 3:30 A.M. on 14 February, elements of the CCF 360th Regiment of the 120th

Division had reached their attack positions north of Wonju. The first assault hit the unprotected right of K Company, 38th Infantry. In less than half an hour, the Chinese had swept the weary and worn soldiers of King Company off Hill 342, the dominant terrain feature at Wonju. The Chinese followed up this initial attack with pressure on the entire left flank. I Company, 38th Infantry, was hit hard and pushed off Hill 255. The Netherlands Battalion was shoved off Hill 325, but the stubborn Dutch stormed right back in a counterattack. At daylight, the issue there still was in doubt. Farther left, C Company, 9th Infantry, reported repulsing Chinese attacks, and the 1st Battalion, 9th Infantry (1/9), reported that its heavy mortar platoon had been ambushed in the gap between the Dutch and the 1/9 Infantry and lost all its equipment. The 2d Battalion, 38th Infantry, was taken out of reserve and, with a platoon of tanks from the 72d Armor, moved 4,500 yards to the west to bolster the relatively weak 9th Infantry defenses on the left flank of the Wonju position. The 2d Battalion, 187th, was alerted to be prepared to move into the gap created by the withdrawal of the 3d Battalion, 38th Infantry.[12]

By 9 A.M., the Chinese controlled the commanding terrain north and northwest of Wonju. The gates to the city were swinging open.

Concurrently, during the early morning hours of 14 February, 7 miles south of Chip'yong-ni at the crossroads village of Chuam-ni, two other 2d Division units were undergoing a nightmare. The 2d Division Reconnaissance (Recon) Company had been screening east of Route 24 when one of its platoon positions was attacked early on Tuesday. The division directed the 9th Regiment to reinforce the Recon Company. The remainder of 2d Recon moved to support its beleaguered platoon and was joined there by Company L, 3d Battalion, 9th Infantry, of the 2d Division. The combined force came under the command of Maj. Harlan C. Stine, the 3d Battalion's executive officer. This force established a defensive position on a road about 2 miles east of Chaum-ni, where it was promptly attacked by elements of the CCF 116th Division. Late Tuesday afternoon, the combined force withdrew to the crossroads at Chuam-ni. The units should have been withdrawn completely, but the 2d Division still believed that the unit could perform a credible job of blocking enemy activities from the crossroads position and could hold out until the British 27th Brigade advanced to its positions. Unfortunately, the British were advancing too slowly on Route 14, and it would take three days for the 27th Brigade to get anywhere near Chuam-ni. That misreading of the tactical situation by 2d Division headquarters would have ghastly consequences.

At about 5 A.M., Wednesday, 14 February, a regiment of the CCF 116th Division, which had surrounded the tiny force, struck the two-company perimeter. The firefight continued until midmorning. 1st Lt. Harvey Land, a platoon leader with the 2d Recon, remembered that, at first, the troops were holding their own: "Then the ammunition began playing out. All the .50-caliber ammo was gone and the mortar shells had been fired. One tank was useless and there was very little .30-caliber ammo left."[13]

Major Stine realized that the outgunned unit could not stay where it was. The survivors would have to run a gauntlet, but there was no other choice. The order was given to pull out. It was an almost impossible task to break hard contact in daylight and conduct a fighting withdrawal, but somehow the little force did it. The CCF, aware that there would be a withdrawal, had prepared a gauntlet. The two companies fought their way south.

Land remembered, "There were Chinese everywhere, firing from ridges on both sides of the road, lying in ditches to shove torpedoes under the passing vehicles. The soldiers at the rear walked backwards, firing as they did."[14]

The Chinese also had blown a bridge about 2 miles south of Chuam-ni. This cost the unit a number of wheeled vehicles that could not get around the obstacle. And, as had happened north of Hoengsong, the men who paid most dearly were the nonambulatory wounded who were abandoned. The casualties were horrendous, with a total of 212. The 2d Division Graves Registration later recovered 114 bodies in the combat area. The commander of 2d Recon, Capt. Antonio L. Baca, was killed. Major Stine was so severely wounded that he was evacuated to the United States. Lieutenant Land escaped without a scratch.[15]

The Chinese claimed in an after action report, captured later, that they had "annihilated" two companies of the 23d Infantry.[16] They had the unit identifications wrong, and this was the last "victory" that the Chinese could claim in the Fourth Offensive.

EIGHTEEN | First Decision at Wonju

Wednesday, 14 February, was Valentine's Day. It had no intrinsic meaning except to those soldiers who kept treasured letters and pictures from wives and sweethearts—creased, folded, wrinkled, and sometimes stained. The day meant absolutely nothing to the Chinese. It should have. For the Chinese, it was the day of three lucks, all of them bad.

Standing in the way of the CCF moving through the swinging gate into Wonju were the paratroopers of the 187th Airborne RCT, the Rakkasans,[1] who believed that the best defense was an aggressive offense. That was the CCF's bad luck number one. By 9 A.M., the weather at Wonju, which had been miserable to that point, cleared and provided good visibility to aerial observers—bad luck number two. Finally, for the first time since the Chinese had entered the war, the Americans had massed artillery—in this case, a whole lot of artillery.

Artillery forward observers went flying Wednesday morning to take advantage of the high, broken cloud cover. Over the Som River, which looped and curved its way through the mountains northwest of Wonju, one observer, Lt. Lee R. Hartell, spotted what looked like a heavy tree line along a sandy beach of the river. After a second look, he and his pilot realized that the "tree line" was moving; a huge column of Chinese marching four abreast and accompanied by pack animals. Hartell and the pilot estimated that the columns were two divisions in strength, approximately 14,000 men, and Hartell immediately called for artillery. The first shot was a white phosphorus marking round, and, from that, Hartell radioed in range and deflection corrections and called for a "fire for effect."[2]

Thanks to General Stewart's foresight and preparation, the artillery at Wonju was able to deliver a tremendous amount of fire. The batteries fired all of their VT-fuzed ammunition first. The VT (variable time) fuze, introduced during the latter part of World War II, was a proximity device that used radio waves to trigger a detonation at a uniform 65 feet above the ground, the optimal height for shrapnel effect on troops in the open. Air bursts also could be obtained by the use of time fuzes, which normally take some adjustment to obtain the correct altitude. At Wonju, it didn't much matter.

Hartell, whose parent organization was the 15th Field Artillery Battalion, gained a measure of revenge for his comrades who had died in the valley north of Hoengsong. Parts of the enemy column had started to peel away from the main body of troops and were headed for the Netherlands Battalion positions. These segments received special attention from the guns.

The 2d Division historian wrote of the event:

> Thunderous barrages roared across the hills as tons of shrapnel poured into the plodding troops. Thousands of shells wrecked havoc never before seen on any army as the pilots reported the river running red with the blood of the massacred troops. Still they came, marching into the rain of death, heedless of the carnage around them as they crawled forward.[3]

The firing continued for three hours. General Haynes called Stewart to inform him that he would have to stop because his ammunition was running low, but Stewart would have none of that; "Keep firing until the last shell has been used." Stewart and Haynes then arranged for an immediate ammunition resupply. As the guns maintained their deadly roar, Haynes called Stewart again and said that his guns were overheating. Stewart's reply: "Keep firing until the gun barrels melt."[4]

Stewart knew instinctively that American forces never again would be presented this kind of target and every Chinese soldier killed along the Som was one less that UN soldiers would have to face later.

The division historian continued his narrative of death:

> Hour after hour the unbelievable slaughter mounted as dog-tired,
> exhausted artillerymen slammed an endless stream of shells into the
> exposed masses of Chinese who continued to press forward. Then
> the staggering losses began to tell. The once-full ranks were now thin,
> blasted, shocked remnants without leaders, without hope. Slowly, as
> though dazed, the remains of the ranks broke. Now only unorganized
> bands of useless bodies, they tried to escape north out of reach
> of the murderous guns. The cracking rain of steel followed them
> northward and the air strikes took up where the artillery could not
> reach.[5]

The four hours of massed artillery fire that is believed to have
killed five thousand Chinese soldiers and wounded thousands more
became legendary among artillerymen as the "Wonju Shoot." In
reference books, it is regarded as "the single most lethal use of
artillery of the Korean War." As a footnote to this event, six months
after the Wonju Shoot, Lieutenant Hartell, while serving as a forward observer on the ground, was killed when he called in artillery
fire on his own position, which was being overrun. He was awarded
the Medal of Honor for his heroism.[6]

The resupply of ammunition and petroleum products by truck
convoys on icy, poorly maintained roads was a slow process. The
artillery needed a quick buildup of depleted stocks. This meant that
the 2d Division turned once again, as it had all during January, to
the Far East Air Force Combat Cargo Command for aerial resupply.
The 314th Troop Carrier Squadron, a C-119 (flying boxcar) outfit
flying out of Ashia Air Force Base in southern Japan, was the principal delivery unit. Members of the 187th Parachute Maintenance
Detachment packed the cargo chutes, rigged the cargo for drop,
and rode the aircraft to the destination as cargo kickers.

Cpl. David V. Carr was a cargo kicker on a C-119 loaded with
artillery ammunition for the Wonju area. His pilot told him on the
flight in from Japan that the artillerymen had been bitching about

the loads being scattered on the drop zone. This time, he wanted to drop them right in their laps. He told Carr that he would swoop into this valley, and, right over the artillery positions, he would pull up, firewall the throttles, and Carr would dump the load. Carr said, "Yes, sir" and went back to the cargo compartment. He rerigged the load so that the four separate pallets would be "daisy-chained." Instead of the static lines of each pallet's chutes being attached to the aircraft, they were attached to the load in front of them. The last pallet out would have the static lines of its four chutes attached to the aircraft. When they opened, the static lines on the next packet of chutes opened and so on. Carr said that the artillerymen gaped with astonishment as the chutes on the last pallet popped just in time to stop the free fall before it hit the ground. Carr said afterward, "They wanted it in their lap, they got it in their lap."[7]

At Wonju during the February battles, Combat Cargo dropped 3,023 tons of cargo, mostly ammunition and gasoline. Over at Chi-p'yong-ni, 400 tons of ammunition were dropped during the three critical days of the battle.[8]

Probably nothing illustrated the vast disparity in the war-fighting capabilities of the two major combatants as did logistics. When UN forces in Wonju needed a resupply of ammunition, it was delivered by air from Japan within hours. The Chinese resupply of large-caliber mortar ammunition from Manchurian bases could take weeks through a convoluted system of rail, truck, and coolie transport that had to dodge marauding American fighter-bombers on the way south.

The Chinese antidote to their enemy's massed artillery and its technology-driven resupply system always had been simplicity itself: put the infantry forces on the run and the artillery will run with them. The CCF regiment on the high ground just outside Wonju was poised to do exactly that even as the Som River ran red with the blood of their comrades. The 2d Battalion, 187th Airborne RCT, had been placed under the 38th Infantry's operational control early that Wednesday morning and given the mission of reoccupying the hills from which the 3/38 had just been driven.

1st Lt. James H. Nix, leader of the 3d Platoon of E Company, remembered the rude awakening from the warm depths of the new mountain sleeping bag that he had just been issued. "It was just a few ticks short of 0500 hours on Valentine's Day," he remembered. "It was cold and dark and we were briefed in almost funeral quality voices. The Chinese had hit the 38th Infantry and overrun their positions by 0400 hours. We were to reoccupy those positions." He said that, while the briefing was conducted, the troopers were fed a hot breakfast and were packing their gear into the appropriate bag. In the 187th, the sleeping bag, extra socks, letters, and one extra fatigue uniform went into the "A" bag, which stayed with the company supply truck. Such gear as a shelter half or poncho, extra boots and underwear, and some ammunition went into the combat pack that stayed with the paratroopers until they actually entered the assault. All other gear was stored in "B" and "C" bags, which, Nix said, nobody had seen since arriving in Korea.[9]

For the troopers of the 2/187, the early part of the day was a case of hurry up and wait. Fox Company originally had been deployed on a ridgeline due west of Wonju and very close in. No one in authority yet had any idea of the nature of the threat or the precise direction from which it was coming. After the 2/38 and the tanks had been deployed farther west to shore up defenses within and to the left of the Netherlands Battalion, the 2/187 was moved by truck and foot to the foot of Hill 255. Its first mission was to take back the territory recently lost by the 38th Infantry.

Fox Company had the initial mission of attacking into the gap between the previous locations of the Netherlands Battalion and I Company, 38th Infantry. The objective was the hamlet of Ch'a-myon-ni, located in a valley between Hill 255 on the northeast and Hill 325 on the southwest. Capt. George E. Pickett IV, the company commander, had an additional mission of providing left-flank security for E Company, which would be assaulting Hill 255. He fulfilled it by detailing his 3d Platoon as a base-of-fire element on a finger running off a ridgeline on Hill 255. The 1st and 2d Platoons started the assault as soon as supporting fires from battalion mortars and

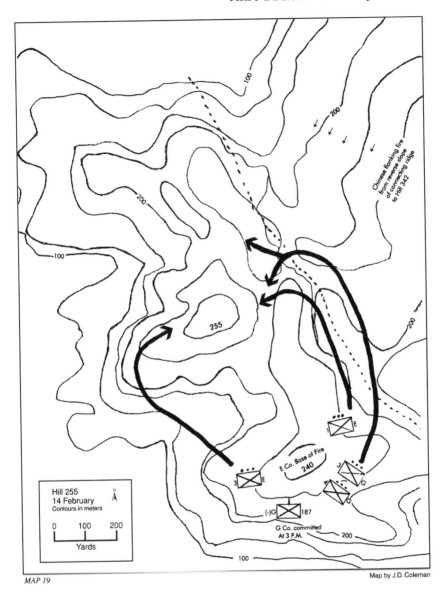

Chinese flanking fire from reverse slope of connecting ridge to Hill 342

255

E Co. Base of Fire
240

Hill 255
14 February
Contours in meters

N

0   100   200

Yards

(-)G   187

G Co. committed
At 3 P.M.

MAP 19

Map by J.D. Coleman

75-mm recoilless rifles lifted. Both platoons were stopped in their tracks by a heavy volume of fire from Chinese positions on high ground just north of the village.

Pickett's assaulting platoons maneuvered to higher ground to the west of the village. This tactic worked, and Fox Company made contact with F Company, 38th Infantry, that was trying to replace the Dutch on Hill 325. The Dutch, having been told they would be relieved by a 38th Infantry unit at 6 A.M., left the hill promptly at that time, while their relieving unit was still enjoying a leisurely breakfast in the valley. The Chinese wasted little time in flowing into the empty holes on the hill. The two F Companies ended up making a tandem but uncoordinated attack on the crest of the hill and its northern ridgelines. The Chinese stubbornly resisted the 38th Infantry unit.

1st Lt. Joel Nyquist, a forward observer from the airborne artillery who had been loaned to the 38th Infantry, was with the lead platoon attacking the crest of 325. He remembered Company F of the 38th as a unit filled with replacements, some of whom still had clothing tags on their field gear. There was only one officer platoon leader. Nyquist said that the company commander, Capt. John H. Nelson, finally decided to move against the hill and addressed one of his NCO platoon leaders. When he told the NCO to lead off with his platoon, the sergeant replied: "F— you." Nyquist, coming from an airborne outfit, was at first shocked but later recalled that the sergeant didn't even have the courtesy to say "sir." Nelson did nothing to the NCO, cast a sort of apologetic look at Nyquist, and then turned to his second lieutenant. The lieutenant responded with a "Yes, sir," and began moving his platoon up the hill. Nyquist thought at the time that it probably was going to be a long and trying day.[10]

The lieutenant's platoon was held up by Chinese fire about 400 yards from the crest of the hill. At that point, Nyquist saw a squad of troops from the 2d Battlion, 187th (easily identifiable by the white split half-moon drop zone assembly markings on their helmets) drive the Chinese off the hill. The troopers were casually picking off running enemy soldiers when a U.S. 38th Infantry machine gun opened up on the Rakkasans. Nyquist raced over to the machine gunners and stopped their firing before they caused casualties, but the paratroopers quit the hill in disgust. Nyquist was correct in his surmise that it would be a long day. That night, after surmounting difficulties in obtaining supporting artillery fire, he was badly wounded and evacuated.[11]

Meanwhile, the remainder of Fox 187th continued its attack and drove the Chinese away from the vicinity of Ch'amyon-ni. As the Fox Company command group and weapons platoon were displacing forward, the company and the adjoining American and Dutch units were strafed, napalmed, and rocketed by three South African F-51s. Fox Company escaped harm, but the Netherlands unit sustained one killed and sixteen wounded in the attack and had to be replaced by another Dutch unit. An investigation led officials to believe that the flight was directed by Chinese using captured American radios and recognition signals.[12]

Capt. Jack B. Shanahan's Easy Company's first mission was to attack and secure Hill 240 as a first step toward moving onto Hill 255. Hill 240 was about 600 yards south of the knob that was the crest of Hill 255. That particular terrain feature (823 feet in elevation) was on an elongated hill mass perpendicular to, but part of, the more dominating mass that rose in multiple ridgelines to Hill 342, a distance of about 2,000 yards. A way of understanding the terrain is to envision a large typewritten numeral 1. The base would be the Hill 255 mass, and the top of the numeral would be Hill 342. The body of the numeral would be the multiple ridgelines climbing from the lower hill to the higher. The hill mass that was E Company's objective measured about 1,200 yards in length at the 200-meter contour line. It varied in width from 200 to 500 yards. The knob that was the highest point on the hill mass was situated on the westernmost portion of the widest part of the mass, and the western approach was almost clifflike. A glance at a map would lead to the conclusion that the terrain at the various elevations was relatively flat. In reality, the map would not reveal the myriad folds, knobs, ravines, and terrain breaks, all of which provided concealment and cover for a determined enemy.

E Company's second platoon, flanked by the third on the left and the first on the right, attacked Hill 240. The attack proceeded without incident until the platoons were about 100 yards from the military crest, where they met troops from the 38th Infantry who were in the process of withdrawing. Captain Shanahan turned them around, and the combined force swept across the hill and exchanged fire and hand grenades with Chinese troops that had been advancing toward Wonju. After securing the hill, Shanahan released the 38th Infantry soldiers to return to their units.[13]

Hill 240 provided Shanahan an ideal location for his fire support. His attack plan used the 2d Platoon, reinforced by a section of heavy machine guns and a recoilless rifle from H Company, as the base of fire element on Hill 240. The plan then called for the 1st and 3d Platoons to assault Hill 255 after they made hooking movements that would bring them to the objective from opposite directions. The 1st Platoon, under 1st Lt. William J. Dolan, had the right-flank movement, and Lieutenant Nix's platoon was to swing to the left. The plan called for a mortar and artillery concentration that would pound the objective for five minutes before "zero hour"— 2:30 P.M. Shanahan's fire support plan also brought in an air strike that splashed napalm on the Chinese defenders.[14]

Just before reaching its line of departure, Nix's platoon encountered a group of five soldiers, members of Company M, 38th Infantry, who had been separated from their unit since before 4 A.M. Two of the men were recalled reservists and had arrived in their units with rifles still coated with grease (cosmoline) two hours before darkness the day before. Nix said that he decided it would be fruitless to try to send these men back to his company headquarters. Also, because one of the men was a "rocker sergeant" (staff sergeant), he designated them as his fourth rifle squad. Just before it was time to jump off, Nix's platoon was hit with three rounds of friendly fire, either from a tank or from a recoilless rifle situated on its left rear. Lt. Rudy Parrizo, his artillery forward observer, quickly got on the horn and had the firing squelched. The three paratroopers wounded by the friendly fire were able to walk, so Nix pointed them in the direction of the battalion aid station. Just then, Nix saw artillery rounds detonating on top of Hill 255 and Shanahan yelled into the radio to his two platoons, "That was your preparation. Go!"[15]

Both platoons used two squads abreast in their assault. In the 3d Platoon, Nix placed himself with the left flank squad and his platoon sergeant, M.Sgt. Joe Cummins, with the right flank squad. On the north side of 255, Dolan's platoon slid down into a covered draw that was out of sight of the CCF positions. Dolan placed a 3.5-inch bazooka on the left of his two-squad skirmish line. His first squad would be his reserve and would follow the skirmish line in a diamond formation. The weapons squad leader, in control of the light machine gun, was given the mission of roaming within the formation to positions where his squad could best support the advance of the platoon. The company commander had given Lieutenant Dolan an SCR-300 radio for communications because of the unreliability of the smaller platoon radio. When the platoon left the security of the draw and moved into the open, the enemy let it advance 50 yards before opening up with a hail of rifle and automatic weapons fire. Not only was the fire coming down from the heights of Hill 255, but also on the platoon's right from the reverse slope positions on the ridgelines leading to Hill 342. Dolan's radioman was the first casualty, and the SCR-300 radio was shot off his back and ruined. On Hill 240, Shanahan could see what was happening and sent another radio to the platoon.[16]

On the left flank of the attack, as soon as Nix's platoon emerged from the draw where it had been concealed during its approach, his men were hit by a hailstorm of grenades. Nix said that everyone hit the ground, but when he realized that they were concussion, rather than fragmentation, grenades, he prodded everyone to their feet and they stormed the ridge crest that was the source of the grenades. This crest was actually not so much a ridge but rather a bulge along the 220-meter contour line on a finger extending to the west from the crest of Hill 255. The men were showered with grenades again, and again they hit the dirt. Then, the platoon began receiving rifle and machine-gun fire from the direction of Hill 255. Nix made some adjustments in his firepower by redirecting the light machine-gun and BAR team to the right while he took two squads of riflemen to assault what he called the crest of ridge 220. Before his platoon took the hillock, he learned that Cummins, his platoon sergeant, had been hit and was down.

"I arrived at his side about the same time as did a litter team," Nix said. "As they moved him on the litter, I saw the extent of the wound. Sergeant Cummins had the top of his head blown off. I could see the brain, not bleeding very much, but fully exposed and pulsating with each heartbeat. The men close by saw the sergeant being carried away and their reaction was very much a manifestation of how I felt—sick and lifeless—as if all energy had drained out of my legs and arms. There were other wounded in the same position so I directed my attention to their welfare and, in a few seconds, felt my strength return."[17]

Nix's platoon was now down to about 60 percent strength. Sgt. 1/C Sam Spence, the platoon guide, took over the duties of Sergeant Cummins with the right flank squad.

On the other side of the hill, Dolan's platoon was engaged in a vicious fight. The machine gunner was killed while moving his weapon to a new position. The assistant gunner pushed aside the dead gunner and fired the gun. Dolan described the action to the X Corps historian: "The medic was collecting ammunition from the casualties, distributing it and treating the wounded. All my leaders were either on line or in front of their men. The wounded were either crawling down the hill or firing from the position where they had fallen. The walking wounded, of their own accord, continued the assault. Some men were hit as many as three times before they left the hill."[18]

Back near the base of the fire hill, the men of G Company had been held as the battalion reserve. It became clear to the battalion commander, Lt. Col. John Connor, that Easy Company would have to have some help and he ordered G Company out of reserve and into the fray. The company received two missions: (1) take over the base of the fire mission on Hill 240 because Shanahan had to commit his 2d Platoon to assist Nix's depleted force and (2) maneuver some men to reinforce Dolan's platoon. Captain Cook, G Company commander, kept his 1st and 2d Platoons on Hill 240 as base of fire, and these platoons soon had a bridge of fire crossing the narrow ridge connecting the two pieces of high ground. He then directed his 3d platoon and the weapons platoon, which had been hastily organized as a fourth rifle platoon, to make an end run around to the right. This movement, he believed, would take some of the heat off of Dolan's platoon by diverting some of the fire that was coming from the positions farther up the ridges to the north. Cook and his command group would move with the flanking platoons.[19]

From Hill 240, there was a steep, north-facing slope down to a narrow valley, and a steep slope on the north side of the valley rose to a ridgeline at about the same elevation as the hill that the platoons had just left. Once that terrain was gained, the two maneuver units would swing to the left and hit Hill 255 on the right flank of Dolan's platoon. As the platoons neared the top of the first ridge, the inevitable shower of grenades sailed over the crest. To the author, who was with Cook, it resembled a flight of blackbirds. These were concussion grenades. They could kill if they detonated close to a man, but the lethal range of fragmentation was small and the troopers weathered this storm in good shape. The Chinese were also firing mortars, which are terror weapons to infantrymen on the receiving end. Artillery rounds could be heard almost from the moment that the shell left the tube right up until the impact. Veterans could detect from the pitch of the sound if the rounds would be close, and a soldier had a split second to get on the ground and try to pull himself up under his helmet. Mortar rounds made only a very soft "pfffft" sound just before exploding. One could hear the soft sound only if it was a dud, and the next sound would be a dull "thunk." Chinese mortar fuses were notoriously unreliable. Troopers lying on that shale slope were grateful for shoddy workmanship in communist arsenals, but enough rounds exploded to inflict casualties on the men of George Company.[20]

On the west face of Hill 255, the 3d Platoon advanced methodically by fire and maneuver. Nix had exhausted the ammunition for his carbine and pistol, so he grabbed a BAR from one of his men who had just been wounded. He snagged three of the 38th Infantry troops and moved to the extreme left flank of his platoon. From there, he could see the Chinese on the steep slopes of the north and west sides of Hill 255 and proceeded to pick them off one by one. At the same time, his platoon kept advancing up the hill. Sgt. Jimmy Jones, leader of the third squad, received a head wound as his squad was cresting a ridge top close to the objective and was knocked unconscious. An aid man bandaged his wound and advised him to lie down until he could be evacuated. Instead, Jones reassumed command of his squad and led his men on another charge against the enemy. In the fierce hand-to-hand fighting that ensued, he killed nine Chinese soldiers.[21]

In Lieutenant Dolan's sector, the Chinese contested every inch of ground that the Rakkasans gained. The 1st Platoon troopers were wounded repeatedly, and still they pressed upward. With fire support from Hill 240 within 70 yards of the platoon, Dolan called for a recoilless rifle shot at an enemy bunker and then led the platoon in an assault on the positions near the top of the hill. It was a brutal fight, the paratroopers killing Chinese at point-blank range, shooting and bayoneting them, and crushing skulls with rifle butts. During the assault, the Chinese showered the paratroopers with grenades, as well as mortar fire. The Rakkasans countered with a grenade barrage of their own. Men of the platoon tossed all the grenades that they carried. When their supply was exhausted, they took grenades from the enemy dead. As soon as they tried to cross the crest, however, they were beat back by machine-gun fire from the right of the platoon.

With nineteen men still in the fight, Dolan decided to withdraw slightly to take care of his critically wounded men. The G Company assault had not yet reached a point where it could relieve the pressure on Dolan, and his meager force had to beat off a counterattack from his right that seriously wounded his platoon sergeant, M.Sgt. L. B. Cook. Dolan was hit but not wounded, the slug hitting a grommet on his pistol belt; the impact knocked him down. The last two men who remained standing tried to continue the attack, but they could not hold the ground that they had gained. Dolan crawled to his radio to call for artillery fire on the crest and reverse slope, which were about 70 yards ahead of his tiny group. As he completed the call, a burst of machine-gun fire knocked the radio handset out of his hand, sheered off the antenna, and lodged four slugs in the set itself.[22]

The Chinese final protective fires coming from well dug-in positions made the topping of Hill 255's crest a very hazardous business.

After resting for fifteen minutes and getting an ammunition resupply, they received help in the form of 1st Lt. David N. White's seventeen-member 3d Platoon from G Company.

White's platoon and Lieutenant Epps' 4th Platoon had fought their way to a position where White could reinforce Dolan while Epps, concurrently, could keep the Chinese off the right flank of the assaulting paratroopers. The journey to reach that point had not been easy. Cpl. Harry Stewart, normally a 60-mm mortar squad leader, carried the machine gun that had been issued to the ad hoc rifle platoon that morning. It had a tripod but no pintle, so Stewart fired from the hip. After weathering the storm of grenades and mortar fire, Stewart closed in on a square hole that housed a .50-caliber machine gun and a number of Chinese soldiers firing .45-caliber submachine guns. Sgt. 1/C Ira Taylor was killed by a burst from one of the latter weapons. Stewart boldly walked toward the enemy position as he fired the machine gun from his hip. In his recommendation for Stewart's Distinguished Service Cross, Epps wrote that he did not know how many Chinese soldiers Stewart had killed, but he had seen a half-dozen enemy soldiers jump out of their hole and run down the hill only to be dropped by Stewart's fire.[23]

When two other Weapons Platoon men, Sgt. Johnny Bramblett and Cpl. Ken Fortna, dropped into the hole, which Bramblett remembered as being deep and square, they found that the .50-caliber machine gun would not fire. They still had enemy to shoot at, so Bramblett made a quick diagnosis of the stoppage, hastily adjusted the headspace, and proceeded to fire the ammunition remaining in position.[24]

With both of Easy Company's platoons now reinforced, the assault on the crest was under way for the third time. Enemy resistance was comparatively light as the Chinese slipped away to fight another day. Sergeant Jones's squad then swept onto the objective. While Jones was assigning defensive positions, he was wounded again and evacuated. Company E had suffered a total of sixty-three casualties, of which eighteen were killed. Company G had two men killed and eighteen wounded. In comparison to the enemy, the losses to the attacking forces had been small. The Chinese, fighting from the advantage of fortified positions on the high ground, lost far more— 450 enemy dead littered the hilltop and its approaches.[25]

The companies hastily organized defensive positions. As darkness fell, along with more mortar rounds, Fox Company was firmly tied in with the Netherlands Battalion and Easy Company, now the new owners of Hill 255. George Company established positions on E Company's right flank to protect against any Chinese incursion down Hill 342. The Chinese had occupied that hill all day.

Because the 2d Battalion was obviously going to spend the rest of the day in the conquest of Hill 255, the 3d Battalion was ordered at 3 P.M. to assault and occupy Hill 342. It was probably too much to expect that the Chinese juggernaut could be stopped and shoved back in just one day. The 187th would need a second day to complete its business.

18. These are the survivors of the First Platoon of G Company when the company reached Chech'on on 22 February. Even though wounded, Master Sergeant Valent still stands resolutely in front of his troops.

19. Lt. Gen. Matthew B. Ridgway, Eighth Army commanding general, briefs the press about the progress of Operation Thunderbolt, the first offensive the Eighth Army had staged since Ridgway assumed command.

20. In the foreground is the hamlet of Saemal, north of Hoengsong. The road is Route 29, the MSR upon which Second Division units were trapped by overwhelming Chinese forces. The CCF had ambushes between Ch'angbong-ni and Saemal, but it was the valley between Hoengsong and Saemal that was dubbed "Massacre Valley."

21. Cpl. John J. Zupko (right), a medic attached to the 15th Field Artillery Battalion, was credited with rescuing thirty wounded soldiers while salvaging this 105mm howitzer during the battalion's nightmare withdrawal from Massacre Valley. Zupko picked up wounded and piled them in the truck that was towing the artillery piece. Wounded were even placed on the trails of the tube. At left is Pfc. Henry Rarim of 2d Infantry Division Artillery.

22. South Korean first lieutenant Choi Beu Hon (right), in Korean peasant garb, traces on a map the route he followed in leading four Americans to friendly lines after they were surrounded by Chinese. Lieutenant Choi was attached to B Battery, 15th Field Artillery Battalion, 2d Infantry Division, when it was trapped by the CCF in Massacre Valley. Listening to his story are M.Sgt. Vance Snyder (left) and ROK first lieutenant Be Su Gung (center) of Headquarters Battery, 2d Division Artillery.

23. A C-119 of the Far East Air Force's Combat Cargo drops supplies at Chip'yong-ni. Aerial resupply was vital during the winter when South Korean roads, barely adequate under the best of conditions, were ice-covered and treacherous. In this

instance, aerial resupply was even more crucial because Chip'yong-ni remained surrounded by Chinese forces for several days.

24. First Lt. Wilbur Webster (left), D Battery, 82d AAA Battalion, and Capt. Carroll D. Harrod of Headquarters Battery, 49th Field Artillery Battalion, are pictured after their escape from their Chinese captors on 12 March 1951. After their capture near Ch'angbong-ni on the night of 11 February, they had been marched slowly north with other wounded soldiers. After eluding their captors, they walked into the front lines of the 7th Cavalry Regiment, 1st Cavalry Division, northeast of Chip'yong-ni.

U. S. ARMY

25. The Chinese attacked down this ridge toward the G Company positions at Chip'yong-ni. The camera sees approximately what Cpl. Eugene L. Ottenson's machine gunners could see. The folds in the ground provided excellent cover for CCF soldiers crawling into hand grenade range. Number 9 marks the direction of the Chinese assault. Number 10 is Corporal Ottenson's squad location. When the CCF finally overran Ottenson's position, it was only a matter of time before the Chinese occupied all of G Company's positions. This photo was shot by an Eighth Army historical team in the fall of 1951.

26. This is the rear area of Company G at Chip'yong-ni. The Eighth Army historical team was able to locate positions even though the huts had been razed. Position Number 1 is the location of the G Company command post. Number 2 is the 1st platoon CP, an unusually long distance from the platoon positions, which were on the low hill to the left of the vehicles on the MSR. Number 3 is a position of a 155mm howitzer, from Battery B, 503d Artillery. Number 4 is the location of the Battery B squad tent. The cut made by the MSR passing through the hill on the left is just beyond the two vehicles.

27. This is the cut where the MSR from Koksu-ri entered the Chip'yong-ni perimeter. Number 18 shows the machine-gun position manned by artillerymen. Number 19 indicates the location of an antitank minefield laid by the CCF. Number 20 denotes the protective wire positions set up by the defenders. Number 21 is the right flank position of the 1st Platoon of Company G. The 23d Infantry tanks ultimately moved south on this road to a point where they could bring fire on the Chinese positions on the reverse slope. The tanks of Task Force Crombez came up this road.

28. Lt. Gen. Edmund M. Almond, X Corps commander, congratulates ROK Brig. Gen. Choi Yong Hee, following the presentation of a Silver Star to the commander of the ROK 8th Division. The ceremony at X Corps headquarters in Ch'ungju came after Ridgway strongly suggested to Almond that he improve his relationships with ROK generals working for him.

29. Sfc. Joseph W. Maiser displays the medals that will be awarded to members of the 187th Airborne RCT during ceremonies held at Chech'on following the conclusion of the Wonju campaign.

30. Brig. Gen. Frank S. Bowen, 187th Airborne RCT commander, receives the third oak leaf cluster to the Silver Star from Lieutenant General Almond.

31. Lieutenant General Ridgway (second from the right) greets Lt. Col. Ralph Monclar (left), commander of the French Battalion. Lieutenant General Almond is second from the left. The names of the other two men in the foreground are unknown. Ridgway was at X Corps headquarters at Ch'ungju to present the French Battalion with a special battle streamer for its outstanding service during the battle at Chip'yong-ni. This photo of Ridgway clearly shows that what some people thought was a second hand grenade on his web gear, was, in fact, a World War II first aid packet issued to paratroopers. Ridgway is also wearing paratrooper pants.

32. Gen. Paul Freeman, a spry and fit 81 years of age, appears at the February 1985 dedication of the monument honoring the defenders of Chip'yong-ni. He is returning to his seat following an emotional speech that paid tribute to the fallen soldiers of the 23d RCT. To the left of Freeman is the sterling silver Korea Bowl, made from melted-down Combat Infantrymen's badges donated by the men of the 23d Regiment during the Korean War.

33. At the conclusion of the Chip'yong-ni monument dedication, the participants pause for photographers. Standing between the honor guard soldiers are, from left, Mr. Chi Kap-Chong, Chairman of the UN Korean War Allies Association; Gen. Paul Freeman, whose 23d RCT made the gallant stand against overwhelming Chinese forces; Mr. François Dureau, former French liaison officer to the UN Command's Military Armistice Commission; and Maj. Gen. Henry Doctor Jr., commanding general of the 2d Infantry Division at the time of the ceremony.

34. Wilbur Webster (center) renders honors at the 1998 dedication of the monument honoring the men of the 2d Infantry Division who perished in Massacre Valley in February 1951. Webster, a member of D Battery, 82d AAA Battalion, was instrumental in getting the monument erected and dedicated. The inscription reads in part: "We dedicate the memorial to those soldiers who gave their lives in this battle. Their noble spirit, bravery and faith to preserve freedom and peace in the world will be remembered forever with this memorial in our beautiful land of Korea."

NINETEEN | Climax at Chip'yong-ni

Although thousands of Chinese had died no more than 18 miles to the east, the defenders of Chip'yong-ni knew nothing of that battle. They spent Valentine's Day preparing for what they knew could be an overwhelming Chinese attack at nightfall.

For a period, it appeared as though the weather around Chip'-yong-ni would benefit the Chinese. Low cloud cover partially shut down tactical air support and aerial resupply for most of the day. The incessant mortar and artillery fire precluded any kind of aerial evacuation of casualties, which gave Colonel Freeman a reasonable excuse to defy General Almond's order to turn over his command to Colonel Chiles and be evacuated.

Help for the garrison, however, was on the way. General Ridgway was well aware that any defensive position could be reduced if an attacker had enough manpower and determination. He had no doubt about Chinese manpower and was not about to underestimate his enemy's determination. Consequently he gave his IX Corps commander, Maj. Gen. Bryant Moore, the mission of reinforcing the 23d RCT. Moore, in turn, gave the mission to Col. Marcel Gustave Crombez, commander of the 5th Cavalry Regiment of the 1st Cavalry Division. Despite the name and the shoulder patch featuring the head of a horse, the 1st Cavalry Division was a "straight-leg" infantry division. The 5th Cavalry was chosen because it was in corps reserve and situated near Yoju, the logical jumping-off point for any move to Chip'yong-ni.

Crombez received his mission late on Wednesday. By the time he had assembled his task force, it was dark. It consisted of the three organic infantry battalions of the regiment, plus two battalions of field artillery and a company of combat engineers. His armor punch consisted of Company D, 6th Tank Battalion, equipped with M-46 Pattons armed with 90-mm guns, and two platoons of the division's 70th Tank Battalion, which had the Sherman "Easy Eights."

The task force went as far as Hup'o-ri, about 9 road miles south of Chip'yong-ni on Route 24-A, where it held up all night until emergency repairs could be made on a bridge.[1]

The fact that the task force was not organized until late on Wednesday meant that the garrison at Chip'yong-ni would have to spend another night alone and face whatever the Chinese could throw at it. Freeman knew that the earliest he could expect ground reinforcement was late Thursday afternoon.

A rational presumption might be made that, during daylight hours diligent efforts to improve fighting positions all along the perimeter were made. Perhaps they were. Certainly, prudent commanders would have changed the locations of their automatic weapons. That may have been done in some cases, but there was no evidence of any such steps in the critical G Company area. Capt. Edward C. Williamson of the Eighth Army Historical Section conducted detailed interviews with G Company personnel, and no one indicated that positions were improved during the day. Most of the troops entertained hopes that the Chinese would abandon their efforts to storm the perimeter.[2]

In the G Company sector, however, the company commander, 1st Lt. Thomas Heath, met with two officers from the 155-howitzer battery position—Captain Elledge and Lt. Arthur Rochnowski—to coordinate mutual defense. They decided that the center of the company front, Lieutenant McGee's 3d Platoon, was the most likely spot for an attempted Chinese penetration. Rochnowski agreed to set up three outpost positions and three BAR teams on the 3d Platoon's right flank. These positions would be in addition to the two .50-caliber machine guns to be manned by artillerymen on the MSR boundary between G Company and the French Battalion. He said that, if necessary, he would send some of his artillerymen to fight with Heath's troops and strip away men from the howitzers and fire them with skeleton crews. The tubes were in a shallow bowl immediately behind the low hills that constituted G Company's defense line.[3]

Most of the Air Force's tactical air strikes that afternoon were diverted to punishing the stragglers from the Wonju Shoot or supporting IX Corps units in a major push against the CCF Thirty-Ninth Field Army positions to the west of Chip'yong-ni. Freeman did get three air strikes late in the day and twenty-four C-119s dropped supplies of artillery and mortar ammunition, but he was unhappy with the resupply. There was a shortage of illumination rounds for all calibers of weapons, and the .30-caliber rifle ammunition came loose packed in boxes rather than in clips. The clips, made of thin metal, hold eight rounds and must be fully loaded to keep the rounds from falling out. At night, it is extraordinarily difficult for an infantryman, in a hole under fire and with cold, numb fingers, to reload an M-1 clip from a box of loose rounds. Consequently, word went out to the rifle companies to fire only when they had a target and to make every effort to conserve ammunition.[4]

The first enemy action of the evening occurred at 8:30 P.M. when K Company on the eastern extremity of the perimeter received a mortar barrage. The Chinese had been dropping mortar rounds sporadically all day, so this particular barrage carried no special significance; however, it was followed by a thunderous barrage of mortar, artillery, and self-propelled heavy guns that struck all parts of the perimeter with an emphasis on the RCT command post. The CCF plan this night was more coordinated. The enemy kept pressure all around the perimeter to pin defenders in place and to preclude reinforcement of the sectors where the Chinese hoped to make a breakthrough. The CCF concentrated on two locations in an attempt to penetrate the perimeter. As the cacophony of bugles, horns, and whistles echoed around the perimeter, the Chinese assault groups from Hill 506, on the east, struck K Company, and from

Hill 397 on the south, the Chinese came in a column of companies down the long finger that pointed straight into G Company's positions.

The Chinese knew with some precision where to attack. The first blow was directed against the machine gun in the 3d Platoon's sector, and, within minutes, the gunner was wounded. His place was taken by Cpl. Eugene L. Ottesen, who kept his gun firing well into the night before he was eventually overwhelmed.[5] Ottesen, whose body was never found, had a "US" prefix to his service number, which indicated that he was a draftee. Beginning in February throughout the 2d Division, the men plucked from civilian life by the reinstated draft were appearing as fillers in infantry outfits. Casualty reports for the period of Chip'yong-ni reveal that twenty-one casualties were draftees.[6]

The fighting was all around the perimeter, but no fight was so desperate as in Company G's sector, and, in that sector, no men were so desperate as those in Lieutenant McGee's 3d Platoon. The Chinese had hit the left-flank squad of the 1st Platoon on McGee's right—just across a small saddle on the ridge that served as a tie-in point between the two platoons—and had killed or driven out the occupants of two of the fighting positions. The enemy then set up a machine gun in one of the holes and began firing down the line at 3d Platoon positions. Because of that fire, McGee suspected that the 1st Platoon had lost some foxholes in its sector. He called the company commander on the telephone.

"Heath," he asked, "is the first platoon still in position?"

Heath, in turn, called the master sergeant, the acting platoon leader, who, unknown to Heath, had remained holed up in the platoon CP, a hut just a stone's throw from the company CP hut. The sergeant telephoned Sgt. 1/C Donald R. Schmitt, the platoon sergeant, who had positions on the right of the 1st Platoon line. Schmitt looked around and replied that the line was holding. That information was then relayed to Heath. When McGee heard Heath's response, he was still dubious. He and his platoon sergeant, Sgt. 1/C Bill C. Kluttz, yelled over at the 1st Platoon sector but received no answer. The machine gun firing at him from the 1st Platoon area was troublesome, but of more pressing concern were the numbers of Chinese in and around 3d Platoon positions. McGee could see four Chinese over and to the rear of the position of one of his squad leaders. He yelled at the sergeant, "There are four of them at the rear of your hole. Toss a grenade up and over." McGee said he knew that they were CCF because they were on their hands and knees and he could see the shovels on their backs.

About that time, the enemy machine gun on their right cut loose with a burst, and the squad leader was unable to rise up and throw a grenade. So McGee grabbed his BAR and with his runner, Pfc. Cletus Inmon using his M-1, killed the first Chinese to penetrate in that sector. Looking to his front, McGee spotted a dozen or so enemy soldiers crawling from a dry creek bed toward the sergeant's hole. McGee and Inmon opened up with their weapons, but the enemy soldiers kept working their way uphill, crawling and throwing small potato masher–type grenades. McGee yelled at the squad leader to toss some grenades at the Chinese advancing on his position, but the man was more interested in keeping his head down. There were three men in his hole, another sergeant and a private. The squad leader and the other sergeant jumped out of their hole and ran toward McGee's. The sergeant was hit as he ran, but the squad leader dropped in on top of McGee and Inmon. With the man on top of him, McGee could neither see nor fire.

"Get the hell out of here and get back with your squad," he yelled. The sergeant did not budge, but after a second order delivered more harshly and profanely, he climbed out of the hole and was shot through the shoulder. The luckless private that remained in the squad leader's hole was killed by a Chinese satchel charge. McGee called for litter bearers to evacuate the two sergeants.

Besides trying to provide leadership to his platoon, McGee was busy simply defending his position. The Chinese were advancing on him the same way that they were attacking all across the line— using cover of overhead machine-gun fire from the high ground to the south of the perimeter, crawling, throwing grenades and, when closing next to a fighting position, tossing in satchel charges. McGee's BAR, usually a reliable weapon, was jamming every tenth round. He used his pocket knife to extract the jammed cartridge case, but he dropped the knife while extracting a case and could not find it in the dark. He picked up his carbine and had to pound home the bolt to overcome the frozen oil on the works. With the carbine, he killed a Chinese soldier just as he raised onto his knees to hurl a grenade.

When Ottesen's machine gun had been silenced to McGee's left, and attempts to fill the gap between Ottesen and McGee had failed as Chinese bullets and grenades struck down the men trying to make the countermoves, McGee knew that he badly needed help. With wire communication to company headquarters now cut, McGee sent a platoon runner, Pfc. John Martin, to Lieutenant Heath for help. At this point Heath finally believed McGee that the left of the 1st Platoon line was gone.

When Martin delivered McGee's plea for more people, Heath stepped outside the CP hut and shouted to Lieutenant Rochnowski for help in restoring G Company's positions. The battery commander soon assembled fifteen men and turned them over to Heath. Martin was given the task of guiding the men to the 3d Platoon positions. As the reinforcements crossed the crest of the hill, the enemy opened up on them with automatic weapons and mortar fire. A mortar round killed one of the artillerymen and wounded another, and the survivors turned and fled back down the hill. Martin then returned to the company rear to pick up the company's wire team carrying an ammunition resupply and guided them to the battle area.

Heath, meantime, stopped the fleeing artillerymen at the bottom of the hill, reformed them, and led them back toward McGee's platoon. By now, the enemy was in full possession of the Company G positions near the saddle, and the line had erupted into a frenzy of firing. Near the top of the hill, the terrified redlegs again broke and ran. Heath went down the hill after them and grabbed a couple of them by their clothing. He yelled, "Goddammit, get back up on that hill! You'll die down here anyway. You might as well go up on the hill and die there."

The cowering artillerymen knew better; they were not planning on dying anywhere. They had dug their personal protection holes even deeper during the day, and they fervently believed that they could weather the storm if they could just get back into their holes or even their squad tents.

By 2 A.M., the Chinese had enough men in the saddle on the hill to begin firing at the artillery positions in the bowl behind the main line positions. Lt. Carl F. Haberman, Company G's Weapons Platoon leader, quickly displaced his 60-mm mortars to a ditch about 100 yards farther to the rear and kept them firing. Then, he returned to the artillery positions and entered a squad tent to find it filled with artillerymen.

"Hell," he said, "a squad tent won't stop bullets." He persuaded a half-dozen men to follow him outside, but they refused to climb the hill.[7]

Not all of the artillerymen were so craven. Those given special infantry training that included the firing and maintenance of machine guns acquitted themselves well in the fight. The segregated units had it tough enough just to get by in a peacetime Army. Being assigned to a segregated unit in Almond's X Corps was one of the least desirable fates for black soldiers in 1950 and 1951. Given training, leadership, and a feeling of belonging in an outfit that took care of its men, black soldiers thrived and performed competently, sometimes heroically, when called upon.[8]

The enemy attack continued without letup. It was not the stereotypical "human wave" attack but a persistent, gnawing assault that progressed from one hole to the next. Sometime between 2:30 and 3 A.M., G Company lost the rest of the hill. Sergeant Schmitt and the remainder of the 1st Platoon came down from the west end of the company's sector. In the 3d Platoon, a machine gun being manned by Sergeant Kluttz finally jammed and could not be cleared. That was the last straw. He and Lieutenant McGee yelled to the survivors of the platoon to throw what hand grenades they had remaining and to scoot over the crest of the hill toward the company CP.

Heath reported the loss of his position to his battalion commander, Lt. Col. James Edwards. Because a break occurring anywhere on the perimeter was serious, Edwards ordered a counterattack and promised to send help. His problem was that he did not have much to send. His battalion reserve consisted only of the support platoon of Company F. The platoon had already spent a squad in an earlier attempt to restore the line between the 3d and 1st Platoons. After ordering the support platoon to move to George Company's area and report to Lieutenant Heath, Colonel Edwards called Colonel Freeman, who still had B Company and the Ranger Company as a reserve. With a pitched battle still raging in his 3d Battalion area, Freeman did not feel comfortable in committing his entire reserve in G Company's area, so he piecemealed the reserve, sending a platoon of rangers and a tank. While waiting for the reserve to get to his position, Heath took what was left of his company and established an improvised line on a 4–5-foot high rib of ground that crossed the artillery position in the bottom of the bowl. Because he knew that the company officers had their hands full, Edwards sent a battalion staff officer, Lt. Robert Curtis, to command the reserve force.

When he arrived at the area, Curtis had an immediate problem with the Rangers. The commander of the Ranger Company had accompanied his platoon and refused to permit it to be attached to any other unit, to participate in a conventional infantry counterattack, or even to take orders from anybody but the regimental commander. So Curtis had to call Edwards, who sent out another staff officer, Capt. John Ramsburg, to take command of the small force.[9]

Dr. Kohen remembered that the 2d Battalion had a bootleg quad-50. "We were on the road somewhere and came across this abandoned quad-50. So Colonel Edwards told his folks to take it with us. Every time we had an inspection we had to hide it," he said. At Chip'yong-ni, Dr. Kohen remembered Colonel Edwards turning to Captain Ramsburg and saying, "John, I want that hill back. If we don't get that hill back, we're all dead. You take that group and the quad-50 and you get that hill back."[10]

Ramsburg found out that the M-16 halftrack had been accidentally run into a ditch and would be useless for the counterattack. After getting a resupply of radios from Battalion Headquarters, Ramsburg formed the two platoons into assault units. The Fox Company platoon was to orient on the old 3d Platoon positions, and the Ranger Platoon would aim for the former positions of the 1st Platoon on the right side of the G Company hill. Ramsburg had the G Company mortars moved up to where he could communicate by voice. The base mortar fired one round that detonated right on top of the ridge.

"That where you want 'em?" one of the mortarmen shouted.

"That's exactly right," Ramsburg yelled back. "Now sweep that hill in both directions."

He asked for a five-minute concentration, and, three minutes into it, he had his two machine guns open up on the hill in front of them. The firing brought immediate retaliation from the Chinese. A dozen or so mortar rounds crashed into the assembly areas of the assault platoons and wounded six men, including the leader of the F Company platoon.

Nevertheless, the counterattack still kicked off in good shape, but it was crippled by fire from the right flank. Ramsburg could not tell if it was friendly fire from the French positions or was from the Chinese who had occupied positions on that flank. The Rangers suffered the most casualties from this attack. Then, in spite of specific orders not to fire without orders, one of the tanks let loose with a long burst of .50-caliber machine-gun fire. Concurrently, the left-flank platoon began receiving accurate machine-gun fire from its left flank. It came from a position the attackers had believed to be held by friendly forces. The fire from the flanks, plus that from the top of the ridge, decimated the attacking platoons and the counterattack collapsed. Lieutenant Heath, taking over from an injured Ramsburg, was nearly to the crest when he was shot in the chest at about the same time as the Ranger Platoon leader was killed. Heath survived that wound but would be killed in action in September.

While these events were playing out, Captain Elledge persuaded a tanker to pull the 2d Battalion's quad-50 out of the ditch. It was operable, so Elledge loaded it with ammunition. When he learned that all of the Americans had pulled back from the former G Company positions, he obtained permission to fire at any targets of opportunity on the hill. M.Sgt. Andrew E. Reyna, the section leader (two tanks) of the Regimental Tank Company, asked Elledge to provide covering fire for his tanks so that he could roll into the artillery battery's supply area and recover sixteen wounded men who had been left behind.

While Elledge pounded the hilltop with fire from his guns, Reyna and his crews drove their tanks under the fire to the base of the hill, carried the men from the supply tent, and loaded them on the tanks for the return trip to safety. Elledge had been firing so steadily that, in the first gray light of morning, artillerymen across the road could see heat waves shimmering around his four guns. As the daylight intensified, Elledge saw the Chinese point an empty 75-mm recoilless rifle at his position. With the breech open, he could see daylight though the tube. By the time that the Chinese had slammed a round into the breech, Elledge had traversed the M-16 turret in that direction and tore the men and gun apart with the concentrated fire from four machine guns.

Elledge and the tanks, three of them by now, continued pounding the hill. An artillery officer yelled for a gun crew to man a howitzer. A half-dozen men scrambled over the road embankment, turned around a 155 howitzer, and fired six white phosphorous shells at the hill. For observers behind the howitzer, the "flash-bang" time was nearly instantaneous.

Everyone expected the Chinese to pull back during the daylight hours, but this unit, later identified as an element of the 344th Regiment, 115th Division, of the Thirty-Ninth Field Army, was under orders to stay, dig in, and prepare for further assaults after dark. The Chinese organized a stout reverse-slope defense, a technique for which they were justly famous.

While the CCF soldiers were digging in and Colonel Freeman was trying to decide what to do about the penetration in G Company's sector, the relief column from the 5th Cavalry had run into strong Chinese resistance. The 1st and 2d Battalions attacking north had been stopped near Madu-ri, a town about 6 miles south of the Chip'yong-ni perimeter. Colonel Crombez, with several generals nipping at his heels, realized that a conventional attack would never reach the perimeter in time to be of any value, so he opted for an armored punch. Crombez selected the twenty-four tanks in his original task force and a squad of engineers to remove land mines from the roadway. Then, in one of the more controversial tactical decisions of the war, he designated Capt. John C. Barrett's L Company of the 3d Battalion, 5th Cavalry Regiment, to ride on top of the tanks.[11]

Lt. Col. Edgar J. Treacy, Jr., 3d Battalion commander, was stupefied by the idea of having his 160 infantrymen ride exposed on the tanks. Both he and Barrett vigorously protested that the order violated Army doctrine and that casualties could be calamitous. Crombez was not persuaded, but did make a concession that he would stop the tanks so that enemy fire could be suppressed. Crombez, however, denied Treacy's personal request to ride the tanks and ordered him to take charge of the resupply truck convoy and bring it in when the road to Chip'yong-ni was clear.[12]

Barrett and the tank company commander, Capt. Johnny M. Hiers, briefly conferred to work out a system of signals so that the infantrymen, who would dismount to fight off close-in CCF attacks, could be given enough warning to permit them to remount the tanks.

The Patton tanks, with their 90-mm main guns, were to lead the armored column. Crombez, wearing a cavalry-yellow scarf, climbed into the fifth Patton in line and closed the hatch. He did not emerge from the tank until the column was inside the perimeter of Chip'-yong-ni. Only the engineers rode on the first four tanks in the column. L Company troops spread out on all but the final four tanks. Captain Barrett climbed on the fifth tank. Treacy had made an alteration to the plan when he directed Barrett to load his service and supply truck, carrying a half-dozen Korean augmentees to serve as litter bearers. The truck, to follow the last tank, would be available to pick up any wounded men that could not remount the tanks after a firefight. Treacy then disregarded Crombez's order to remain with the truck convoy and climbed on board the fifth tank with Barrett.[13]

The column moved out at 3:45 P.M. All went well until it reached Koksu-ri, 2 miles north of the starting point. There, the Chinese, using mortars, machine guns, satchel charges, and bangalore torpedoes, attacked the column. The tanks shuddered to a halt, and the infantrymen dismounted to fight off the attacks. Without warning, Crombez ordered the column to move out. Most of the men were able to scramble on board the tanks, but about thirty men, including some wounded, were stranded. Barrett shouted to the men, "Stay by the road! We'll come back for you." Both Treacy and Barrett were furious at Crombez and, according to Clay Blair's interview with Barrett, Treacy told him that when it was all over, he intended to bring formal charges against Crombez.[14]

The truck following the tanks picked up three wounded men, but the truck was drawing so much fire that the remainder of the wounded opted to stay where they were. After both officers in the group were wounded by mortar fire, M.Sgt. Lloyd L. Jones organized the stranded men and led them back toward their own lines.

About a mile past Koksu-ri, the column once more was halted because of CCF fire. Again, the infantrymen left the tanks, and some of them deployed some 50 yards or more from the road in order to accomplish the protection mission. Once again, the tanks lurched forward without warning and left behind an even larger group of men, including Colonel Treacy, who had been lightly wounded. Barrett was unable to get on the fifth tank but managed to clamber on board the eighth or ninth tank in the column.[15]

At Chip'yong-ni, once Freeman was assured that the 5th Cavalry would have a relief force in the perimeter by nightfall, he consented to evacuation. Before he turned his command over to Colonel

Chiles, he ordered the full RCT reserve—Company B and the remainder of the Ranger Company—to restore the G Company sector. Freeman also ordered that the attached engineer company be constituted as the new regimental reserve. He then boarded a helicopter and flew to a hospital at Ch'ungju, where Ridgway met and congratulated him. Freeman believed that after a brief recuperation from his wound he, like Mike Michaelis, would be returned to Korea and given a star. Instead, he was hijacked by the Army's Chief of Information and became a spokesman for the Army efforts in Korea. This move did not hurt his career, which ended with four stars.[16]

The counterattack by Captain Pratt's Baker Company was unsuccessful. By midmorning, when the attack finally kicked off, the Chinese had well-prepared fieldworks, and they repulsed the first efforts. Some dispute remains over how the counterattack was conducted. Edwards, the battalion commander, in an informal report on the action that he wrote for Freeman's information, claims that Pratt initially attacked with only one platoon instead of conducting a coordinated attack. Pratt himself hotly disputed that assertion in his 1992 book. A reliable corroboration of Pratt's contention was provided by one of his platoon leaders, 1st Lt. Richard S. Kotite, in a letter to historian Appleman in December 1951. Kotite wrote that his platoon was on the left (aiming at the George Company center), and the platoon of Lt. Maurice Fenderson had the right flank. The platoons took heavy fire up to the crest of the ridge. Kotite said that, when his platoon went over the crest, his men found themselves in a cross fire laid down by three machine guns. The platoon had to pull back to about 5 yards below the crest, where it exchanged grenades with the enemy. Fenderson's platoon was cut to pieces, and, later, when Edwards ordered B Company to pull back, Pratt combined both platoons.[17]

The Americans tried again and again to take the hill, but the dug-in Chinese were too strong for the depleted company to overcome. Priority for air strikes was now Chip'yong-ni, and fighter-bombers from the Air Force, Navy, and Marines, converging on the beleaguered perimeter, flew 131 sorties. Chinese attackers around the perimeter were driven into hiding except on the critical south sector, where CCF soldiers defiantly fired rifles and automatic weapons at their aerial tormentors. After what seemed a particularly effective napalm run, Edwards sent his forces back up the hill, but they were again stalled below the crest as they exchanged volleys of grenades with the Chinese.

Edwards decided that the only way to dislodge the Chinese was to get his tanks far enough south on the MSR so that they could bring direct fire on the reverse slope. Earlier in the day, on the first sortie by the tanks, a box mine that had been planted by the CCF in the road cut by the artillery's old machine-gun position disabled a tank. Edwards sent some members of his Pioneer and Ammunition (P&A) Platoon to locate and extract mines, but the CCF fire did not allow them to get close to the mines. Then, Edwards tried to send the tanks with the P&A Platoon, but Chinese rocket-launcher teams forced the tanks to withdraw again. Finally, Edwards put together a mini task force consisting of tanks, P&A men, and the Ranger Company to provide infantry protection for the Pioneers. Edwards said that the Ranger Company commander objected to his troops being used in that manner. Edwards told him either to do what he told him or to report to the rear under arrest. The task force moved forward, and Chinese bazooka men were gunned down when they popped out of holes to fire at the tanks. The tanks traveled down the road to a point where they could deliver devastating fire on the reverse slopes. Company B then made a final counterattack and carried the hill.

Edwards wrote that just at that psychological moment—about 4:30 P.M.—the relief column from the 1st Cavalry, chasing about 250 Chinese in front of them, came into view. With the fire from 23d Infantry tanks added to the oncoming task force, most of the 250 Chinese perished. "This panicked the whole Chinese Army," Edwards wrote, "and they all got out of their holes and ran away from us. I never saw a sight like that and never expect to see another like it. Every hill around the perimeter had running chinks on it!

The Air Corps (sic) was striking, the artillery shooting, the flak wagons barking, every mortar and recoilless firing and every rifleman shooting! There were more targets than we had weapons. What a day! That broke the seige."[18]

That the Crombez task force made it to the perimeter in as good a shape as it did boiled down to the heady and courageous act of one soldier. About a mile south of the perimeter, for about a distance of 150 yards, the road passed through an extremely steep cut with sheer embankments as high as fifty feet. The Chinese made an all-out effort to stop the task force at that point by concentrating mortar and bazooka fires. The first tank was hit by a bazooka round that wounded the occupants, but the tank made it through the pass, as did the second and third tanks. The fourth tank, in which the tank company commander, Captain Hiers, was riding was struck by a 3.5-inch bazooka round that penetrated the armor and exploded the ammunition in the turret ready racks. The men in the fighting compartment, including Hiers, were killed. The driver, Cpl. John A. Calhoun, was badly burned. The first instinct for many men would have been to forget about driving a tank and take care of the burns, but Calhoun ignored the searing pain. Gunning the engine, he drove the tank through the cut and then off the roadway so that the rest of the column could continue.[19]

After the Chinese fled, Crombez drove his tanks into the perimeter and basked in the accolades of the Chip'yong-ni defenders. Captain Barrett, however, nursed a rage born of knowing that his company had been destroyed. Of the 160 infantrymen who had started, only 23 remained, and, of these, 13 were wounded. Barrett's frustration increased when Crombez elected not to make a return trip with only one hour of daylight left. It snowed the next morning, and Crombez delayed his return until about 11 A.M. He did not require any troops to ride on the tanks for the return unless they volunteered; no one volunteered. Instead, an artillery liaison plane maintained continuous cover for the column as it moved south. The observer in the plane was instructed to call for artillery VT shells directly over the buttoned-up tanks in the event of enemy attack.

No Chinese were spotted on the return trip, nor was a shot fired.[20] The potential for use of VT fuzes begs the question—why would not that tactic have worked for the sprint north the previous day?

Although contemporaries at the time (Edwards called it "an awfully stupid maneuver") criticized the use of infantry on the tanks and no tactical analysis in later years found merit in the action, Crombez nevertheless prospered somewhat. Ridgway awarded him a Distinguished Service Cross despite his having remaining buttoned up in the tank for the entire trip. Even though Crombez was older than the average regimental commander at that time, Ridgway permitted him to remain in command of the 5th Cavalry for several more months. Blair noted that Crombez's career went nowhere after Korea; nevertheless Ridgway's support assured him of a star before his retirement.[21]

As was their wont, the Chinese conducted a critique of the Chip'-yong-ni fight and published it as part of a collection of combat experiences. As with most of these documents, it was captured later. This is what the Chinese had to say about Chip'yong-ni:

1. In the conduct of the entire campaign, or the battle command, we have underestimated the enemy. In view of their past characteristics in battle, *we expected the enemy to flee at Chipyong-ni, after the enemy at Hoengsong was annihilated.* (Emphasis added)

2. Unfamiliarity with the situation. We thought the enemy had merely field works when they had organized key points of defense and other such defense work as bunkers, wire entanglements, et cetera, with tanks, acting as mobile fortresses. We not only did not organize, coordinate, and have the attacking units under a centralized command, but even two regiments of the same division failed to coordinate their movements, resulting in a "You fight, I rest" attitude.[22]

Chip'yong-ni represented a major American victory over the Chinese. It also revealed a fundamental flaw in Chinese tactics—lack of flexibility. The Chinese were masters at detailed planning in advance of an operation, but, once it was under way, they lacked the tactical doctrine to make critical changes to meet new operational requirements. And, even if some commanders could see a need for modification, the Chinese lacked the tactical communications systems necessary to effect meaningful changes. When the encirclement and ambush tactic did not work on the first night, the Chinese had ample forces in the area to have overrun Chip-yong-ni. In their position, that's what Ridgway would have done, what he thought the Chinese would do, and why he was willing to overlook the obvious faults of Crombez in favor of obtaining the benefit of reinforcement of the Chip'yong-ni perimeter.

The 23d Regiment paid a stiff price for its defense of the perimeter, but nothing like what might have occurred had Ridgway permitted the 23d to run a gauntlet to Yoju. The casualty list compiled after the war and after all American prisoners had been returned showed that the 23d Infantry Regiment sustained 66 dead, of which 7 died in communist captivity. There were 179 wounded, but mitigating that number was the fact that 121 men were returned to duty, some within a week of their wounding. The dead included 6 men who had died of wounds, part of the blame for which might have been the inability to evacuate seriously wounded men to a surgical hospital. The artillery units had much lighter casualties—a total of 5 killed and 22 wounded.[23]

Although the CCF had to forsake its plans for the 23d RCT at Chip'yong-ni, it by no means had abandoned its Fourth Offensive goal of capturing Wonju. The Sixty-Sixth Field Army, lurking just northeast of Wonju, had escaped the abattoir of the Wonju Shoot, and a reinforced regiment still owned a part of the high ground north of Wonju.

TWENTY | **Final Decision at Wonju**

At the time that General Stewart ordered a company of the 3d Battalion, 187th Airborne RCT, to assault Hill 342 on Wednesday afternoon, 14 February, he was not blessed with supernatural prescience. Stewart knew that Chip'yong-ni had weathered the first night of CCF assaults, but he didn't know if the 23d RCT was going to survive enemy attacks that night, the next night, or even the next night. The architect of the Wonju Shoot knew that the Chinese had been badly hurt in that artillery holocaust, but, at that time, he did not have an inkling of how badly. He also knew that the Netherlands Battalion had taken some severe hits and that his left flank was vulnerable with only the 1st Battalion, 9th Infantry, plus the 2d Battalion, 38th Infantry, and a platoon of tanks, out there for security. He did know that it had cost the Wonju defense the better part of a very good rifle company just to reoccupy the first of the hills seized by the Chinese early that morning. That intelligence told Stewart that the Chinese planned to stay on the high ground and probably reinforce their forces there. Moreover, intelligence reports indicated a CCF buildup 3–4 miles north of Wonju. An ROK lieutenant, who had escaped, told debriefers that the Chinese intended to attack down the Wonju River bed.[1]

So Stewart had to play it safe and not strip the defensive line straddling the MSR that had been established the day before. All of these factors finally led to the conclusion that he could spare only one rifle company from that position. Everyone else had to stay put and watch for a possible Chinese end run to the east or the west. Wonju, with its strategic value, was still the prize.

Sometime during the day on Wednesday 14 February, X Corps directed General Bowen, 187th Airborne commander, to assume command of all 187th and 2d Division troops in the area. The G-3 and S-3 journals are silent about the time that Bowen's assumption of command occurred. The only official indication in the record is in the end-of-day summary of the 2d Division's G-3 Journal: "The importance of unified command in the vital Wonju area was recognized and, by mutual consent, CG 187th Abn. RCT was placed in command of all 2d Div-187th Abn personnel in the Wonju area."[2] Stewart was released from his tactical responsibilities to devote full time to the Hoengsong inquiry.

Capt. William E. Weber had spent a good part of his career in the 187th, beginning in the latter part of World War II, when it was known as a glider infantry regiment assigned to the 11th Airborne Division in the Philippines. As a first lieutenant at Fort Campbell, Kentucky, he had commanded L Company of the regiment. Now, as a captain, he commanded K Company of the 187th, the designated assault force for the attack on Hill 342.

At midafternoon Wednesday, Lt. Col. Delbert E. Munson, 3d Battalion commander, passed the mission along to Weber. King Company was in a very good position to begin the attack. Its defensive position was 1,500 yards south and slightly east of the objective. It was 4 P.M. by the time that Item Company had replaced K Company on the old defense positions so that Weber's company could move to its attack positions at the foot of the hill.[3] Air strikes had begun a half hour earlier to soften up Chinese positions on both the forward and reverse slopes of Hill 342. When darkness shut down the air strikes, the 674th Field Artillery Battalion, the organic field artillery for the airborne regiment, began to plaster the crest and forward slopes of the objective, while K Company moved upward from the line of departure. The company followed a north-south ridgeline that originated in the lower ground. This ridgeline, like so many in Korea, had paralleling ridges off the main ridgeline. Hill 342 actually consisted of the three highest parallel ridges that bisected the long ridgeline. Each had a peak, close to its center,

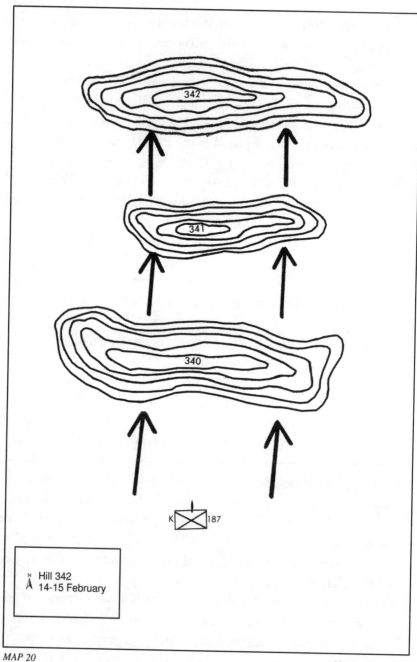

MAP 20

Map by J.D. Coleman

that sloped away east and west, gently at first and then sharply. The three objective peaks were known to K Company as 340, 341, and 342, the first two being intermediate objectives. Each peak was about 60–80 yards in straight-line distance from each other, but the ground distance of walking down into the draw and back up the top of the next peak, of course, was considerably greater.

Although harassed by long-range small-arms fire, the company made fairly rapid progress up the ridgeline until just before reaching the crest of Hill 340. There, at about 5:30 P.M., enemy resistance stiffened and the attack was stalled by extremely heavy fire from well-concealed entrenched machine guns and riflemen. During the attack on Hill 340, Pvt. Robert E. Sullivan moved farther west to reach a vantage point from which he could fire on CCF positions with his BAR. Although he was exposed to intense enemy fire, Sullivan continued to deliver suppressive fire that allowed his platoon to advance until he was mortally wounded.[4]

Weber asked Munson for permission to wait until darkness and conduct a night attack on the objective. When Munson agreed, Weber used the time to work with his artillery forward observer to bring suppressive fire on suspected enemy positions and had ammunition redistributed among the assault elements.

Weber advanced up the mountain with two platoons abreast, his 1st, under Lieutenant Overgaard, on the left and the 2d Platoon on the right. Before jumping off on the final assault, Weber reinforced the left-flank platoon with a squad from his 3d Platoon to compensate for the loss of eight men who had been wounded or killed during the first push up the mountain.

The assault went well and fairly quickly. The company had seized Hill 340 and then 341 by 9 P.M. Forty-five minutes later, Weber's Company K was "king" of Hill 342. Attacking against what was estimated to be a CCF company, K Company sustained eight casualties—one killed and seven wounded. When Weber reported the seizure of the objective, Munson told him, "You're sure to be counterattacked so make a good tight perimeter and call for illumination periodically." Weber set about establishing a perimeter defense that incorporated Hill 341 as well as 342. He set his 60-mm mortars in a draw behind 340 and located his command post in a hole on the reverse slope of 342, about 30 yards down from the crest.

Weber sent out patrols in front of his positions. All was quiet on the east side of his positions, but the patrols on the north and west sides reported a lot of enemy activity farther down the hill. Weber's forward observer placed artillery fire into the areas where the Chinese seemed to be milling around, but no one could ascertain the results. K company positions received a couple of short rounds that shook them but did not hurt anyone.[5] Short rounds occurred with some frequency during the early months of the war. A great deal of the artillery ammunition was from World War II stocks warehoused on Okinawa. Powder charges did not always burn uniformly, and even the best redlegs (artillerymen) in the business could not control defective ammunition.

On Hill 342, a lot of holes already had been dug. The 38th Infantry had started digging in, and then the Chinese had improved those positions. When Sgt. 1/C Charles O. ("Pop") Brooks and his light machine-gun team arrived on the hill, they found a hole with a dead Chinese soldier in it. They threw him out and took over the hole for themselves. Brooks said that the hole was too small for the three of them, and, because it was very cold, they kept warm by digging. As they dug deeper and tunneled forward toward Chinese positions, they created a protective cave. Brooks had let the other two men, Pfc. Randal Stenson and Cpl. Earl Putt, take the first rest while he stayed awake. He was wide awake around 3 A.M. when he saw a Chinese soldier loom up out of the night only 10 or 15 feet from his hole. Suddenly, the perimeter began receiving mortar fire, and covering machine-gun fire lashed K Company positions. Men in different parts of the perimeter had various perceptions of the attack. In some places, the assault was accompanied by the usual cacophony of bugles, whistles, and horns. At Brooks's position, the Chinese soldier, firing as he came, rushed the hole. Brooks ducked into the cave as the enemy soldier fired into the hole and passed on.[6]

A battalion of Chinese infantrymen, using standard CCF assault procedures, began overwhelming assaults on the north and west portions of the perimeter. The operations journals called these attacks *banzai* attacks, which, in truth, they were not. True banzai attacks, made by the Japanese during World War II, had featured fanatical charges by masses of men. The Chinese assaults included a lot of men, but their attacks did not present such lucrative targets as a mass of men charging into machine guns. The Chinese, using cover of darkness, crawled on hand and knees to get in position to throw grenades or to use a rifle or submachine gun. They would take one hole and then methodically attack the next hole while someone stayed behind to improve the conquered hole. When one soldier was killed or wounded, another took his place and then another and another. This seemingly limitless manpower and the CCF profligate use of it in attacks spawned the common usage of the terms *human wave* and *banzai* attacks.

On top of 342, Weber's company was learning how badly the Chinese wanted the hill back, and the Chinese were learning just how tough this band of Rakkasans was. In the 2d Platoon manning the northwest sector, Pfc. Russell H. Bowers, a rifleman, was in a position that the Chinese wanted to penetrate. Although he was the target of grenades and automatic weapons fire that seriously wounded him, Bowers kept a steady volume of fire on the advancing enemy with his rifle. His fire was so intense and accurate that the Chinese were forced to withdraw and concentrate their attack on another sector of the defensive perimeter. Despite his painful wounds, Bowers continued to fire on the enemy until he was killed by a mortar round.[7]

The Chinese increased the intensity of their attack on the north slope and made several penetrations of the line. Captain Weber ranged around his positions and exposed himself to enemy fire as he worked to help his platoon leaders.[8] Weber was trying to defend too much ground with too few men. After a second savage assault on his 3d Platoon, where numerous penetrations were made, Weber realized that he would have to pull back to the second peak 341 and form a much tighter perimeter there.

The machine gun operated by Corporal Putt was laying down a steady stream of fire when a grenade detonated in his hole. Brooks had his left foot blown off, both Putt and Stenson were also wounded, and the machine gun was knocked out of service.[9] Sgt. 1/C Thomas R. Wilcynski helped to save the 3d Platoon from destruction by setting up a strong squad position to cover the platoon's withdrawal to 341. The withdrawal was a dicey affair because of the number of wounded men who had to be carried or dragged to the other hill. When the pullback was complete, Wilcynski sent back the cover squad and remained on the hill as he fired furiously at the enemy until the squad completed the move. Wilcynski then moved back to Hill 341 to help organize its defense and, in the process, beat back another CCF assault.[10]

The Chinese did not give K Company the luxury of time in pulling back and reorganizing on Peak 341. They followed closely behind the withdrawing troopers and threw grenades at them. In a penetration of the 1st Platoon's positions from the west, a Chinese grenade landed in the hole occupied by Weber and his artillery forward observer. Weber recalls the incident with great clarity:

> I had the SCR-300 with me because my radio operator had already been hit. I have this memory of reaching down to grab this grenade and pitch it out of the hole and it went off. It took the arm and, of course, blew our radios away as well. Gary Chow [M.Sgt. Y. S. ("Gary") Chow, the first sergeant] came up and wrapped something around my arm. But you know, I didn't feel anything.[11]

Even with his right arm shattered, Weber continued to command his company. About twenty minutes later, another grenade or a mortar round landed in his CP and shattered his lower right leg. That pretty much was the end of the fight for Weber. His troops carried him back to where the company mortars were located and made him as comfortable as possible. Weber does not remember who took command of the company. There were two lieutenants remaining unwounded. Pfc. Donald F. ("Don") Boor remembered a Lt. Naughton taking charge and going around telling people, "We're not going to let those bastards on the same hill with us." In fact, Capt. Corwin Boak, Jr., the executive officer, had taken over until he was also wounded.

Weber later said that, after a while, it was not a unit battle but a lot of individual fights. An example of an individual seeing a need and filling it was Private Boor. A .57-mm recoilless rifle gunner, whose weapon was useless in close-quarter combat, Boor loaded up on grenades and dueled with the Chinese. When a machine gun in his sector stopped firing, Boor, who had been a machine gunner before being handed a .57, pulled the machine gun back from the line of fire and diagnosed the stoppage as caused by incorrect headspace. After making the adjustment, he put the gun back on line and fired it. He moved his position repeatedly in order to maintain a steady volume of fire.[12]

The violence on the hill was easily visible from the positions of E and G Companies down the ridgeline to the west on Hill 255. Lieutenant Epps, who had been wounded in the thigh but had elected to stay with his platoon overnight, was awake with pain. During that long night, he could see Hill 342 rock with explosions. Epps was amazed at the tremendous volume of fireworks and explosions. The intensity of the battle astounded him, and he remembered it as the most terrible firefight that he had ever witnessed in three wars.[13]

Pfc. Lou Richards, a K Company rifleman, in remembering the battle, said that his company could not have survived without the efforts of I Company. The Item Company Rakkasans formed a daisy chain to move ammunition up the hill to the K Company position.[14]

The mountain was too dark and too steep to try to carry litters off of it, so Weber and the seriously wounded men lay shivering in the bitter cold. Sergeant Chow performed triage on the wounded, Weber remembered. If a man was slightly wounded and could walk and shoot, Chow had the medics patch him up and then sent him back on line. Consequently, some men were wounded more than once.[15]

At dawn, the Chinese broke off the attack and attempted to fortify and defend the Hill 342 peak, but a counterattack by the bloodied remnants of K Company drove CCF soldiers off the peak.

While King Company was undergoing its ordeal, G Company was directed to send a combat patrol up the ridgeline from Hill

255 toward Hill 342. The objective was a piece of high ground about 700 yards west and south of Hill 342. The purpose was both reconnaissance and, if feasible, to make a spoiling attack on the area from which most of the CCF assaults on the K Company perimeter seemed to be originating. The patrol, composed of the company's 2d Platoon led by 1st Lt. Earl K. Wooley, jumped off at 4:30 A.M. and moved quickly up the ridgeline. There were four peaks on the long ridgeline. The platoon easily reached the third peak after shooting a number of Chinese soldiers who were still in their holes. The reaction from the fourth peak was violent. Hand grenades showered the platoon, and machine-gun fire from reverse slopes pinned down the troopers. During the ensuing firefight, the enemy began flanking movements on both flanks of Wooley's platoon and he received permission to withdraw to the company's positions on Hill 255. Under cover of long-range machine-gun fire from G Company, Wooley's platoon made the withdrawal in good order.[16]

Even though the gambit with the combat patrol was seemingly less than fully successful, that patrol, combined with the K Company attack on Hill 342, sent a message to the Chinese commanders at Wonju. The Americans were not only tenaciously defending their territory, but they were audaciously attacking at night, heretofore exclusively a Chinese tactic.

Meanwhile, to the left of the 187th's positions, Fox Company, 38th Infantry Regiment, rediscovered its pride in being an American fighting force. After twice being pushed off Hill 325 and recapturing the high ground three times, it had dashed Chinese plans to use the terrain for a thrust into the left flank of the Wonju defenses. Fox's commander, Captain Nelson, won a posthumous Distinguished Service Cross for his gallantry during the attacks and counterattacks.[17]

During the morning, L Company, 187th Airborne RCT, jumped off on an attack to seize Hill 203, a promontory about 400 yards west of the Wonju River and due east of Hill 342. Concurrently, Item Company moved up and replaced King Company on Hill 342.

Daylight also permitted litter bearers to move the wounded off the hill. For some wounded men, the wait for evacuation had been as long as eight hours.[18]

Captain Weber was one of the most seriously wounded. Capt. Warren Belt, commander of the Regimental Medical Company, was at the regimental collecting station when Weber was brought in. He said that the surgeons there expected Weber to lose both an arm and a leg. They were correct, but the loss of his right arm and lower right leg did not stop Weber from remaining on active Army duty and ultimately retiring as a colonel.[19]

There were not enough litters remaining on the hill to evacuate Sergeant Brooks, so his fellow troopers improvised a litter by using a blanket and two M-1 rifles. Private Boor helped to carry Brooks down the mountain with the rifle and blanket litter. When Brooks reached the bottom of the hill, the first sergeant of I Company came up to him and said, "You put on quite a show up there last night, sarge. I guess I should have let you keep those rations." Brooks said that I Company's topkick was referring to an aborted raid on C-rations that Brooks had staged during the company's move into the Wonju defense line. There were no hard feelings, Brooks said. Everyone acknowledged that paratroopers had no scruples about scrounging to feed, arm, or comfort their comrades.[20] Some units raised the techniques of scrounging or "midnight requisitioning" to an art form. Sergeant Valent and his platoon, also known as "Jumpy and his forty thieves," were notorious in the 187th.

At noon on 15 February, G Company attacked northeast up the ridgeline toward Peak 342. When it reached the third of the four peaks where the 2d Platoon had been earlier that morning, CCF resistance became vicious. The 1st Platoon, led by Sergeant Valent, made a direct assault on the peak, while Wooley's platoon made a flanking movement to the right and attacked the fourth and highest peak from the east. Soon, both peaks were seized by G Company troopers. The 3d Platoon passed through the other two platoons and began moving toward Hill 342 with the aim of linking up with Item Company. The platoon began receiving heavy automatic weapons fire from positions hidden in the folds of ground below the summit of the peak just taken. Lieutenant White, the 3d Platoon's leader, charged a machine-gun position, got the drop on the gun crew with his carbine, and killed both men. A second machine gun, 50 yards from the first, opened up on White and wounded him in the chest. Despite his serious wounds, White crawled to within 15 yards of the second gun and, before dying of his wounds, threw a white phosphorus grenade into the Chinese position and knocked it out. He was posthumously awarded the Distinguished Service Cross for his heroism. Pfc. Robert W. Minkler, who was also assaulting the second gun, was killed by a shot from a Chinese rifleman close to the second gun.[21] By late afternoon, G Company troops had driven the Chinese from the ridge between Hills 255 and 342 and Wooley's 2d Platoon had made physical contact with Item company's positions on Hill 342.

With L Company's seizure of Hill 203 earlier in the day, the 187th had moved the Wonju defense line west of the river 1,000 yards north onto the dominant high ground. During the afternoon of the 15 February, the 2d Battalion, 9th Infantry, replaced the 2d Battalion, 38th Infantry, and the Netherlands Battalion, thus solidifying the defensive line west of Wonju.

During the next two days, aggressive patrolling north of the new defensive positions revealed that the Chinese had begun withdrawing north toward Hoengsong. The prisoners captured by the Rakkasans on the high ground identified their unit as the 360th Regiment, 120th Division, Fortieth CCF Field Army. They said the entire regiment had been on Hills 255, 342, and the ridgelines between, and their mission was to secure the high ground and then seize Wonju itself. Assaults by three U.S. airborne rifle companies, with no more than 150 men each, had wrested the hills from control of a Chinese regiment, numbering as much as 2,000 men.

The Chinese portion of the Fourth Offensive slammed into a wall at Wonju and the People's Volunteers were sent reeling back north. The Sixty-Sixth CCF Field Army, with three divisions that had hardly been taxed in the battles above Hoengson, was positioned to attack the right flank of the Wonju defenders. That they did not and rapidly retreated north without making contact seems clear evidence that General Peng had folded his hand. Even as the retreat progressed, Peng was called back to Peking to report to Chairman Mao about the situation in Korea.

To the east of Wonju, however, the North Koreans were pushing ROK units back toward Chech'on. Some of the withdrawals were deliberate, as Ridgway wanted to straighten out the lines to reduce the vulnerability of the ROK forces on the east coast that had forged farther north than any other UN unit. General Yu, ROK III Corps commander, permitted his units to withdraw without maintaining contact. This was counter to Ridgway's instructions, and he angrily directed the KMAG chief, Brig. Gen. Francis W. Farrell, to position himself where he could personally ensure that ROK units did not withdraw without remaining in contact with and punishing the enemy. The NKPA V and II Corps units drove hard toward the south. The ROK III Corps elements began throwing up stronger defenses and stopped the North Koreans well in front of the NKPA objective of Yongwol.

In the X Corps sector, Brig. Gen. Kim Pak Il, I Corps commander, who, with his staff, had been loaned to General Almond by Ridgway to reorganize and command the ROK divisions in X Corps, had a tough task. Kim struggled to reorganize the remnants of the ROK 5th and 8th Divisions and use them in a defense line north of Chech'on. The North Korean 6th, 7th, and 12th Divisions found the weak spots in the defensive line and penetrated to within 5 miles of Chech'on. To keep Chech'on from falling and to protect the vital MSR to Wonju, Almond committed the U.S. 7th Division's 31st Infantry to back up the ROK 5th division. With the 7th Division's 32d Infantry providing close-in defense of Chech'on and one battalion of the 17th Infantry on the MSR in the danger zone, the NKPA threat was stabilized.[22]

No commander in the Wonju defense line had any illusions that the Chinese had quit the field for good. They believed that the CCF had merely pulled back a few miles to the Hoengsong area to reorganize. For the defenders, the respite was welcomed. It provided an opportunity for small-unit leaders to take stock of their men and equipment and to write recommendations for awards.

Under the best of circumstances, awards and decorations in line infantry units tended to be uneven. Much depended on how commanders at battalion and regimental levels felt about the desirability of awards and the emphasis that they placed on the process. Command emphasis varied widely even within the same regiment. The writing ability of small-unit leaders in preparing recommendations for awards also played a part. Most soldiers recognize these differences and understand that one commander's conception of what merits a Silver Star is but a Bronze Star or a pat on the back in the estimation of another commander. Although they do not like it, most soldiers can accept this situation. What tends to gum up the works is senior commanders entering the picture. General Almond was constantly handing out instant awards. In Vietnam they were known as *impact awards*; with Almond, they could have been better termed *impulse awards*.

On 19 February, the 1st Platoon of E Company, which consisted of survivors of the assault on Hill 255, was directed to report to Regimental Headquarters and draw fatigues suitable for standing in formation for an awards ceremony to be conducted by General Almond. Somehow, Almond had the idea that the conquest of the hill was solely the work of one platoon. Platoon member John O. Morris remembered that Almond started by giving two members, who were to be recommended for Medals of Honor, interim awards of the Silver Star (both awards were later downgraded to Distinguished Service Crosses). After he presented the awards, Almond asked Lieutenant Dolan about the dead and wounded in the platoon. Dolan referred to his notebook and replied, "Sir, I had nine men KIA [killed in action] and seventeen WIA [wounded in action], and many of them will be recommended for awards." According to Morris, Almond then said, "I hereby award the Silver Star to all the killed and wounded."[23]

When Almond returned to his headquarters, he directed that E Company be written up for a Distinguished Unit Citation. Probably because of Almond's actions in decorating the 1st Platoon en masse, the staff officers writing up the recommendation concentrated on the actions of Dolan's platoon. Consequently, the special report on Hill 255 in the X Corps command report is the story of only the 1st Platoon.[24]

Fred Waterhouse, in his Rakkasan history, wrote that Colonel Connor, 2d Battalion commander, enthusiastically supported the citation for Company E, but he also felt that the entire battalion should have received a citation. Connor was not present during Almond's visit to the E Company platoon and did not have a chance to plead his case. Later, he wrote, "I was unable to explain to the general that it was the concerted effort of the entire battalion, with G Company as the flanking force, which accomplished the mission."

In an interview with Waterhouse in 1989, Normand O. LeBrun and John Maneri, both E Company riflemen, said that G Company should have received the citation. Both asserted that E Company could not have taken the hill without the flanking attack of G Company.[25]

LeBrun, a trooper in the 1st Platoon, did not receive a Silver Star. He left for his rest and recuperation (R&R) leave the morning after the battle and missed Almond's awards ceremony. LeBrun said that Lieutenant Dolan told him he had put him in for the award.[26] One possible reason for the oversight was that Dolan was killed in action a little more than a month later.

There is no mystery as to why Colonel Connor was not present at the awards ceremony for a platoon in his battalion. He and the remainder of the 2d Battalion were on vehicles heading southeast out of Wonju for the town of Sillim ni at the time that Almond was conducting the awards ceremony. The 2d Battalion was headed for a confrontation with the same North Koreans who had just clobbered the ROK 5th Division. This fact begs the question: Why would a corps commander strip away a rifle platoon from an already understrength rifle company which he had just ordered back into combat. The answer lies in a 1990s term—*photo op*. General MacArthur, accompanied by an entourage of newsmen, was scheduled to visit the Wonju front the following day. In fact, the X Corps

Daily Journal for 19 February carried the entry that the Corp's public information staff was concerned about seven unaccompanied newsmen who showed up unannounced at the 187th Command Post that morning.[27]

Almond apparently got what he wanted. In the X Corps files, a true copy of an adulatory news story is attached to the report of the attack on Hill 255 by E Company's 1st Platoon. There was no identification of the news medium from which it was taken, but it clearly was a news story and not a X Corps press release.[28] Moreover, the story reflected Almond's new rank. General Ridgway had pinned Almond's third star on him on 14 February.

Later, on the day that he decorated the E Company platoon at Chip'yong-ni, Almond also decorated a number of enlisted men, as well as Colonel Monclar, the French Battalion commander. A clue to the frenzy of award giving to enlisted troops might be a story that appeared in *Time* magazine. Although it'appeared in the 19 February issue, most public information officers were aware of unfavorable stories before they actually hit the street. This particular story ripped General MacArthur and Air Force Lt. Gen. George Stratemeyer for their overly generous bestowing of Distinguished Service Crosses and Silver Stars. The article made the point that rear-area senior staff officers were generously rewarded with medals for heroism where no real heroism was apparent. And, at the same time, enlisted men gave their lives heroically with a possible posthumous reward of a Bronze Star, if that.[29]

Almond was incensed by the story that denigrated MacArthur and, on 21 February, directed his public information officer (PIO) to draft a letter to the editor of *Time* magazine to refute the article on medals. Almond wanted to enclose pictures of him decorating enlisted men. His PIO submitted a memorandum recommending that the letter not be sent because the Department of Defense would likely respond. Two days later, the PIO log reflected that a draft letter was given to Almond and that it was dispatched.[30] No record of the letter appears in the files, and *Time* did not see fit to print the letter, although the magazine did print a number of other letters.

Captain Shanahan made sure that members of the other platoons were appropriately recognized. Lieutenant Nix was awarded the Distinguished Service Cross for his actions on the west approaches to Hill 255, and several members of his platoon earned Silver Stars and Bronze Stars.

An interesting postscript to the Hill 255 story relates to the five 38th Infantry soldiers who were drafted by Nix as a fourth rifle squad for his platoon. Nix said that all five men did a good job for him and all wanted to stay with the platoon. He arranged for them to get airborne physicals from Capt. Robert Bernstein, the 2d Battalion surgeon. Four of the men passed and stayed with the 187th. They qualified as parachutists when the regiment pulled back to Taegu to prepare for the 23 March combat jump.[31]

MacArthur did indeed visit the Wonju front on 20 February. When he arrived at Suwon that morning, he had been briefed by Ridgway about Operation Killer, which was scheduled to begin the next day. At an impromptu press conference at the X Corps advance command post later in the day, MacArthur declared "I have just ordered a resumption of the offensive."[32]

Because MacArthur had absolutely nothing to do with the planning of Killer, Ridgway was both surprised and dismayed by MacArthur's announcement. It long had been MacArthur's practice to fly to Korea in advance of a major operation and, in effect, fire the starter's gun. Ridgway ruefully remembered that it was "an unwelcome reminder of a MacArthur I had known but had almost forgotten."[33]

TWENTY-ONE | Transitioning to "Killer"

Even as the guns were blazing around the Wonju hills and before the tanks of Task Force Crombez started for Chip'yong-ni, General Ridgway, sensing that the Chinese had shot their bolt, was planning to institute a counteroffensive.[1]

Before he launched an offensive, however, Ridgway needed to straighten up the lines west of Chip'yong-ni. The Chinese were still strongly defending the salient that protruded deep into IX Corps territory. Ridgway wanted that bridgehead reduced and then wanted the IX Corps to extend to the east through the town of Hajin, about 3 miles northwest of Chip'yong-ni. The Chinese Thirty-Eighth Army had been stubbornly resisting IX Corps and I Corps attacks. Then, two days after the relief of Chip'yong-ni, the CCF, without fanfare, melted away. When probes by the 5th RCT of the 24th Division revealed that the Chinese appeared to have withdrawn from the salient west of Chip'yong-ni, Ridgway directed Maj. Gen. Bryant Moore, IX Corps commander, to advance and seize the high ground along a line running from his left boundary with I Corps through Yangp'yong to the village of Hajin. Because Ridgway already had moved the IX Corps boundary east to the Som River, about 6 miles from Wonju, Moore proposed attacking north with the British 27th Brigade, the ROK 6th Division, and the U.S. 1st Cavalry Division to seize the high ground overlooking the Seoul–Wonju railroad from Hajin to the Som River.[2]

Although intelligence was sketchy on the whereabouts of the Chinese units that had not been consumed in the flames of Wonju and Chip'yong-ni, nobody in the U.S. Eighth Army thought the

Chinese had left the country. Ridgway believed that he now had a handle on the rhythm of Chinese war-making—attack until initial momentum is lost, pull back slightly, organize good defenses, rest and refit, then attack again. Consequently, he wanted to disrupt that rhythm by counterattacking quickly and denying the Chinese any respite in which to prepare new attacks. He also wanted to destroy the North Korean forces that had pushed a salient deep into X Corps territory in the Chech'on area. On 18 February, Ridgway developed the concept for his counteroffensive. It would feature twin thrusts to pinch off enemy forces in the Chech'on salient. One would go north from Wonju toward Hoengsong and be conducted by IX Corps, and the other, to the east, would be a X Corps drive from Yongwol to beyond P'yongch'ang. These parallel thrusts would meet at some point north of Hoengsong and P'yongch'ang and pinch out the escape routes of the NKPA and CCF forces trapped within the salient. Ridgway named the offensive "Killer."[3]

His first battle was a contest of wills. When the code name was heard at the Pentagon, there was an immediate negative reaction. Gen. Collins, Army chief of staff, sent Ridgway a prompt but courteous protest that the word *killer* would be difficult for the Army's public relations apparatus to deal with. Ridgway responded politely but, nevertheless, kept the code name because it perfectly described the objectives of his offensive. He later wrote, "I did not understand why it was objectionable to acknowledge the fact that war was concerned with killing the enemy." In his book, *The Korean War*, Ridgway wrote that he later learned that severe political pressures were being put on the Army and the Administration at the time. Not surprisingly, Ridgway had a strong opinion on the issue: "I am by nature opposed to any effort to 'sell' war to people as an only mildly unpleasant business that requires very little in the way of blood."[4]

Ridgway had to fight several other internal battles as well. Even as he was developing his concept for an offensive, he received the staff recommendations he had requested in late January on the terrain lines that the Eighth Army should attempt to occupy during the spring and summer months. If Ridgway had expected to see lines drawn toward and along the 38th Parallel, he received a substantial shock when he looked at the staff plans. Incredibly, the staff recommended that the Eighth Army abandon offensive operations, defend in place until spring, and then voluntarily withdraw to the old Pusan Perimeter. Ridgway instantly disapproved the proposal and directed his staff that, henceforth, they were to think primarily in terms of the offensive. According to Clay Blair, the officer who ultimately took the fall for the defeatist plan was Brig. Gen. John Dabney, Ridgway's G-3.[5]

Another internal issue that Ridgway had to resolve to ensure that his fighting forces remained intact was to salve the wounded feelings of ROK generals who resented the bullying tactics of General Almond. Ridgway did not wait for a conference with Almond, who was not at his headquarters. He cornered Col. John S. Guthrie, Almond's chief of staff, at the X Corps advance airstrip at Wonju. Ridgway told Guthrie to convey to Almond that the ROK commanders of the 8th, 3d, and 5th Divisions, which were attached to X Corps, "were very resentful of the way they are treated in X Corps. He told Guthrie that the UN command was heavily dependent on the ROK units as battle partners and losing the ROK Army's cooperation would have serious consequences. Guthrie was to inform Almond that he wanted the situation promptly corrected.

The import of Ridgway delivering a rebuke to a three-star general through a subordinate was not lost on Almond. In late February and early March he scheduled some awards ceremonies for ROK commanders, a tactic at which Almond was particularly good. The second part of Ridgway's strategy to keep the ROK commanders on board took place at a conference at Eighth Army Headquarters in Taegu late in the afternoon of 16 February. In attendance at this meeting was Gen. Chung Il Kwon, chief of staff of the ROK Army; Sihn Sung Mo, South Korean defense minister; Ambassador Muccio; and selected Eighth Army staff members.

Ridgway led off by praising General Chung for being present during the crisis with the ROK 5th Division near Chech'on the preceding day and noted that it was his belief that the senior commander always should be present at the crucial moment in battle. He said that, at present, he was not going to try to fix responsibility for the mistakes that had been made—it was too early for that. (Although not stated in the command summary, Ridgway apparently was referring to the Hoengsong debacle.) He asked that all commanders examine the action to learn a lesson to see what could be done immediately and from a long-range view to improve battle performance. He also reminded the conferees of the importance of maintaining major unit integrity. "We are fighting a numerically superior enemy," Ridgway said. "We must make up for it by good footwork, by maximum use of movement, combined with fire power. If a division has good reconnaissance, continuous reconnaissance with proper reporting to proper authority, there is no excuse for its being destroyed." Ridgway also bore down on the recent loss of vast quantities of military equipment. He said that it was a "grave offense against everyone in the Army and it would not be tolerated." Ridgway earlier had told ROK officials that unless they could demonstrate that they could protect their artillery, he was not going to give them any more.

When Minister Sihn and General Chung had an opportunity to respond to Ridgway's lecture, they relayed the complaints of their division commanders over the way they were being handled in X Corps. The record states that Ridgway responded that "we must use every resource at our disposal to compose that difference." He stressed that there must be no friction between commanders. While the record does not say so, it is likely that Ridgway told Sihn and Chung that he had directed his corps commanders to be more sensitive to the concerns of the ROK commanders. At the same time, he issued a "buck-up" request to be relayed to General Yu, ROK III Corps commander. Yu had been making noises about getting his 3d and 5th Divisions back from X Corps control. Ridgway asked General Chung to tell Yu that he would get the divisions back as soon as the current crisis was over. He also asked Chung to help him ensure that Yu understood the gravity of the situation in the P'yongch'ang–Yongwol corridor and that even minor offensive movements by the ROK 7th and 9th Divisions could pay enormous dividends. Both South Korean leaders appeared satisfied when they left the meeting.[6]

Now that coalition warfare responsibilities had been satisfied, Ridgway could turn to the task of cranking up his counteroffensive. There was nothing complicated about the plan. He intended to shift the IX Corps–X Corps boundary to the east so that Wonju and Hoengsong would be in the IX Corps sector. To hammer that sector, Ridgway planned to commit the well-rested 1st Marine Division. At twenty-five thousand men, it was the most powerful force in the Eighth Army. Ridgway knew that the 2d Division was in no shape to conduct an offensive against the Chinese field armies that he believed were waiting in the Hoengsong area. Moreover, because he had promised General Smith, 1st Marine Division commander, that he would never be required to have his Marines serve under General Almond again, Ridgway had no choice but to move X Corps to the east. The 2d Division felt betrayed by the X Corps commander.[7]

Even General Stewart was unaware of the real reason why X Corps was moved out of the Wonju–Hoengsong axis. Years later, he wrote that when the Marines moved over the locations where Support Force 21 had bled and died and saw the bodies and destroyed equipment, "they assumed that the 2d Division had suffered a humiliating defeat and were not backward in expressing their contempt. I think that the Corps Commander's act in this instance was reprehensible, unnecessary and shameful."[8] Although Almond was blameless in this incident, the fact that a brigadier general thought him capable of such a malicious act speaks volumes about his reputation in the command.

Intelligence officers in Eighth Army Headquarters were aware that an estimated seven new armies were entering Korea, but they could not, with any precision, pinpoint whether these new forces were moving south to engage UN forces. Ridgway adopted a prudent course by crediting the new enemy reserves with the capability of appearing at the front within any twenty-four–hour period. In an "eyes only" (to be read only by the addressees) memorandum to Corps commanders, Ridgway cautioned them to take proper precautions while advancing in Operation Killer. They must maintain major units intact, make proper use of terrain, and have solid lateral security and carefully coordinate movements within and between corps. With the memory of Almond's Operation Roundup in mind, he sternly warned the senior commanders against "being sucked in and destroyed piecemeal, whether by ruse, or the temptation to your own aggressiveness to pursue beyond your capability of providing powerful support, or of timely disengagement and local withdrawal."[9] There would be no more Hoengsongs on Ridgway's watch.

Because the ROK 6th Division and the British Commonwealth Brigade were already in position to the right of the U.S. 1st Cavalry Division, those units would attack in their current zones. The 1st Cavalry would fill in between the British and the 24th Division. When the Marines advanced, there would be a solid line of forces on their flanks. The U.S. 2d Division, on the X Corps left, would cover the Marines' right flank. To the right of the 2d Division would be the U.S. 7th Division and then three ROK divisions.

In order to give commanders in the Eighth Army a clear picture of where Ridgway wanted to be when Operation Killer concluded, a phase line designated as "Line Arizona" was drawn on planning maps. This line ran from Yangp'yong (near the big bend of the Han River) to the east as it passed north of Chip'yong-ni, Hoengsong, and P'yongch'ang and ended on the coast near the town of Samch'ok.[10]

The 187th was to revert to X Corps reserve at Chech'on when the Marines moved through its positions at Wonju. Its mission was to be prepared to support the 7th Division's attack, if required; however, Ridgway informed Almond that he was not to commit the unit without Ridgway's prior approval. The Eighth Army Commander intended to move the Rakkasans back to Taegu for refresher jump training in preparation for a parachute assault north of Seoul. The string on the 187th was effective upon the launch of Killer, scheduled for 10 A.M., 21 February.

Until that deadline, however, the 187th was Almond's to do with as he wished. Almond was obliged by the Eighth Army to return the ROK 18th Regiment, which had been on the right flank of the Wonju defense line, to its parent division, the ROK 3d Division. He also needed to release the two 17th Infantry Regiment battalions that had been attached to the 187th to provide depth to the Wonju defense. The 3d Battalion, 187th, was shifted to the right of the regiment's 1st Battalion to relieve the ROK 18th Regiment. Almond, however, wanted one battalion from the 187th to conduct offensive operations south and east of Wonju, about halfway to Chech'on. There was a troublesome North Korean force just northeast of the town of Sillim-ni that had overcome efforts of ROK elements to halt its advance toward Chech'on. The 2d Battalion was tabbed for the mission.

Early on Monday morning, 19 February, the 1st Battalion, 9th Infantry, moved in to relieve the 2/187. The company that was to relieve G Company arrived and milled around while G Company platoon leaders walked their 9th Infantry counterparts to their positions. The 9th Infantry company commander, a first lieutenant, stayed in the command post area until his platoon leaders returned. The men at the G Company command post were heating their breakfast C-rations over a small fire when the 9th Infantry platoon leaders returned. One of them asked their commander what they should do in the event of a major Chinese attack. His response was, "You How Able" (he was using the phonetic alphabet as a euphemism for "haul ass").

Captain Cook, the G Company commander, nearly dropped his can of rations. Cook, more than anyone around the fire, knew the horrendous human cost to seize and hold the hills north of Wonju. Many of his close friends from his days as a platoon sergeant in E Company were, at that moment, lying in a Pusan mortuary.

The platoon leader persisted in questioning his commander and asked what to do with the crew-served weapons. The response was, "Leave 'em." It was nearly the last straw for Cook. Paratroopers, like Marines, do not intentionally leave their weapons, their wounded, or their dead behind. Cook rose from his seat on the ammunition box and appeared as though he wanted to leap across the fire and throttle his counterpart. He controlled himself, but his baleful glare caused the 9th Infantry troops to withdraw to another location until G Company had vacated the territory.[11]

The 2d Battalion was loaded on trucks by 9 A.M. and, by noon, was unloading just outside Sillim-ni. There, the battalion was joined by B Battery, 674th Field Artillery Battalion, plus a battery of 155 howitzers and a platoon of 4.2-inch mortars. The battalion then picked up a platoon of tanks from the 72d Tank Battalion and began marching east along a road that many of the men remembered mostly as an improved goat trail. The assigned objective was what X Corps called "Objective P." It consisted of two large hill masses that towered over the road passing between them. Hill 687 (2,254 feet) was on the north side of the road and Hill 738 (2,421 feet) on the south.[12] There was reputed to be anywhere from one North Korean company up to possibly a regiment on the mountains. Whatever the opposition, just trying to climb those steep, snow-covered slopes would be challenging in itself.

Fox Company was leading the battalion column. At about 4 P.M., the company's lead platoon received fire from a finger that jutted down from Hill 738 on the south (right) side of the road. Because F Company's assigned objective was Hill 687 on the north side of the road, Captain Pickett, company commander, immediately directed his company to deploy rapidly to the left side of the road and begin movement toward the company objective behind a low finger that paralleled the road. It was a long haul, about 3,000 yards, from where the company deployed off the road. In remembering the engagement, 1st Lt. Donald L. Roberts, 2d Platoon leader, said that the initial contact did not amount to much; the North Koreans probably did not have more than a squad on outpost duty.

Pickett and his platoon leaders studied the crest of Hill 687 with binoculars and could see no signs of enemy soldiers. Because no fire had yet come from the objective hill, Pickett pushed his company hard to get to the heights before the enemy could find out what

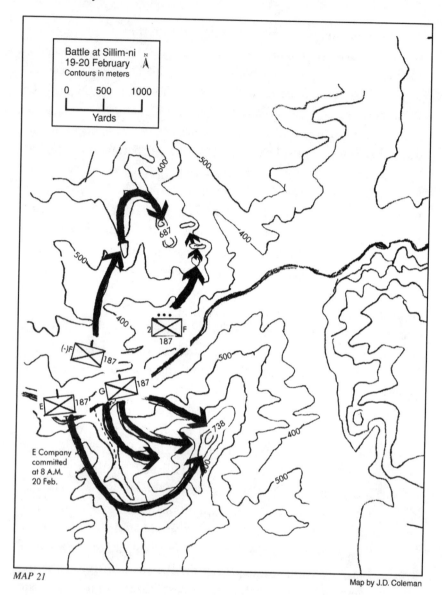

Battle at Sillim-ni
19-20 February
Contours in meters

0   500   1000

Yards

687

2 F 187

(-)F 187

G 187

E 187

738

E Company
committed
at 8 A.M.
20 Feb.

MAP 21

Map by J.D. Coleman

he was up to. He split the company, led two platoons up a ridge
on the southwest side of the objective, and sent Roberts's platoon
to a position on the southeast side. There, the platoon could mount
a diversionary attack or serve as the company reserve, if necessary.
Without drawing enemy fire, the two assault platoons made it to a

north-south ridgeline that paralleled the objective ridge. The two ridgelines were about 500 yards apart and separated by impossibly steep slopes and a narrow valley. The ridges on which the company and the objective were located, however, were part of a larger hill mass to the north that towered another 800 feet higher than either ridge. So Picket decided that the best way to attack Hill 687 would be to work his company up the ridge that he currently occupied to the head of the valley and then move over and down the slope to seize the objective. As soon as most of his assault force was on the parallel ridgeline, it began receiving long-range automatic weapons fire from across the ravine. In his after battle report, Pickett wrote that, because he had been pushing his company hard to get to the objective quickly, his troops were in not in a good attack formation. He pulled the company behind the cover of the ridgeline and organized it for a night attack.[13]

Meanwhile, his 2d Platoon had moved swiftly to its first objective, a knob on a ridgeline southeast of Hill 687. The platoon still had received no enemy fire. With Captain Pickett's last words to him— "Get on your objective before dark"—still fresh in his memory, Roberts rapidly pushed onto the next ridge, which also was not defended. When he was ready to move onto the next ridge, which was his final objective, he was surprised that it appeared very much a dominant terrain feature, second only to the Hill 687 itself, and a feature that the North Koreans were quite likely defending in strength. Roberts had lost radio contact with Pickett, but with darkness rapidly approaching, he had to press on. He left one squad as a base of fire and, with two squads in a column formation to save time, headed down a steep draw between the two ridges. Deep snow impeded progress of the assault teams, and it now was very dark as Roberts and his squads began struggling up the steep slope to objective three.

Roberts has vivid memories of that moment. "Like a clap of thunder, two light machine guns, sub-machine guns and rifles opened up over our heads, aiming at the base of fire element on objective two," he wrote later. Roberts said he was about seventy-five yards from one of the machine guns. He habitually carried solid tracer ammunition in his carbine magazine to mark targets, and he put a stream of tracers on the machine gun. That shut off the guns momentarily, but then there was a swift and violent reaction to the tracers. The North Korean fire went right down the middle of his assault group and split it in two. With no cover and being hopelessly outgunned, the trailing squad returned uphill to the base-of-fire squad's location.

Roberts and the remaining squad, led by S.Sgt. Clarence B. Sprouse, slid to their left and avoided a head-on collision with the enemy force. The squad moved silently and undetected onto the ridgeline and headed west toward the summit of Hill 687. Roberts assumed that the remainder of the company would have been on the objective by this time and had driven the North Koreans down the ridgeline where they collided with his force. The company was not there yet, but the squad surprised a half-dozen North Koreans with a Maxim heavy machine gun on a wheeled mount. Without a shot being fired, the paratroopers captured two of the gunners before the remainder fled. They removed the bolt from the gun and pushed it over a cliff. The squad then followed Roberts down a secondary ridge to the location of the rest of his platoon.[14]

Meanwhile, Pickett had moved his two platoons north to the con-necting ridge, crossed over to a position directly north of the ob-jective, and assaulted south. The platoon on the east side of the objective ridge received small-arms fire from the south, as well as from NKPA positions on a ridgeline another 300 yards farther east. By 10 P.M., Fox Company had control of the crest of Hill 687 but not the main ridgeline where Roberts had stirred up a hornets' nest. Pickett reported that it was his decision to make a night attack.[15]

Not entirely.

Colonel Connor, the battalion commander, was under intense pressure from General Bowen to keep the attack moving. Bowen, in turn, was reacting to pressure from Almond, who wanted to take Objective P before the kickoff of Killer, and he was obligated to return the 187th units to Eighth Army reserve. Fox Company was in a position from which a night attack was feasible and possible, even without supporting artillery fires. George Company was not so lucky.

After the enemy outpost was routed, Captain Cook was ordered to immediately assault Hill 738, the G Company objective. Cook and his executive officer, Capt. John R. D. Cleland, were profoundly concerned about attempting to assault the mountain that loomed white and ghostly in the rapidly darkening skies. They wanted to hunker down for the night and, following artillery and tactical air preparatory fires, conduct a coordinated assault early the next morning. The battalion commander insisted that the assault take place that night and get under way immediately. There is nothing in the records of Bowen's S-3 journal or in the X Corps G-3 journal that would justify the haste. Once again, generals and colonels were demanding that soldiers give more than their leaders had a right to ask.

Cleland later enumerated all the things that were not done that night: "There was not even a rudimentary reconnaissance of the terrain or the enemy positions. There was no fire plan, no coherent plan for maneuver or mutual support from F Company to our left and no registration of artillery or mortars before we started off, willy-nilly, climbing that hill. We started that action in a disorganized way, dispersed three platoons over unknown territory just as it was getting dark and things never got better."[16]

Even though there was formidable fire support available, the company proceeded after a last-light air strike and some fire from the company's own mortars. Johnny Bramblett remembers getting two new mortars from battalion supply, along with four new members of the mortar squad. He said that the new tubes still had cosmoline in them and he had no opportunity to properly clean them so he set them up at the base of the hill and fired a few rounds with maximum charges to burn out the grease.[17]

Each of the three rifle platoons had separate ridgelines to climb toward the summit of 738. The climb was hellish. The grade was very steep, and the north-facing slopes had knee-deep snow. The temperature was plummeting to the low teens. Troopers were sweating with the exertion, and, as soon as North Korean resistance stalled the advance, their damp garments began to freeze. The 3d Platoon was on one of the two main ridges that, at first, appeared to lead to the summit. Cleland remembered that a couple of hours after dark, the company found a deep ravine that bisected the ridge-line. The ground dropped off precipitously and, with extremely heavy enemy fire coming from above, the company was stalled. The North Koreans were shooting at the paratroopers from the top of the hill about 200 yards away. With the attack bogged down at this point, Cook directed a 57-mm recoilless rifle to fire at a machine gun across the ravine. Pfc. Virgil Clemmons clambered up, lined up a shot, and fired. Whether he hit anything was unknown because green tracers immediately lanced through G Company positions close to where the recoilless back blast illuminated the area. Cook took a slug in the lower left side. He pressed his pile liner into the wound with one hand while he notified Battalion Headquarters that he had been hit and was turning the company over to Captain Cleland. This happened at about 9:45 P.M. A medic put a field dressing on the wound, then refusing to permit anyone to assist him, Cook began to slip and slide down the hill toward the battalion aid station.[18]

Cleland knew that there was no way the company could assault the summit from the ridge that it was occupying. In fact, he was risking the company by simply standing fast. While he and Capt. Robert F. Hewett lay prone and scanned the mountaintop to their front, Hewett was shot in the leg and had to be evacuated. Cleland shifted the main effort to the next left ridgeline after rounding up stragglers and people who were lost. By the time Cleland had things sorted out and the company poised for an assault, it was after midnight.

The company jumped off with Sgt. Lewis Sperduto leading and firing a light machine gun from his hip. Machine-gun fire attracts a lot of enemy attention, and Sperduto was killed during the assault. Another part of the company attack featured the BAR team of Pfc.

Olaf Pulver and Pfc. Morrison, who delivered continuous fire into the North Korean positions. A bullet to the head mortally wounded Pulver, but Morrison kept the BAR firing. The assault again stalled in the face of overwhelming firepower from the top of the hill.[19]

Cleland pulled the company back into a coiled position, where the men could rest and reload, and gathered up strays, particularly from the leaderless 3d Platoon. Then, he sent the Rakkasans struggling back up the hill. He was leading the company up the ridgeline when an enemy machine-gun burst hit one arm, spun him around, and shattered the other arm. G Company men close to the captain recalled that they had to pry his .45 pistol from his left hand, and, very carefully, a grenade clutched in his right hand. A 2d Platoon rifleman, John Hare, was detailed to help Cleland down the hill. With both arms broken, the captain needed assistance to wade through the deep snow and to protect himself when he slipped and fell. Hare partially solved the problem by making a supporting sling out of empty ammunition bandoleers. He looped them under the captain's armpits and over his own neck and shoulders.[20]

With the departure of Cleland from the mountain, the succession of command gets murky. The battalion's S-3 journal states that Captain Hewett took command. Cleland, however, distinctly remembers that Hewett, who was the 3d Platoon leader, had been wounded earlier. Troopers remember that Sergeant Valent of the 1st Platoon, although wounded, assumed control of the company until Lieutenant Wooley, the 2d Platoon leader, could move from another ridgeline to the ridge where the main body was located. This is consistent with the memory of Capt. John Miley, who became the fourth and final commander that night.[21]

Miley reorganized the company, established three routes of attack on the summit, and waited until daylight to call in artillery and then air strikes. Mixed loads of high explosives and white phosphorus seemingly left the defenders stunned. When the barrage lifted, G Company assaulted up three separate ridgelines, but several hundred NKPA soldiers came out of their bunkers and stalled the assault just below the crest of 738. There matters stood for most of the morning, with both sides exchanging grenades and sporadic rifle and automatic weapons fire. Colonel Connor committed his reserve, E Company, at 10 A.M. Captain Shanahan took his company on a long end run around the west and south of the mountain and found a good avenue of approach up a long ridgeline from the south. Although E Company was barely two platoons strong after its ordeal on Valentine's Day, its final assault, coordinated with George Company, finally knocked the North Koreans off the summit.

While the two companies were staging for a final assault, Fox Company, across the road on Hill 687, finally secured all the ridgelines of its objective just before 2 P.M. Once the high ground was taken, the North Koreans abandoned their positions on the hills on the north side of the road. The two-company assault on the summit of Hill 738, combined with the faltering morale of defenders who could see their comrades fleeing from the other hills, finally resulted in the enemy being swept from the hill. Afterward, hundreds of North Koreans poured out of lesser hills and peaks to the east and north and ran pell mell onto a road in a narrow valley just to the east of the two mountains, where the tank platoon was waiting. Scores of North Korean soldiers perished under the withering fire of the tanks. On top of the ridges, the Rakkasans blazed away at the fleeing troops with rifles, machine guns, recoilless rifles, and mortars.

Prisoners taken by the 187th told intelligence interrogators that Hill 687 had been garrisoned by a battalion of the 3d Regiment, NKPA 7th Division. Hill 738 was defended by a reinforced battalion of the 1st Regiment, NKPA 12th Division. The North Korean grip on the Chech'on salient was shattered, and the way was clear for Operation Killer to proceed without troublesome opposition from NKPA forces. The cost to G Company was high—seven men were killed and more than thirty wounded. Two men from Fox Company died that night, as did a machine-gun platoon leader from H Company.

The regimental medical teams had to handle the wounded and the dead at distances far greater than their normal evacuation techniques

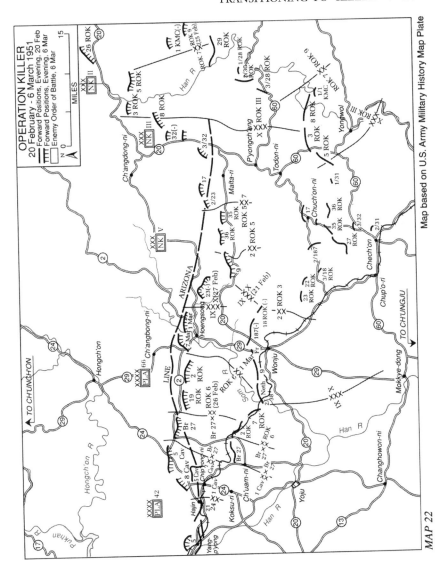

MAP 22

allowed. Capt. Warren Belt, who commanded the 187th Airborne Regimental Medical Company, remembered that litter jeeps from the battalion aid station and the 187th Airborne regimental ambulance platoon moved the wounded to the MSR at Sillim-ni, a distance of about 8 road miles. There, they were transferred to enclosed ambulances for the 15-mile trip to the regimental collection station at Wonju. Because the 187th did not have a graves registration unit, the medical company also processed the evacuation of the forty-two men who died in the battles around Wonju.[22]

General Almond had extracted the last measure of offensive capability from the paratroopers. Per orders of General Ridgway, the 187th was pulled off-line when Operation Killer kicked off the next day and, on the last day of February, transported to Taegu, where it prepared for a combat parachute assault north of Seoul.

George Company had the dubious honor of being intensely involved with the first and last battles of the Communist Fourth Phase Offensive.

TWENTY-TWO | **In the Final Analysis**

The great Chinese–North Korean Fourth Phase Offensive, upon which Chinese planners had hung great expectations, began with a bloody bang on 11 February and ended with less than a whimper fifteen days later. Sometime late in that period, General Peng was summoned to Peking for a consultation with Chairman Mao. He explained to Mao that the Korean War could not be quickly won. In his memoirs, Peng wrote, "The Chairman gave a clear instruction for conducting the War to Resist U.S. Aggression and Aid Korea: 'Win a quick victory if you can; if you can't, win a slow one.' That is a clear and flexible principle."[1]

Peng's memoirs were in reality a treatise that he wrote over a period of sixteen years (1958–1974) while undergoing extreme interrogations by the Red Guards who had set upon him with Mao's acquiescence. Consequently, the memoirs are suspect of being self-serving. Nevertheless, careful reading can result in the gleaning of some truths, some obvious and some hidden. Most historians have taken Peng's words at less than face value. Gen. Paik Sun Yup, in his book, wrote, "Analysts believe that in fact Mao reprimanded him sharply."[2]

Mao had postulated ten principles for warfare. Although they reflect the Chinese Communist experience with revolutionary warfare on Chinese soil, they nevertheless represent the doctrine that Peng and his subordinate commanders carried into Korea.[3] (These principles are reproduced in Appendix II.) By placing pressure on Peng to capture Seoul quickly during the Third Phase Offensive, Mao had violated one of his own principles: "Take small and medium cities and extensive rural areas first; take big cities later." Through necessity, Peng had violated another Mao principle. Whether or not he was "reprimanded" for that is problematical. What is more likely is that Peng started the process to modernize and regularize the Chinese Army.

China scholar John Gittings wrote in 1967 that "The Korean War speeded up the process of modernization and encouraged a drift away from the revolutionary model. This was followed by two years of 'regularization,' in which conscription, systems of ranks and awards, and all the other trappings of a professional army were introduced."[4]

Peng also might have tried to explain to Mao that the Americans had learned from earlier mistakes, as did Chiang Kai-shek during the encirclement campaigns in Kiangsi Province during the early 1930s. After sustaining humiliating losses in his first four attempts to encircle and root out the communist stronghold in Kiangsi Province, Chiang revived a mid-nineteenth century strategy that employed a string of blockhouses aimed at the heart of the enemy's stronghold. This fortified line of communications strategy isolated an area by gradually connecting key points with occupied lines of fortifications, across which no one would be permitted to travel without permits. The goals of this network were to reduce communist mobility, remove their capacity for surprise, act as a source of physical security for those who accepted Nationalist rule, and impose an economic blockade. The Nationalists moved slowly but steadily, often marching no more than two or three miles in a day, and refused to be diverted when communist elements attempted to lure them into traps. Thus the communists' area for maneuver began to shrink. It took a year, but the Nationalists prevailed. On 15 October 1934, the communists pulled out of their Kiangsi soviet and began their celebrated "Long March."[5]

Although Peng could not know about Ridgway's warning to corps commanders, prior to Operation Killer, to avoid moves that would cause a UN unit to become trapped and lost, he was, however, well aware of how Ridgway conducted his offensives in the western sector. The Americans did not use blockhouses, but massed artillery, tanks, and tactical air strikes, combined with closely coordinated and patient infantry advances, served the same purpose. The CCF had nothing to match American resources, as Peng knew full well when he reported to Mao. This why some sinologists believe that Peng laid his career on the line and forcefully argued for seeking immediate and substantial materiel assistance from the Soviet Union, as well as massive troop reinforcements for use in Korea. Becoming unduly indebted to the Soviet Union was a heavy price for Mao and the Politburo to pay for success in Korea. The Chinese leadership in Korea also knew by then that Americans would stand and fight and, at the earliest opportunity, aggressively carry the fight to their enemies.

In 1953, a training manual published by the People's Liberation Army paid lip service to Mao's early 1950 assertion that America was a paper tiger, but it carefully stressed that the paper tiger had serious teeth:

> The American army is politically a reactionary military organiza-
> tion of the imperialists, and basically is a "paper tiger." But it is an
> army with modernized equipment and fighting power. Its training
> and equipment are very different from that of the reactionary nation-
> alist (i.e. Kuomintang) troops. To destroy thoroughly such enemy
> troops, it is necessary to build up a strong modernized national
> defence army, and responsible officers should give an all-out and
> correct understanding of the American army to every soldier of
> the PLA.[6]

The Chinese had also learned another reason why Mao's princi-
ples of war could not always be exported. The civilian populations of both North Korea and South Korea had been indifferent and sometimes hostile to the exhortations of the commissars. With their extended supply lines interdicted by U.S. air attacks, the CCF had to resort to foraging, a fruitless task in a barren and frigid landscape, by then nearly devoid of people.

For all of these reasons, the leadership of the Chinese People's Volunteers was aware that, as it pulled troops back from contact on the central front, the People's Volunteers no longer had the capability to win the war and, given the changing nature of U.S. tactics, could very well lose it. This is what Gen. Robert E. Lee knew when he moved the remnants of his army across the Potomac and back into Virginia.

Calling the battles in the central sector the Gettysburg of Korea is not hyperbolic. There are too many similarities to dismiss the comparison lightly. Coming off four decisive victories in his previous five general engagements with Union armies, Lee was supremely confident in the ability of his tough, lean veterans. Peng's peasant soldiers had routed UN forces in two engagements in North Korea and had recently prevailed in the relatively easy recapture of Seoul.

General Lee counted on the continued mediocre performance of the Union's generals and combat forces. The Chinese counted heavily on the continued poor showing by UN forces, especially U.S. troops and their leaders.

The Confederates positioned themselves for a battle at Gettysburg by sidestepping the Federal Army defending Washington and stealthily marching deep into Pennsylvania. The Union movement to Pennsylvania was a reaction to Lee's penetrations. Peng took five of his field armies from north of Seoul and sidestepped away from the preponderance of the UN strength in the western sector to the more vulnerable central sector. As soon as he was aware of the danger posed by the Chinese, Ridgway began moving troops to counter the threat.

For sheer intensity of small-unit combat, Joshua Chamberlain's 20th Maine defense of the Union left on Little Round Top was the stuff of legends. A comparable action was G Company's defense of its position and the subsequent counterattacks by the Americans at Chip'yong-ni. Another action, even though this was an attack, could be the assault of the 187th rifle companies against a Chinese regiment on Hills 255 and 342. Chamberlain won a Medal of Honor at Little Round Top. No Medals of Honor were won either at Chip'yong-ni or at Wonju, but a number of Distinguished Service Crosses, the nation's second highest award for valor, and a plethora of Silver Stars were awarded.

There are, of course, an enormous number of disparities, and historians could make arguments about the comparisons listed above. But, the one overarching comparison was that as Gettysburg was the high-water mark of the Confederacy, so Wonju was the limit of advance by the Chinese Communist forces. When Lee returned to Virginia, there were many bloody battles yet to be fought and many men yet to die before Appomattox stilled the guns. For the Chinese, there was one spasmodic episode in late April and early May, the Fifth Offensive, which resulted in hideous Chinese casualties, followed by stalemated trench warfare for two more bloody years.

An examination of the Chinese posture prior to the Fifth Phase Offensive reveals some insights into Mao's alleged guidance to Peng. Mao sent three fresh army groups—the Third, Ninth and Nineteenth—to Korea. The attack to capture Seoul on the western front in late April featured 270,000 Chinese soldiers, which demonstrated the continued reliance of the Chinese on the "man over weapons" doctrine.[7] The massive assault there, and later in the eastern sector, well might have been Peng's response to Mao's guidance of "winning a quick victory." Certainly, Peng tried every battlefield tactic and strategy that had worked before, but he was checked at every turn. Some historians contend that the repulse of the Chinese Fifth Phase Offensive was the turning point in the war, but the die actually had been cast two months earlier at Wonju.

Although unseasonable rains prevented General Ridgway from achieving all of the goals that he had set for Operation Killer, the offensive featured the kind of grind-it-out, patient movement of infantry units that had typified the advances in the western sector. When Ridgway terminated Killer, he segued into Operation Ripper, which was designed to return UN forces to the neighborhood of the 38th Parallel. As the political questions of UN advances above the 38th Parallel were resolved, Ripper became Rugged and then became Dauntless.

Along the way, President Truman grew weary of the posturing from the Dai Ichi Building in Tokyo and relieved MacArthur on 11 April. Ridgway was elevated to commander in chief and his replacement as Eighth Army commander, Lt. Gen. James A. Van Fleet, arrived in Korea on 14 April. The transition from a Ridgway Eighth Army to a Van Fleet Eighth Army was virtually seamless, mostly because Ridgway initially put Van Fleet on a tight leash.[8] Operation Dauntless continued without pause.

Not only had Mao committed additional ground troops for General Peng, but he also deployed the People's Air Force to Manchuria to support future ground activities. In addition to more MIG-15s, the CCF acquired from its Soviet allies enough Ilyushin (IL-10) ground-attack planes to equip at least two air regiments. Because of the fear of large-scale retaliation by the United States, the Chinese high command had forbidden the use of Manchurian air bases for launching attacks on UN troops and installations. This forced the air commander, Liu Ya-lou, to begin developing Korean air fields on which to base his attack aircraft. In mid-April, just prior to the airfields receiving PLA aircraft, the U.S Air Force destroyed them. The Chinese Fifth Phase offensive would have no air support.[9]

For his Fifth Phase Offensive, Peng hurled three fresh army groups at Seoul and allegedly promised its capture to Mao as a May Day present. General Van Fleet's units conducted a skillful fighting retreat that bled the CCF fearfully in the process. When the first impulse of the offensive ended, the Chinese did not have Seoul and they had lost an estimated 75,000 killed and wounded. American casualties were less than half those sustained during the Chinese Second Offensive in November, and there were no bugouts.[10]

The second impulse of the Fifth Phase Offensive struck with two army groups (175,000 soldiers) on the east central and eastern sectors. It had been preceded by a short lull while Peng again attempted to sidestep what he believed to be the main strength of the Eighth Army—I Corps and IX Corps in the west. His target was the eastern flank of X Corps in Korea's mountainous spine. This was an area also heavily populated by ROK units, and the South Korean units again bore the brunt of the initial Chinese assaults. This time, however, American units had contingency plans for such possibilities. The South Korean units took heavy punishment, but, even though the overall defensive lines stretched and some units gave up ground, UN forces eventually recoiled and finally held. Then, as the Chinese offensive began sputtering, Ridgway, from Tokyo, suggested to Van Fleet that he mount a counteroffensive designed to take UN forces into what was known as the "Iron Triangle." As inexorable as Grant driving on Richmond, so did the Ridgway–Van Fleet army advance and stabilize the lines, reoccupy ground temporarily lost, and seize new territory above the 38th Parallel.

Once it became clear to the Chinese high command that there was no longer any possibility of quick victories, Mao ordered his army to turn the war into one of sheer endurance.[11] The following two years of truce talks and bloody battles etched the names of battlegrounds—Heartbreak Ridge, The Punch Bowl, Pork Chop Hill, and others—into the public consciousness. In the end, Mao did not win a slow victory; however, except for an enormous human toll, he did not lose either.

Although Van Fleet commanded the Eighth Army, no one doubted that it was really Ridgway's army. It bore his stamp, and its offensive spirit was directly attributable to him. As Mao had given Peng a "clear and flexible principle," Ridgway had given Van Fleet his, one he had been following since assuming command of the Eighth Army on 26 December: "Real estate is not important, destroying the enemy army is."

In just fifty-four days after assuming command of a defeated army, Matthew Bunker Ridgway had turned that army around. He had rid the army of most of its weak and incompetent leaders (some were untouchable[12]), established firm principles by which he wanted the army to conduct itself, and, by constantly stressing the offensive, infused the men with a self-confidence they were unaware they possessed. Clay Blair quoted General of the Army Omar Bradley, who wrote about Ridgway: "It is not often in wartime that a single battlefield commander can make a decisive difference. But in Korea, Ridgway would prove to be the exception. His brilliant, driving, uncompromising leadership would turn the tide of battle like no other general's in our military history."[13]

Even the most inspiring and charismatic leader who does not have tactical smarts, however, can lose battles. Ridgway had outgeneraled Peng Teh-huai, one of the world's most experienced combat leaders, and reestablished the reputation of American arms. Although Ridgway had made sound tactical decisions throughout his time in Korea, his decision to insist that the 23d RCT remain at Chip'yong-ni and fight might have been the most significant one of the war. Had Ridgway acquiesced to the requests of General Almond and 2d Division leaders, the 23d RCT would have been destroyed by the division-sized ambushes prepared by the Chinese. With Chip'yong-ni abandoned, it would have been almost impossible for General Stewart to retain the concentration of artillery that he did at Wonju. Without the decimation of the two Chinese divisions at Wonju, that crossroads town would have quickly fallen, and the North Korean thrusts to Chech'on would have driven a wedge even deeper into South Korean territory. When the Eighth Army staff presented Ridgway with its plan for phased withdrawals to the Pusan Perimeter, despite his preference for the offensive, he would have had little choice but to take whatever steps he could to save his army.

Ridgway was a heroic figure of olympian proportions. His army also had heroes. Some of them are described in this book; too many are not. There were also antiheroes, many of them senior officers who made some egregious decisions that killed far too many young men of many nationalities. Fortunately for the United States and Korea, other senior officers, including General Stewart and Colonel Freeman, also made some good decisions that preserved the victory. And there were enough good soldiers to aid the truly great soldiers in the line outfits to overcome the handicaps of the bad decisions. In the Wonju campaign, countless examples of inspired leadership and bravery were demonstrated throughout the ranks of infantry and artillery battalions by majors, captains, lieutenants, sergeants, and privates who seized the moment. Their gallantry, initiative, and perseverence in those ice-covered mountains of central Korea composed a story of epic proportions.

Tragically, the story was quickly forgotten. The Wonju campaign featured the forgotten battles of a forgotten war. Even given the drama of the cavalry riding to the rescue at Chip'yong-ni, how many Americans remember it? A poll of Americans who are old enough to remember the Korean War might, when prompted, dimly recall Pork Chop Hill or Heartbreak Ridge if, indeed, they can remember anything about that war. Obscure Korean place names, such as Hoengsong, Wonju, and even Chip'yong-ni, simply do not register on most Americans' memory screens.

The heroes and their comrades who fought their hearts out in Central Korea in February 1951 wrote their story in blood and misery. Their struggle might have been forgotten, but it was not in vain. Theirs is the story of the Korean Gettysburg.

APPENDIX I | **News Story about X Corps Award**

"With X Corps in Korea—The living and the dead of a 41-man platoon of the 187th Airborne Infantry Regiment were honored for bravery today by Lt. Gen. Edward M. Almond within sight of a battle scarred hill which they retook from the Chinese Reds five days ago, with more than 50 percent casualties.

"Standing at attention, in a little clearing surrounded by the rubble of war, 15 soldiers who came through the battle unscathed, heard the X Corps Commander tell them 'No soldiers have withstood more vicious an onslaught than did you men here.'

"Only the occasional boom of rear artillery broke the chill morning quiet as General Almond pinned Silver Stars on the breasts of four, awarded Bronze Stars for Valor to eight, recommended the Distinguished Service Cross for three and cited the nine dead and 17 wounded for Silver Stars.

"They were members of the 1st Platoon of Company E, which fought its way through 400 yards of exposed terrain in a terrifying barrage to sweep to the top of a hill designated on maps as 225 (sic) and vital to the UN fortifications.

"It was their assignment to make a frontal assault across that gridiron of death. They were to fight to the crest of the steep hill, which until recently was just another hill in a country of hills, pushed its way into American history when the company swept it clear of strongly entrenched Red Manchurian forces, killing 451 of the enemy defenders.

"With a quiver in his voice that he made no attempt to conceal, General Almond told the thin line of brave men that 'your feat marks the highlight of this campaign . . . yours is a fine regiment, with a fine commander and fine men. I would have no hesitation in giving it the most important assignment of the Corps mission.'"

A TRUE EXTRACT COPY:

Carl J. Wright Jr

Capt. Arty

APPENDIX II | Mao's Ten Principles of Revolutionary Warfare

1. Attack dispersed, isolated enemy forces first; attack concentrated strong enemy forces later.
2. Take small and medium cities and extensive rural areas first; take big cities later.
3. Make wiping out the enemy effective strength our main objective; do not make holding or seizing a city or place our main objective. Holding or seizing a city or place is the outcome of wiping out the enemy's effective strength, and often a city or place can be held or seized for good only after it has changed hands a number of times.
4. In every battle, concentrate an absolutely superior force (two, three, four and sometimes even five or six times the enemy's strength), encircle the enemy forces completely, strive to wipe them out thoroughly, and do not let any escape from the net. In special circumstances, use the method of dealing the enemy crushing blows, that is, concentrate our strength to make a frontal attack and an attack on one or both of his flanks, with the aim of wiping out one part and routing another so that our army can swiftly move its troops to smash other enemy forces. Strive to avoid battles of attrition, in which we lose more than we gain or only break even. In this way, although inferior as a whole (in terms of numbers), we shall be absolutely superior in every part and every specific campaign, and this insures victory in the campaign. As time goes on, we shall become superior as a whole and eventually wipe out all the enemy.

5. Fight no battle unprepared; fight no battle you are not sure of winning; make every effort to be well prepared for each battle; make every effort to insure victory in the given set of conditions as between the enemy and ourselves.

6. Give full play to our style of fighting—courage in battle, no fear of sacrifice, no fear of fatigue, and continuous fighting (that is, fighting successive battles in a short time without rest).

7. Strive to wipe out the enemy when he is on the move. At the same time, pay attention to the tactics of positional attack and capture enemy fortified points and cities.

8. With regard to attacking cities, resolutely seize all enemy fortified points and cities which are weakly defended. At opportune moments, seize all enemy fortified points and cities defended with moderate strength, provided circumstances permit. As for strongly defended fortified points and cities, wait till conditions are ripe and then take them.

9. Replenish our strength with all the arms and most of the personnel captured from the enemy. Our army's main sources of manpower and materiel are at the front.

10. Make good use of the intervals between campaigns to rest, train and consolidate our troops. Periods of rest, training, and consolidation should not in general be very long, and the enemy in so far as possible be permitted no breathing space.

NOTES

Nearly all unit operational and intelligence reports and associated documents from the Korean War are preserved in the National Archives and Records Administration (NARA) repository in College Park, Maryland. These documents are in Record Group 407 which includes hundreds of numbered boxes. Unless indicated otherwise, military records cited in these notes are located in the NARA repository.

Introduction: February 1951—The Month of Destiny

1. Mossman, *Ebb and Flow*, 325. This publication, the U.S. Army's official history of the period, asserts that Gen. Peng Teh-huai replaced Lin Piao as commander of Chinese forces "in either January or February." Virtually all other histories, however, contend that it was Peng who led Chinese forces across the Yalu River in October 1950 and who remained as commander in chief of the CCF for the entire period of the Korean War.

2. X Corps Periodic Intelligence Report (PIR) 138, 11 February 1951, 1.

    This report was being prepared even as the Chinese massed for their assaults. It listed three North Korean divisions in contact with ROK and 2d Division units, with the possibility of the CCF 198th Division reinforcing the NKPA elements.

3. X Corps PIR 138, 4. This portion of the intelligence reports the massing of Chinese troops north and west of Chip'yong-ni and the potential of a Chinese thrust through that outpost.

Chapter One: The *Inmun Gun*

1. Sawyer, *Military Advisors in Korea*, 45–95.
2. Sandler, *The Korean War*, 181–9.

3. Paik, *From Pusan to Panmunjom*, 7–15.

4. Fehrenbach, *This Kind of War*, 78; Sandler, *Korean War*, 328. Both works use the quote but do not attribute it to a specific MacArthur document or speech.

5. Gugeler, *Combat Actions in Korea*, 3.

6. Gen. Creighton W. Abrams, U.S. Army Chief of Staff, address to annual meeting of the Association of the United States Army, Washington, D.C., 16 October 1973. Transcript from audio recording in author's possession.

7. Blair, *Forgotten War*, 87–8.

8. Ibid., 320.

9. Waterhouse, *The Rakkasans*, 47.

10. Blair, *Forgotten War*, 336–7; Ferhrenbach, *This Kind of War*, 225.

11. Appleman, *South to the Naktong, North to the Yalu*, 607–10.

12. Blair, *Forgotten War*, 353–8.

13. Fehrenbach, *This Kind of War*, 214.

14. Hoyt, *On to the Yalu*, 191, 195, 205, 259, 261–3; Appleman, *South to the Naktong*, 721–8.

15. Fehrenbach, *This Kind of War*, 217–23.

16. Spur, *Enter the Dragon*, 117–9.

Chapter Two: Bugles, Whistles, and Shepherd's Horns

1. Appleman, *South to the Naktong*, 673–4.

2. Blair, *Forgotten War*, 377.

3. Ibid., 391; Appleman, *South to the Naktong*, 762.

4. Appleman, *South to the Naktong*, 763.

5. Ibid., 768.

6. Ibid., 767.

7. Quoted in Mossman, *Ebb and Flow*, 47.

8. Quoted in Gugeler, *Combat Actions in Korea*, 61–2.

9. Blair, *Forgotten War*, 434–5.

10. Whitson and Chen-hsia, *Chinese High Command*, 263–87.

11. Quoted in Appleman, *South to the Naktong*, 720.

12. Whitson and Chen-hsia, *Chinese High Command*, xxiii. In the Preface, Whitson discusses the translation of the word *Chun*. He notes that the literal translation has traditionally been *army* and remains so in

most official U.S. government documents. He maintains, however, that the term *army* has long been abandoned by both the Chinese Nationalist and Communist translators when they refer to a unit consisting of three divisions. Nevertheless, even though many CCF documents refer to these units as *corps*, some still refer to them as armies. Although some American unit documents used the term *corps*, most referred to the three-division organizations as *armies*. Consequently, the term *army* is used throughout this book.

13. Paik, *From Pusan to Panmunjom*, 105.

14. Fehrenbach, *This Kind of War*, 272.

15. Quoted in Blair, *Forgotten War*, 502.

Chapter Three: Withdrawal from North Korea

1. Appleman, *Disaster in Korea*, 365.

2. Munroe, *Second United States Infantry Division*, 87.

3. Mossman, *Ebb and Flow*, 150.

4. Spurr, *Enter the Dragon*, 4, 239–52.

5. Waterhouse, *Rakkasans*, 59.

6. Ibid., 59–60.

7. Appleman, *Disaster in Korea*, 439.

8. Ibid., 411.

Chapter Four: Ridgway Takes Command

1. Blair, *Forgotten War*, 559.

2. Appleman, *Ridgway Duels for Korea*, 26.

3. Spurr, *Enter the Dragon*, 283–4.

4. Ridgway, *Korean War*, 88–9.

5. Blair, *Forgotten War*, 572–3.

6. Mossman, *Ebb and Flow*, 178–80.

7. Ibid., 180–2.

8. Blair, *Forgotten War*, 578–80.

9. Ibid., 589.

10. Lt. Gen. Edward M. Almond, Oral History, U.S. Army Military History Institute (hereafter USAMHI), 1975, vol. IV, 34.

11. Mossman, *Ebb and Flow*, 186–8.

Chapter Five: The Third Phase Offensive

1. Allied Translation and Interrogation Service (ATIS), Tokyo, translation of captured Chinese document entitled "A Collection of Combat Experiences, issued by Hq. XIII CCF Army Group, 29 March 1951," hereafter referred to as "Collection of Combat Experiences."
2. Mossman, *Ebb and Flow*, 188.
3. "Collection of Combat Experiences."
4. Ridgway, *Soldier*, 210; Mossman, *Ebb and Flow*, 189–91.
5. Mossman, *Ebb and Flow*, 198–201.
6. Blair, *Forgotten War*, 601; Mossman, *Ebb and Flow*, 206.
7. Blair, *Forgotten War*, 603–4.
8. Quoted in Appleman, *Ridgway Duels for Korea*, 90–1.
9. Paik, *From Pusan to Panmunjom*, 118.
10. Appleman, *Ridgway Duels for Korea*, 96.

Chapter Six: Rekindling the Offensive Spirit

1. Blair, *Forgotten War*, 605–6.
2. Herbert B. Powell, Oral History, USAMHI, 1976, vol. III, 70.
3. Mossman, *Ebb and Flow*, 219–22.
4. Quotations in Blair, *Forgotten War*, 614–5.
5. Ibid., 620–43.
6. Appleman, *Ridgway Duels for Korea*, 129.
7. Quoted in Blair, *Forgotten War*, 646–7.
8. Mossman, *Ebb and Flow*, 224–7.
9. Appleman, *Ridgway Duels for Korea*, 130.
10. Powell, Oral History, 73–4.
11. Blair, *Forgotten War*, 585.
12. Mossman, *Ebb and Flow*, 239–40.

Chapter Seven: Thunderbolt and Twin Tunnels

1. Appleman, *Ridgway Duels for Korea*, 141.
2. Mossman, *Ebb and Flow*, 241–2.
3. Ridgway, *Korean War*, 105–6.
4. Blair, *Forgotten War*, 585.

5. James H. Polk, Oral History, USAMHI, 1972, vol. II, 32.

6. Mossman, *Ebb and Flow*, 243.

7. Ibid., 246.

8. Gugeler, *Combat Actions in Korea*, 81–2.

9. Korean War Casualty List, 2d Infantry Division, in author's possession.

10. Gugeler, *Combat Actions in Korea*, 83–97.

11. Paul Freeman, Oral History, USAMHI, 1973, vol. I, 125–6; Blair, *Forgotten War*, 666.

12. 23d Regimental Combat Team (RCT), "After Action Report to Commanding General, 2nd Division, 29 Jan 51–15 Feb 51," 13 March 1951, 1–2.

13. Maj. Gen. George Craig Stewart, "My Service with the Second Division during the Korean War," unpublished manuscript, n.d., 7–8.

14. Freeman, Oral History, 126; Toland, *In Mortal Combat*, 396.

15. Col. Paul Freeman, "Wonju through Chipyong-ni," unpublished manuscript, 14–15.

16. Second Infantry Division Korean War Veterans Alliance, *Bulletin*, Fall, 1997, 1–3.

17. Stewart, "My Service with Second Division," 9–10.

18. Appleman, *Ridgway Battles for Korea*, 210–7; 23d RCT, "After Action Report," 2–3; Freeman, Oral History, 125–8.

Chapter Eight: Thrusts, Counters, Deceptions, and Plans

1. Eighth United States Army Korea (EUSAK) Command Report, February 1951, Section II, Tactical Operations, 44.

2. Blair, *Forgotten War*, 645.

3. Spurr, *Enter the Dragon*, 285.

4. Mossman, *Ebb and Flow*, 249.

5. 23d Regimental Combat Team, After Action Report, 13 March 1951, 3.

6. EUSAK Command Report, 43–47.

7. Headquarters, X Corps, Command Report, February 1951, 3–4.

8. Mossman, *Ebb and Flow*, 251.

9. Stewart, "My Service with Second Division," 11–12.

10. Mossman, *Ebb and Flow*, 254.

11. Quoted in Spurr, *Enter the Dragon*, 285.

12. Russell Spurr, letter to author, May 1999.

Chapter Nine: Operation Roundup Unfolds

1. 187th Airborne Regimental Combat Team, Monthly Narrative Summary, February 1951, 5–6.
2. Blair, *Forgotten War*, 359.
3. Ibid., 122, 127.
4. Waterhouse, *Rakkasans*, 44–5.
5. Author's recollection.
6. Headquarters, X Corps, Periodic Operations Report (POR) No. 131, 4 February 1951, 2.
7. Mossman, *Ebb and Flow*, 126–7; Appleman, *Disaster in Korea*, 333–7.
8. Blair, *Forgotten War*, 687.
9. Munroe, *Second Division*, 97–98.
10. Headquarters, X Corps, Commanding General's (CG) Diary Extracts, 6–8 February 1951.
11. Polk, Oral History, 30.
12. Blair, *Forgotten War*, 32–3.
13. Almond, Oral History, USAMHI, vol. II, 80.
14. Stanton, *America's Tenth Legion*, 8.
15. Blair, *Forgotten War*, 33.
16. Almond, Oral History, USAMHI, vol. III, 68.
17. Powell, Oral History, 84.
18. Quoted in Blair, *Forgotten War*, 648.

Chapter Ten: Prelude to Disaster

1. Mossman, *Ebb and Flow*, 259; Headquarters X Corps, Periodic Intelligence Reports, 5–9 February 1951, 132–7; X Corps Command Report, 4–5.
2. Sawyer, *Military Advisors in Korea*, 153.
3. Quoted in Blair, *Forgotten War*, 722–3.
4. Headquarters, X Corps, CG Diary Extracts, 5–10 February 1951.
5. William M. Mace, interview by author, 23 September 1999.
6. Appleman, *Ridgway Duels for Korea*, 218–9.
7. Polk, Oral History, 32.
8. Ibid., 30.
9. Headquarters X Corps, PIR 138, 10 February 1951, 1–5.
10. Polk, Oral History, 31.
11. Mossman, *Ebb and Flow*, 264–5; Eighth Army, G-2, Estimate of Enemy Situation, 10 February 1951.

12. Mossman, *Ebb and Flow*, 263–4.

13. Headquarters, 2d Division, G-3 Journal, 11 February 1951, 1.

Chapter Eleven: Peng's Plan for the Fourth Phase Offensive

1. Appleman, *Ridgway Duels for Korea*, 227. Appleman quotes a captured document, "A Collection of Combat Experiences," issued by Headquarters, XIX Army Group, PLA, 29 March, 1951.

2. Ibid., 228.

3. Robinson, Preston, and Hogg, *Weapons of Vietnam War*, 95–6. This volume has an excellent section describing Communist weapons, including the M-43 120-mm mortar and the M-37 82-mm mortar, which were important parts of the CCF arsenal in Korea.

4. X Corps, PIR 137, 10 February 1951, 4.

5. X Corps, PIR 135, 8 February 1951, 4.

6. Appleman, *Ridgway Duels for Korea.* 228. Appleman erroneously describes the marching and countermarching of the ROK 10th and 16th Regiments as being part of the Chinese offensive, when, in fact, they occurred two to three days prior to the offensive. (See chapter 10 for a description of these regiments' movements.)

7. The Chinese plans are revealed in the actual execution of those plans, as described in Mossman, *Ebb and Flow*, 267–300. The attitudes of Chinese leadership toward Americans and American generalship are revealed in *Enter the Dragon*.

Chapter Twelve: The Agony of Another Gauntlet

1. Mossman, *Ebb and Flow*, 269.

2. William M. Mace interview by author, 23 September 1999.

3. Mossman, *Ebb and Flow*, 268.

4. Special Report on Hoengsong, Headquarters, 38th Infantry Regiment, 2d Infantry Division, 15 April 1951 (hereafter referred to as Special Report, 38th Infantry), 1.

5. Ibid., 268.

6. Korean War Casualty List, 2nd Infantry Division, (hereafter referred to as 2d Division Casualty list) U.S. Army Records Center, Section II, St. Louis, Missouri, 45–46.

7. Appleman, *Ridgway Duels for Korea*, 226.

8. Mace, interview.

9. Special Report, 38th Infantry, 3; Mossman, *Ebb and Flow*, 270.

10. Anderson, *Warrior*.

11. Mossman, *Ebb and Flow*, 271; 2d Division Casualty List, 107.

12. Wilbur Webster, interview by author, 21 September 1999.

13. Capt. Robert G. Conrad, statement, enclosure with 2d Division Artillery Command Report, February 1951.

14. Ibid.

15. Mossman, *Ebb and Flow*, 271.

16. John Blackwell, interview by author, 19 August 1999.

17. Neil Aiken, interview by author, 18 August 1999.

18. Special Report, 38th Infantry, 6–7; Mossman, *Ebb and Flow*, 272.

Chapter Thirteen: Failed Rescue

1. Headquarters, 2d Infantry Division, G-3 Journal, 12 February 1951.

2. Aiken, interview. Aiken was communications chief of 1st Battalion, 38th Infantry. The author, a field communications chief with G Company, 187th Airborne RCT, can attest to the unreliability of company radios.

3. Details of this encounter from: Special Report, 38th Infantry, 8–9; Tank Company, 38th Infantry, War Diary for 11–13 February 1951; Jack Rogers, interview by author, 22 September 1999; and Reginald J. Hinton, interview by author, 10 September 1999.

4. 2d Division G-3 Journal, 12 February 1951.

5. Headquarters, X Corps, CG Diary Extracts, 12 February 1951.

6. Mossman, *Ebb and Flow*, 274.

7. "Recollections of Oscar Cortez", *Bulletin*, 2d Infantry Division, Korean War Veterans Alliance, summer 1997, 16.

8. Special Report, 38th Infantry, 9–10.

9. Mace, interview.

10. Details of this phase of the action from: Lt. George W. Gardner, "Summary of Combat Actions of A Company, 11–12 February 1951," to Headquarters, 1st Battalion, 38th Infantry; Lt. Col. William P. Keleher, "Summary of Combat Actions of First Battalion, 38th Infantry."

11. Anderson, *Warrior*, 346–347. Reprinted with permission of Jack Anderson.
12. Company G, 187th Airborne RCT, "Lessons Learned in Combat," 13 March 1951. Copy, obtained from Epps family, in author's possession.
13. Mossman, *Ebb and Flow*, 274–5.

Chapter Fourteen: Into the Valley of Death
1. Special Report, 38th Infantry, 11.
2. Mossman, *Ebb and Flow*, 276.
3. Lt. Col. Jack F. Wilhm, interview by Eighth Army Inspector General.
4. Hinton, interview; R. J. Hinton, unpublished memoirs, 11–2, copy in author's possession.
5. Author's recollection.
6. Hinton, interview.
7. Company G, 187th Airborne RCT, "Lessons Learned."
8. John Hare, interview by author, 26 April 1999; John Hare, unpublished manuscript, n.d.
9. Johnny Bramblett, interview by author, 5 May 1999.
10. Tank Company, 38th Infantry, War Diary; Hinton, interview; Bramblett, interview.
11. Capt. James D. Cook, statement in support of recommendation for award of valor medal for M.Sgt. Phillip J. Wilkes, 7 April 1951, copy in author's possession.
12. Company G, 187th Airborne RCT, "Lessons Learned." The author, who was present, remembers standing in a small group struggling to write call signs and frequencies in a notebook without using a light that could reveal a position.
13. Special Report, 38th Infantry, 13.
14. Conrad, statement.
15. Bramblett, interview.
16. 2d Division Casualty List, 225.
17. Special Report, 38th Infantry, 13.
18. Frank Scalzo, letter to author, 18 April 1988.
19. Hare, unpublished manuscript.
20. Netherlands Detachment, United Nations, Periodic Intelligence and Operations Report for period 5 February to 13 February 1951, incorporated in 38th Infantry's Special Report on Hoengsong.

Chapter Fifteen: Revelations and Recriminations

1. Mossman, *Ebb and Flow*, 275; Appleman, *Ridgway Duels for Korea*, 248.
2. Maj. Gen. Joseph P. Kingston, U.S.A. (Ret.), interview by author, 14 May 1998.
3. Appleman, *Ridgway Duels for Korea*, 245.
4. 2d Division Casualty List.
5. Mossman, *Ebb and Flow*, 279; Logistics Annex (tabulation of missing equipment) to 38th Infantry Special Report on Hoengsong.
6. Ridgway quotations in Mossman, *Ebb and Flow*, 280.
7. Almond quotations in ibid., 280.
8. X Corps Command Summary, February 1951, Special Report on Hoengsong.
9. Appleman, *Ridgway Duels for Korea*, 240.
10. Stewart, "My Service with the Second Division," 16–17.
11. Mossman, *Ebb and Flow*, 280–1, quotes the report of the investigation by Brig. Gen. George Craig Stewart.
12. Blair, *Forgotten War*, 696; Appleman, *Ridgway Duels for Korea*, 253–4.
13. Quoted in Blair, *Forgotten War*, 696.
14. Paik, *From Pusan to Panmunjom*, 125–6.
15. Ibid.
16. Webster's story and quotations from interview by author, 21 September 1999.
17. Anderson's story and quotations in *Warrior*, 347–65. Reproduced with permission.

Chapter Sixteen: Establishing the Wonju Line

1. Headquarters, 2d Division, G-3 Journal, 12 Februrary 1951. Entry Nos. 3, 5, and 12.
2. Ibid., Entry No. 89.
3. Headquarters, 187th Airborne Regimental Combat Team, S-3 Journal, 13 February 1951.
4. Munroe, *Second United States Infantry Division*, 86.
5. Stewart, "My Service with Second Division," 13.
6. Ibid., 14–5.
7. Headquarters, 2d Infantry Division Artillery, S-3 Journal, February 1951.

8. Stewart, "My Service with Second Division," 13.

9. Headquarters, 2d Division, G-3 Journal, 13 February 1951. Entry No. 79.

10. Headquarters, Eighth U.S. Army, Command Report, CG Diary Extracts, February 1951.

11. Appleman, *Ridgway Duels for Korea*, 259.

12. Gugeler, *Combat Actions in Korea*, 103.

13. Pratt, *Decisive Battles of the Korean War*, 177–8.

Chapter Seventeen: First Fight at Chip'yong-ni

1. Spur, *Enter the Dragon*, 253.

2. Headquarters, 23d Infantry Regiment, After Action Report for the Period 29 January–15 February 1951; Mossman, *Ebb and Flow*, 285; Gugeler, *Combat Actions in Korea*, 100–1.

3. Freeman, Oral History, USAMHI, Section II, 2–4.

4. Headquarters, 23d Infantry Regiment, After Action Report 13 March 1951; Gugeler, *Combat Actions in Korea*, 106–7.

5. Gugeler, *Combat Actions in Korea*, 105–7; 23d Infantry Regiment After Action Report; Appleman, *Ridgway Duels for Korea*, 264–5; Mossman, *Ebb and Flow*, 287.

6. Roland J. Kohen, interview by author, 6 June 1999.

7. Headquarters, X Corps, Command Report, 14 February 1951.

8. Blair, *Forgotten War*, 699–700.

9. Stewart, "My Service with Second Division," 19.

10. Blair, *Forgotten War*, 107.

11. Appleman, *Ridgway Duels for Korea*, 113.

12. Headquarters, 2d Division, G-3 Journal, 14 February 1951; Headquarters, 2d Battalion, 187th Airborne RCT, S-3 Journal, 14 February 1951.

13. Capt. Harvey Land, interview by Thomas Turner, *Dallas News*, 31 January 1951.

14. Ibid.

15. Mossman, *Ebb and Flow*, 288; Appleman, *Ridgway Duels for Korea*, 291–2.

16. Chinese document quoted in Appleman, *Ridgway Duels for Korea*, 292.

Chapter Eighteen: First Decision at Wonju

1. *Rakkasan* means "falling down umbrella" in Japanese. The name was adopted when the 187th was a member of the 11th Airborne Division on occupation duty in Japan until 1949.
2. Appleman, *Ridgway Duels for Korea*, 296.
3. Munroe, *Second United States Infantry Division*, 107.
4. Blair, *Forgotten War*, 694–5; Stewart Manuscript, 15.
5. Munroe, *Second United States Infantry Division*, 107.
6. Sandler, *Korean War*, 37–8.
7. David V. Carr, letter to author, 30 October 1996.
8. Capt. Annis G. Thompson, *The Greatest Airlift: The Story of Combat Cargo*, Tokyo: Dai-Nippon Printing, 1954, 76.
9. James H. Nix, written reminiscences for author, 13 April 1999; Nix, interview by author, 20 April 1999.
10. Joel Nyquist, letter to author, 27 November 1998.
11. Ibid.
12. Company F, 187th Airborne RCT, After Action Report, n.d.; X Corps, Command Report, February 1951.
13. Company E, 187th Airborne RCT, After Action Report, n.d.
14. Ibid.
15. Nix, reminiscences and interview.
16. "Assault of Hill 255," Special Report Annex, Headquarters, X Corps, Command Report, February 1951.
17. Nix, reminiscences and interview.
18. "Assault of Hill 255."
19. Company G, 187th Airborne RCT, After Action Report; Company E, 187th Airborne RCT, After Action Report, (n.d.).
20. Author's recollection.
21. Silver Star citation for Sgt. Jimmy Jones.
22. "Assault of Hill 255."
23. Waterhouse, *Rakkasans*, 65–6; Company G, After Action Report, 13 March 1951.
24. Bramblett, interview.
25. "Assault of Hill 255."

Chapter Nineteen: Climax at Chip'yong-ni

1. Mossman, *Ebb and Flow*, 291; Appleman, *Ridgway Duels for Korea*, 278.

2. Collection of interviews of G Company, 23d Infantry by Capt. Edward C. Williamson (hereafter Williamson interviews), from the files of the Office of the Chief, Army Military History. Copies in author's possession.

3. Gugeler, *Combat Actions in Korea*, 108

4. Headquarters, 23d Infantry Regiment, After Action Report, 13 March 1951, 4.

5. Williamson, interviews; Gugeler, *Combat Actions in Korea*, 107–10. This narrative, unless otherwise indicated, is based on information from these sources.

6. 2d Division Casualty List.

7. Williamson, interviews; Gugeler, *Combat Actions in Korea*, 110–5.

8. Author's opinion.

9. Williamson, interviews; Gugeler, *Combat Actions in Korea*, 115–6.

10. Kohen, interview.

11. Gugeler, *Combat Actions in Korea* (Task Force Crombez), 128.

12. Blair, *Forgotten War*, 706–7.

13. Gugeler, *Combat Actions in Korea*, 129.

14. Blair, *Forgotten War*, 707.

15. Gugeler, *Combat Actions in Korea*, 130.

16. Blair, *Forgotten War*, 706; Freeman, Oral History, USAMHI, Section II, 4–5.

17. Lt. Col. James Edwards, report of actions to Colonel Freeman; Pratt, *Decisive Battles of Korean War*, 193–204; 1st Lt. Richard S. Kotite, letter to Maj. Roy E. Appleman, 3 December 1951, from the files of the Chief, Army Military History.

18. Edwards, report to Freeman.

19. Gugeler, *Combat Actions in Korea*, 131–2.

20. Ibid., 133.

21. Blair, *Forgotten War*, 709.

22. Quoted in Appleman, *Ridgway Duels for Korea*, 285, translated from the captured Chinese booklet, "Collection of Combat Experiences."

23. 2d Division Casualty List.

Chapter Twenty: Final Decision at Wonju

1. Headquarters, 3d Battalion, 187th Airborne Regimental Combat Team, S-3 Journal, 14 February 1951, Item 223.

2. Headquarters, 2d Infantry Division, G-3 Journal, 14 February 1951, Item 128.

3. Headquarters, 3d Battalion, 187th Airborne RCT, Command Report, February 1951.

4. General Orders No. 68, Headquarters, X Corps, 11 April 1951, awarding a Bronze Star with "V" device to Pvt. Robert E. Sullivan and others.

5. William E. Weber, interview by author, 2 March 1999; Delbert E. Munson, interview by author, 22 June 1999.

6. Charles O. Brooks, letter to author, 2 December 1996.

7. General Orders No. 68, Headquarters, X Corps, 11 April 1951, awarding a Bronze Star with "V" device to Pfc. Russell H. Bowers and others.

8. Ibid., awarding a Bronze Star with "V" device to Capt. William E. Weber and others.

9. Brooks, letter to author.

10. General Orders No. 68, Headquarters, X Corps, 11 April 1951, awarding a Bronze Star with "V" device to Sgt. 1/C Thomas R. Wilcynski and others.

11. Weber, interview.

12. General Orders No. 68, Headquarters, X Corps, 11 April 1951, awarding a Bronze Star with "V" device to Pfc. Donald F. Boor, and others; Donald F. Boor, interview by author, 2 March 1991.

13. Waterhouse, *Rakkasans*, 66.

14. Ibid.

15. Weber, interview.

16. Company G, After Action Report; Earl K. Wooley, interview by author, 2 November 1999.

17. Appleman, *Ridgway Duels for Korea*, 298.

18. Headquarters, 3d Battalion, 187th Airborne RCT, Command Report, February 1951.

19. Warren Belt, letter to author, 23 March 1996.

20. Brooks, letter to author.

21. Headquarters, Eighth U.S Army, General Order No. 318, 17 May 1951, awarding the Distinguished Service Cross to 1st Lt. David N. White; Company G, After Action Report.

22. Mossman, *Ebb and Flow*, 293–4.

23. John O. Morris, "A Personal Reflection," *Rakkasan Shimbun*, summer 1993, 64.

24. Headquarters, X Corps, Command Report (special report), "Assault on Hill 255," February 1951.
25. Waterhouse, *Rakkasans*, 66–7.
26. Norm LeBrun, interview by author, 29 March 1999.
27. Headquarters X Corps, Daily Summary, 19 February 1951.
28. Extract copy of news story. See Appendix I for full text.
29. "Heroism Can Be Easy," *Time* magazine, 19 February 1951, 34.
30. Headquarters, X Corps, Daily Summary, 19 February and 21 February 1951.
31. Nix, reminiscences and interview.
32. Blair, *Forgotten War*, 719–20.
33. Ridgway, *Korean War*, 109.

Chapter Twenty-One: Transition to "Killer"

1. Mossman, *Ebb and Flow*, 301, 305–6; Ridgway, *Korean War*, 110–1.
2. Mossman, *Ebb and Flow*, 301.
3. Ibid., 301–2.
4. Ridgway, *Korean War*, 110–1.
5. Blair, *Forgotten War*, 718, 745.
6. Eighth U.S. Army, Command Report Summary, February 1951, 70–1; Appleman, *Ridgway Duels for Korea*, 301–2.
7. Blair, *Forgotten War*, 723.
8. Stewart "My Service with Second Division," 18.
9. Mossman, *Ebb and Flow*, 305; Blair, *Forgotten War*, 721.
10. Mossman, *Ebb and Flow*, 306.
11. Author's recollection.
12. Headquarters, 187th Airborne RCT, S-3 Journal, 19 February 1951.
13. Company F, 187th Airborne RCT, After Battle Report, 17 March 1951. (Actually more than a true after action report, this report was Captain Pickett's recommendations for the use of fully automatic individual weapons for use in a night attack.)
14. Donald L. Roberts, letter to author, 9 November 1999.
15. Company F, 187th Airborne RCT, After Battle Report, 17 March 1951.
16. Maj. Gen. John R. D. Cleland, USA (Ret.), letter to author, 10 May 1999.

17. Bramblett, interview.

18. Author's recollection.

19. Waterhouse, *Rakkasans*, 69; Cleland, letter to author.

20. Hare, interview.

21. John Miley, letter to author, 21 March 1999. The seeming plethora of captains in the line companies of the 187th resulted from the promotion of all West Point graduates of 1946 to captain in one big group in late January. Cleland had been integrated into the Regular Army one day prior to the class of 1946 and thus had one day's date of rank on the other captains. He had been executive officer of G Company and retained that position. Miley had been first platoon leader in G Company and was transferred to Battalion Headquarters, but Hewett had no place to go and Colonel Connor kept him in G Company as a platoon leader. At the conclusion of the Wonju campaign, the 187th no longer had an excessive number of captains.

22. Warren Belt, letter to author, 24 March 1996.

Chapter Twenty-Two: In the Final Analysis

1. Peng, *Memoirs of Chinese Marshal*, 479–80.

2. Paik, *From Pusan to Panmunjom*, 127.

3. Whitson and Chen-hsia, *Chinese High Command*, 492–3. The importance of these principles merits their quotation in full in Appendix II.

4. Gittings, *Role of Chinese Army*, xiii.

5. Whitson and Chen-hsia, *Chinese High Command*, 268–81.

6. Quoted in ibid., 126.

7. Mossman, *Ebb and Flow*, 379.

8. Toland, *In Mortal Combat*, 438–9; Mossman, *Ebb and Flow*, 367–9.

9. Mossman, *Ebb and Flow*, 378–9.

10. Ibid., 379–97.

11. Toland, *In Mortal Combat*, 466, 483–4.

12. Stanton, *America's Tenth Legion, X Corps*, 320. Historian Stanton wrote that the Army community was badly shaken by MacArthur's dismissal. For purposes of officer corps morale, Army Chief of Staff Collins decided against any action that could be construed as retaliatory toward

MacArthur disciples still in positions of authority or command. Thus, Stanton wrote, General Almond continued to serve as X Corps Commander until he returned home on 15 July 1951 as part of the Eighth Army's normal rotation policy.

13. Blair, *Forgotten War*, 712.

Bibliography

Anderson, Jack M. *Warrior . . . by Choice . . . by Chance*. Mukilteo, Wash.: WinePress Publishing, 1997.

Appleman, Roy E. *South to the Naktong, North to the Yalu*. Washington, D.C.: Center of Military History, United States Army, 1961.

——— *Disaster in Korea: The Chinese Confront MacArthur*. College Station: Texas A&M University Press, 1989.

——— *Ridgway Duels for Korea*. College Station: Texas A&M University Press, 1990.

Blair, Clay. *The Forgotten War: America in Korea 1950–1953*. New York: Times Books, 1987.

Fehrenbach, T. R. *This Kind of War*. Washington, D.C.: Brassey's Inc., 1963.

Gittings, John. *The Role of the Chinese Army*. London: Oxford University Press, 1967.

Gugeler, Russell A. *Combat Actions in Korea*. Washington, D.C.: Center of Military History, United States Army, 1987.

Hastings, Max. *The Korean War*. New York: Simon and Schuster, 1987.

Herbert, Anthony B. *Herbert—The Making of a Soldier*. New York: Hippocrene Books, 1982.

Hoyt, Edwin P. *On to the Yalu*. Briarcliff Manor, N.Y.: Stein and Day, 1984.

——— *The Bloody Road to Panmunjom*. Briarcliff Manor, N.Y.: Stein and Day, 1985.

——— *The Rise of the Chinese Republic: From the Last Emperor to Deng Xiaoping*. New York: McGraw-Hill: 1989.

Manchester, William. *American Caesar: Douglas MacArthur 1880–1964*. Boston: Little, Brown and Company, 1978.

Mossman, Billy C. *Ebb and Flow: United States Army in the Korean War, November 1950–July 1951*. Washington, D.C.: Center of Military History, United States Army, 1990.

Munroe, Clark C. *The Second United States Infantry Division in Korea, 1950–1951*. Nashville: The Battery Press, 1992.

Paik Sun Yup. *From Pusan to Panmunjom*. Washington, D.C.: Brassey's Inc., 1992.

Peng Dehuai. *Memoirs of a Chinese Marshall*. Beijing: Foreign Languages Press, 1981.

Pratt, Sherman W. *Decisive Battles of the Korean War*. New York: Vantage Press, 1992.

Ridgway, Matthew B. *Soldier*. New York: Harper & Brothers, 1956.

―――― *The Korean War*. Garden City, N.Y.: Doubleday & Company, Inc. 1967.

Robinson, Anthony, Anthony Preston, and Ian V. Hogg. *Weapons of the Vietnam War*. New York: Gallery Books, 1983.

Sandler, Stanley, ed. *The Korean War: An Encyclopedia*. New York: Garland Publishing, 1995.

Sawyer, Robert K. *Military Advisors in Korea: KMAG in Peace and War*. Washington, D.C.: Center of Military History, United States Army, 1962.

Spence, Jonathan D. *The Search for Modern China*. New York: W.W. Norton, 1990.

Spurr, Russell. *Enter the Dragon: China's Undeclared War against the U.S. in Korea, 1950–51*. New York: Newmarket Press, 1988.

Stanton, Shelby. *America's Tenth Legion: X Corps in Korea, 1950*. Novato, Calif.: Presidio Press, 1989.

―――― *U.S. Army Uniforms of the Korean War*. Harrisburg, Penn.: Stackpole Books, 1992.

Toland, John. *In Mortal Combat: Korea, 1950–1953*. New York: William Morrow, 1991.

Waterhouse, Fred J. *The Rakkasans*. Paducah, Ky.: Turner Publishing Company, 1991.

Whitson, William W., with Chen-hsia Huang. *The Chinese High Command: A History of Communist Military Politics, 1927–71*. New York: Praeger Publishers, 1973.

Wilson, Dick, ed. *Mao Tse-tung in the Scales of History: A Preliminary Assessment Organized by the China Quarterly*. (Collection of eleven essays; see, specifically, "Mao as Soldier" by Jacques Guillermaz.) Cambridge: Cambridge University Press, 1977.

Windrow, Martin, ed. *The Korean War 1950–53*. Men-at-Arms Series. London: Osprey Publishing, 1986.

Index

Abrams, Creighton W., 8
Aiken, Neil, 124
Air Force, 211
Allen, Levin, 31
Almond, Edward M.: and first battle of Chip'yong-ni, 190; and second battle of Chip'yong-ni, 209; and Fourth Phase Offensive, 105; and awards, 238–39, 244–45; and beginning of war, 13–14, 19; character of, 39–40, 91–94; and Hoengsong, 116, 141, 155; and intelligence, 21, 64, 103; and liberation of Seoul, 10–13; and Massacre Valley, 159–60; and media, 240, 268–69; Mildren on, 97–98; and Operation Roundup, 80, 82, 89–91, 96–97; and other commanders, 42, 59, 61, 175; and Ridgway, 39, 140, 155, 158, 162, 240, 244; and ROK, 52–53; and Saemal, 133–34, 136, 139; and segregated units, 90, 92–94, 215; and Twin Tunnels, 67–68, 70; and withdrawal from North Korea, 34; and Wonju defense plans, 55, 57; and Wonju line, 174
Alston, Leslie, 188
American Corps, 1
Anderson, Jack M., 120, 138–39, 163–70
ANGR-9 radio, 130
Appleman, Roy E., 31, 181; on Almond, 91, 159–60; on Chinese, 34–35; on Chip'yong-ni, 221; on ROK, 52–53

Ashia Air Force Base, 196
awards, 12, 21, 224, 238–41, 244–45

Baca, Antonio L., 192
Baker, Denzil, 153, 179
banzai attacks, 231
Barberis, Cesidio V., 94
Barbey, John C., 115
Barr, David G., 61
Barrett, John C., 219–20, 223
BC-608 radio, 130
BC-610 radio, 130
Belt, Warren, 235, 258
Bernstein, Robert, 241
Blackwell, John, 114–15, 120, 123, 138, 152
Blair, Clay, 10, 12, 86, 97–98, 224; on Almond, 42, 91; on Chip'yong-ni, 190, 220; on MacArthur, 17, 24; on Operation Killer, 244; on Ridgway, 37, 265–66
Blue Boys, 102
Blumenson, Martin, 21
Boak, Corwin, Jr., 232
Boor, Donald F., 232–33, 235
Bowen, Frank S., 33–34, 80, 86, 227, 252
Bowers, Russell H., 231
Bradley, Omar N., 59, 265–66
Bramblett, Johnny, 146, 149–50, 207, 253
British: 27th Brigade, 41, 192, 242; 29th Brigade, 30, 40, 48; and Chip'yong-ni, 180; and Operation Killer, 247

Brodie, Thomas, 49
Brooks, Charles O. "Pop," 230–32, 235
bugout fever, 31, 52
Burrer, Guenther A. "Gunner Burr," 138–39, 165
Byrd, Roy T., 163

Calhoun, John A., 223
Carr, David V., 196–97
casualties: at second battle of Chip'yong-ni, 212, 225; at first battle of Wonju, 208; at second battle of Wonju, 238; definition of, 88; at Kunu-ri, 88; at Massacre Valley, 155–57, 157t; in Operation Killer, 256–58
CCF. See Chinese Communist Forces
Chamberlain, Joshua, 262
Ch'amyon-ni, 201
Ch'angbong-ni, 99
Changjin Reservoir, 14, 19
Chech'on, 237
Chiang Kai-shek, 260
Chiles, John H., 17, 58, 175, 209; and first battle of Chip'yong-ni, 190; and second battle of Chip'yong-ni, 220–21
China/Chinese, 1; and first battle of Chip'yong-ni, 183–93; and second battle of Chip'yong-ni, 209–25; and first battle of Wonju, 194–208; and second battle of Wonju, 226–41; and Fifth Phase Offensive, 263–65; and Fourth Phase Offensive, 112–27; Almond on, 92; American views of, 123; and battle of Hoengsong, 141–54; and beginning of war, 13–15; character of, 34–35; military theory of, 79, 179, 224–25, 231; and Operation Killer, 242–58; plan for Fourth Phase Offensive, 75–84, 101–2, 107–11; plan for Second Phase Offensive, 24–27; plan for Third Phase Offensive, 33, 39, 44, 52; plan for Chip'yong-ni, 100–101; plan for Wonju, 4; prisoners of,

162–66; Ridgway and, 50, 75, 77, 101, 260–61; and Saemal, 131–32, 136–38; view of American forces, 3, 25, 29, 33, 77, 183; and Wonju line, 171–82
Chinese Communist Forces (People's Liberation Army), 1–3; and First Phase Offensive, 16–29; and Fourth Phase Offensive, 104–6; and Third Phase Offensive, 44–53, 84; 4th Army, 18; 13th Army, 63, 65; 38th Army, 27, 48, 78, 83, 101, 242; 113th Division, 45; 114th Division, 45; 39th Army, 3, 48, 83, 101, 104, 211; 116th Division, 43–46, 111, 173, 179–80, 192; 117th Division, 3, 107, 110–11; 40th Army, 3, 48, 83, 104; 120th Division, 3–4, 110, 114, 179, 190–91, 236; 42nd Army, 19, 27, 68, 78, 101, 104; 125th Division, 71, 74, 79; 50th Army, 48, 65, 77, 83, 100–101; 66th Army, 3, 45, 49, 83, 236–37; and Fourth Phase Offensive, 104, 110; 197th Division, 3, 110, 118; 3rd Army Group, 18, 263; 9th Army Group, 18, 25, 27–29, 263; 13th Army Group, 3, 15, 24, 33, 35, 44, 101; 19th Army Group, 263; composition of, 35; discipline of, 45–46, 63–64; 1st Division, 44; 115th Division, 4, 180; 344th Regiment, 218–19; 119th Division, 4; 124th Division, 19; 126th Division, 4; 198th Division, 3, 112; 373d Division, 71; 374th Division, 71; 375th Division, 71; equipment of, 107; forces of, 18; intelligence, 109–10; logistics of, 174, 197, 261; modernization of, 260; in P'yongyang, 31–33; and Twin Tunnels, 71
Chip'yong-ni, 68, 78–80, 100, 171, 173, 185f; first battle of, 183–93; second battle of, 209–25; beginning of, 179–82; Chinese plan for, 100–101, 111; importance

of, 184; plans for, 75–84, 180–81, 210–11
Choe Hyon, 56–57
Choi Suk, 80, 82, 115, 125, 133, 156
Ch'ongch'on, Battle of, 26f, 27–28
Chop'yong-ni, 4
Chou En-lai, 13
Chow, Y. S. "Gary," 232–33
Ch'owon-ni, 125
Chung Il Kwon, 52, 67, 244–45
Ch'ungju, 4, 111
civilian population: Almond and, 93; of Korea, 261; Ridgway and, 49; Stewart and, 70
Clark, Freddie, 132
Cleland, John R. D., 253–54
Clemmons, Virgil, 254
Collins, Joseph Lawton, 58–59, 86, 243
command: Almond and, 91–92; analysis of, 266; at Chip'yong-ni, 209, 220–21; and Massacre Valley, 161; Ridgway and, 39–40, 58, 263–64; at Saemal, 119–20, 129–30; Walker and, 18–19
communications problems, 128–30
Connor, John, 204, 239, 252, 256
Conrad, Robert G., 121–22, 148–49
Cook, James D., 144, 147, 154, 204, 248–49, 253–54
Cook, L. B., 206
Cortez, Oscar, 135
Coughlin, John, 88–89, 159–60; and Massacre Valley, 141, 143–44, 147–48, 152–54; and Saemal, 126, 129, 132, 139–40
Coulter, John, 39–40, 59, 62
Crombez, Marcel Gustave, 209–10, 219–21, 223–24
Crowley, Jack, 151
Cummins, Joe, 203–4
Curtis, Robert, 216

Dabney, John A., 18, 244
den Ouden, M. P. A., 153
Dolan, William J., 202–7, 238–39
Dolvin, Welborn G. "Tom," 54
Donavin, lieutenant colonel, 133

Dorshefski, Joseph, 169–70
Duvall, Herman C., 160

Edwards, Irwin A., 64
Edwards, James, 216–17, 221–22
85-mm main gun, 6
89th Tank Battalion, 54
81-mm mortar, 118–19, 184
82d Airborne Division, 86–87
82d Antiaircraft Artillery Battalion, 89, 121, 136, 139, 151, 157
82-mm mortar, 108
Eisenhower, Dwight D., 91
Elledge, John, 188, 210, 218
Encirclement Campaigns, 24, 260
Ennis, William P., Jr., 116, 134
Epps, Jones, 140, 145–47, 207
equipment: abandonment of, 115, 123, 126, 157–58, 248–49; communications, 129–30
escapees, 163–70

Faith, Don Carlos, Jr., 21, 23
Far East Air Force Combat Cargo Command, 196–97
Far East Command, 17–18, 34
Farrell, Francis W., 237
Fehrenbach, T. R., 9–10, 14, 27, 87
Fenderson, Maurice, 221
Ferenbaugh, Charles B. "Buddy," 61, 64
Fergusson, Robert G., 104–5
15th Artillery Battalion, 88, 119, 121–22, 148–49; and first battle of Wonju, 195; and Massacre Valley, 157; and Saemal, 132–33; and Wonju line, 177
Fifth Phase Offensive, 263–65
.50-caliber machine gun, 69, 123, 145, 150, 188, 207, 210, 217
57-mm antitank gun, 7
57-mm recoilless rifle, 145
Filipino Battalion, 41
First Phase Offensive, 16–29, 20f
1st Cavalry Division, 13, 41, 101, 242, 247; and second battle of Chip'yong-ni, 222; and Third

1st Cavalry Division—*cont'd*
Phase Offensive, 49; and
Chip'yong-ni, 181; and Operation
Thunderbolt, 65; 5th Regiment,
30, 209, 219; 7th Regiment, 30;
8th Regiment, 16–17, 30, 62
I Corps, 14, 16, 40, 54, 100; and
Fifth Phase Offensive, 264; and
First Phase Offensive, 19; and
Fourth Phase Offensive, 101; and
Third Phase Offensive, 48, 50; and
Operation Killer, 242; and
Operation Thunderbolt, 65, 77
503d Artillery Battalion, 89, 119, 138
Fortna, Ken, 207
40-mm Bofors gun, 69
Fourth Phase Offensive, 105–6,
112–27, 113*f*; analysis of, 259–67;
plan for, 83–84, 101–2, 107–11;
prelude to, 95–106
4.2-inch mortars, 70, 184, 249
Freeman, Paul W., 67, 70–71, 88, 173,
266; and first battle of Chip'yong-
ni, 182, 184–86, 189–90; and second
battle of Chip'yong-ni, 209, 216,
221; and Operation Thunderbolt,
79; and Twin Tunnels, 68–69, 73
French Battalion, 41, 67, 87; and first
battle of Chip'yong-ni, 184, 187;
and second battle of Chip'yong-ni,
210; and Twin Tunnels, 68–71, 73

Gardner, George W., 118, 123,
137–38
Garvin, Robert M., 85
Gastenbein, Dean A., 99
Gerhart, George H., 85
Gettysburg, versus Wonju, 262–63
Gittings, John, 260
Greek Battalion, 41
Gugeler, Russell A., 67, 181
Guthrie, John S., 244

Haberman, Carl F., 215
Hajin, 242
Haktam-ni, 124
Han Liqun, 38

Han River, 48, 78
Hare, John, 146, 151, 255
Harriman, William Averell, 37
Harrod, Carroll D., 163–65
Hartell, Lee R., 194–96
Hauck, Larry, 71
Haynes, Loyal M., 115–16, 176, 195
Heath, Charlie, 152
Heath, Louis T., 64
Heath, Thomas, 210, 212, 214–18
Hewett, Robert F., 254–55
Hickey, Doyle, 31
Hiers, Johnny M., 219, 223
Hill, 254–56
Hill 203, 234, 236
Hill 240, 201–6
Hill 247, 57
Hill 255, 178, 191, 198, 199*f*, 201–2,
207–8, 233–34, 236
Hill 255-256, 205
Hill 289, 85
Hill 300, 85
Hill 303, 132
Hill 312, 86
Hill 325, 234
Hill 333, 125
Hill 340, 229–30
Hill 341, 229–32
Hill 342, 178–79, 191, 201, 208,
226–27, 228*f*, 229–31, 233–36
Hill 348 (Pongmi-san), 184, 186
Hill 397 (Mangmi-san), 180, 184,
187, 211–12
Hill 444, 95, 100, 171
Hill 453, 69, 71, 73
Hill 506, 211
Hill 539, 171
Hill 639, 118, 120
Hill 687, 249, 251–52, 256
Hill 738, 249, 253–54
Hill 930, 90, 99, 112, 118
Hinton, Reginald J., 131, 143–45,
147–48, 152
Hodes, Henry, 55, 61–62
Hodges, Warren D., 140, 143
Hoengsong, 3, 87, 89, 237; battle of,
112–18, 113*f*, 141–54, 142*f*;
follow-up to, 155–70

Hoengsong-Hongch'on road, 95
"Hold at all costs" orders, 175–76
Holden, Maurice, 58
Hongch'ong, 163
Howden, James, 130–31
Hsueh Fu-li, 108
human wave attacks, 231
Hungnam, 29, 34
Hup'o-ri, 210

Iho-ri, 67
Ilyushin ground attack planes, 264
Imjin River, 30–31, 44–53
Inchon, 10, 100
Inmon, Cletus, 213
Inmun Gun, 5–15
intelligence: on Fourth Phase
    Offensive, 101–5; on Third Phase
    Offensive, 43, 50; in beginning of
    war, 16–19, 21; Chinese, 109–10;
    on Chip'yong-ni, 78–79, 182; for
    Operation Killer, 242–43, 246–47;
    Ridgway and, 54–55, 63–64, 75; on
    Wonju, 1
Iron Triangle, 264

Johnson, Harold K., 62
Joint Chiefs of Staff, 13, 23, 58–59
Jones, Jimmy, 206, 208
Jones, Lloyd L., 220
Jones, Luther C., 120
Jones, Sherman D., 90, 114, 117

Kallmeyer, Elmer J., 99
Kangnung, 67
Keiser, Lawrence, 57–58
Keith, John W., Jr., 89, 112, 115;
    and Massacre Valley, 141, 149,
    152, 160; and Saemal, 119–20, 124,
    126, 136
Keleher, William P., 88, 118, 120,
    141–42; and Saemal, 122, 124,
    136–38
Kellam, Paul, 147
Kim Il Sung, 6, 31
Kim Pak Il, 237
Kimpo Peninsula, 100

Kingston, Joseph P., 156
Kluttz, Bill C., 212–13, 215–16
Kohen, Roland J., 188–89, 216–17
Koksu-ri, 180, 220
Korea, 2f; climate of, 23, 60, 90, 98,
    107, 109; terrain of, 21, 90, 109,
    174–75, 205–6
Korean Military Advisory Group
    (KMAG), 4
Korean War: analysis of, 259–67;
    beginning of, 5–15; forgetting of,
    4, 267
Kotite, Richard S., 221
Kunu-ri, 87
Kunu-ri–Sunch'on road, 27, 28f

Land, Harvey, 192–93
LeBrun, Normand O., 239
Lee, interpreter, 150
Lee, Robert E., 262–63
Li T'ianyu, 3, 15, 23, 45; and Fourth
    Phase Offensive, 83, 101, 110; and
    Second Phase Offensive, 24–27;
    view of American forces, 77; and
    Wonju, 4, 171
Lin Piao, 75
Lindsay, Jake, 87
Line Able, 34
Line Arizona, 247
Line Baker, 34, 39–41, 43
Line Charlie, 34, 48–50
Line Dog, 34, 48, 50–51, 60
Liu Ya-lou, 264
Lockrem, Arthur, 132
Lowry, Leonard, 122–24, 137

M-24 Chaffees, 85
M-209 converters, 158
M19 dual-40s, 68–69, 89, 136, 151,
    176, 184
M-43 120-mm mortar, 108
M-46 Patton tank, 210, 219
M-15 quad-50s, 68–69, 89, 121, 136,
    151, 156, 176, 184, 186, 216–18
M-1 rifle, 35
MacArthur, Douglas, 7, 10, 13, 29,
    239; and First Phase Offensive,

MacArthur, Douglas—*cont'd*
23–24; and 82d Airborne, 86;
Almond and, 93; end of command,
263–64; and intelligence, 17–18;
and Joint Chiefs, 58–59; and
liberation of Seoul, 12; and
Operation Killer, 241; Ridgway
and, 40, 51; and war aims, 12–14;
and withdrawal from North Korea,
31, 34
Mace, William M. "Sam," 99–100,
114–15, 118–19, 136
MacLean, Allan D., 19
Madu-ri, 219
Maixner, Harold, 89, 117, 124–26,
135–36, 141
Maneri, John, 239
Manual, Delmer, 150
Mao Tse-tung, 6, 33, 237, 263–64;
principles of guerilla warfare, 24,
259–61, 270–71
Marshall, George C., 13, 92–93
Martin, John, 214
Mashburn, William E., 167–70
Massacre Valley, 137, 141–54, 142*f*;
follow-up to, 155–70; monument,
165
McCaffrey, William J., 116
McClure, Robert B., 57–59, 83, 175
McGee, Paul J., 187–88, 210, 212–16
media: and Massacre Valley, 161–62;
and Wonju, 239–40, 268–69
Merton, warrant officer, 143
Messinger, Edwin J., 57, 180
Meszar, Frank, 189
MIAs, 162–63
Michaelis, John H., 49, 54
Michaelis, Mike, 221
MIG-15s, 264
Milburn, Frank W. "Shrimp," 14, 39,
59, 88; and Operation
Thunderbolt, 65, 77
Mildren, Frank T., 97–98
Miley, John, 255–56
Min Ki Shik, 80
Minkler, Robert W., 236
Mitchell, James, 68
Monclar, Ralph, 69–71, 240

Moore, Bryant E., 39, 62, 65, 209,
242
Morris, John O., 238
Morrison, private, 255
Mossman, Billy C., 21, 31, 90, 116
Muccio, John J., 37–38, 51, 244
Mueller, Paul J., 93
Munson, Delbert E., 227, 229–320

Naughton, lieutenant, 232
Nelson, John H., 200, 234
Netherlands Battalion, 41, 87, 89, 95,
132; and second battle of
Chip'yong-ni, 226; and first battle
of Wonju, 195, 198, 200, 208; and
second battle of Wonju, 236; and
Hoengsong, 152–54; and Wonju
line, 176–79
90-mm gun, 210
90-mm main gun, 219
92d Infantry Division, 92–93
IX Corps, 40, 54, 62; and second
battle of Chip'yong-ni, 209, 211;
and Fifth Phase Offensive, 264;
and First Phase Offensive, 19; and
Fourth Phase Offensive, 101; and
Third Phase Offensive, 48–50; and
Chip'yong-ni, 180; and
Ch'ongch'on, 27; Collins and, 59;
and Operation Killer, 242–43; and
Operation Roundup, 79; and
Operation Thunderbolt, 65, 77–78;
and Twin Tunnels, 67; and Wonju
defense plans, 57
9th Infantry Regiment, 2d Division,
27, 57, 95, 117–18, 130, 191; and
second battle of Chip'yong-ni, 226;
and Fourth Phase Offensive, 101;
1st Battalion, 100, 248; 2d
Battalion, 236; and Chip'yong-ni,
180; and Operation Killer, 248–49;
and Wonju line, 171–73, 177–80
Nix, James H., 198, 202–5, 241
NKPA. *See* North Korean People's
Army
North Korea, withdrawal from,
30–36, 32*f*; Ridgway on, 41–43
North Korean People's Army

(NKPA), 1, 98; and second battle of Wonju, 237; and beginning of war, 4–15; II Corps, 38, 55, 56*f*, 60–61, 237; V Corps, 38, 56*f*, 57, 60, 134, 173–74, 237; 4th Division, 8; 6th Division, 57; 8th Division, 100–101; 12th Division, 57; 27th Division, 57; forces of, 6; and Operation Killer, 249, 251–52, 254–56; organization of, 6
Nyquist, Joel, 200–201

Objective P, 249, 252
187th Airborne Regimental Combat Team (Rakkasans), 12, 41, 95; and first battle of Chip'yong-ni, 191; and first battle of Wonju, 194, 198–208; and second battle of Wonju, 226–36, 239, 241; and Third Phase Offensive, 50; Almond and, 91; 1st Battalion, 85–86; 2d Battalion, 60, 197; 3d Battalion, 12, 60; 96th Field Artillery Battalion, 135, 177; 674th Field Artillery Battalion, 135, 177, 227, 249; and Massacre Valley, 143; and Operation Killer, 247–48, 252–53, 256–58; and Operation Roundup, 80, 82; Parachute Maintenance Department, 196; and Saemal, 139; and withdrawal from North Korea, 30, 33–34; and Wonju defense plans, 60; and Wonju line, 176
155-mm howitzers, 46, 88–89, 120, 123, 126, 153, 156, 158
105-mm howitzers, 33, 88, 148, 157–58
120-mm mortar, 108
Onjong, 16–29
Operation Dauntless, 263–64
Operation Killer, 241–58, 257*f*
Operation Ripper, 263
Operation Roundup, 3, 85–96, 161–62; plan for, 75–84, 81*f*
Operation Swarmer, 86
Operation Thunderbolt, 63–74, 66*f*

Operation Thunderbolt II, 76*f*, 77–78
Operation Wolfhound, 54–55, 59
Ottesen, Eugene L., 212, 214
Overgaard, lieutenant, 229

Paddock, Bill, 64
Paik Sun Yup, 7, 27, 30, 44, 51, 259; and Third Phase Offensive, 45–46; on Almond, 162
Pakker, sergeant, 153
Pang Ho Song, 57, 60
Panikkar, K. M., 13
Parrizo, Rudy, 202
Partridge, Earle E. "Pat," 63–64
Peng Teh-huai, 3; and Fifth Phase Offensive, 264–65; analysis of Fourth Phase Offensive, 237, 259–62; plan for Fourth Phase Offensive, 75–84, 101–2, 107–11; plan for Second Phase Offensive, 24–27; plan for Third Phase Offensive, 33, 38, 52; view of American forces, 77, 183; and Wonju, 4, 171
Peploe, George, 88
Pickett, George E. IV, 198–200, 249–52
Pir'yong-ni, 100
Polk, James H., 64, 102–4
Pope, William H., 188
Powell, Herbert B., 55, 61–62, 94
Pratt, Sherman W., 181, 221
prisoners, Chinese treatment of, 163–66
Pulver, Olaf, 255
Pusan, 34
Pusan Perimeter, 8, 8*f*, 244
Putt, Earl, 230–32
P'yongyang, 13–14, 30–36

Quinn, William W., 18, 64
Quirk, James T., 161

railroad, 175
Ramsburg, John, 216–17
RC-292 antenna, 130

Read, Norwood G., 63
Republic of Korea (ROK) Army, 1, 3; and Fifth Phase Offensive, 264; and First Phase Offensive, 16; Almond and, 52–53; and beginning of war, 10, 13; Capital Division, 19, 41, 60, 155; commanders of, 244–45; I Corps, 13, 34, 67, 79, 237; 9th Division, 41; II Corps, 19, 27; 3d Division, 41; 6th Division, 16; III Corps, 41, 45, 67, 79–80, 155, 237; 7th Division, 60; 9th Division, 60; 1st Division, 13, 30, 40–41, 45–48; 2d Division, 41; 3d Division, 19, 55, 80, 96–97, 139, 155; 18th Battalion, 139; 22d Regiment, 96, 133; 23d Regiment, 133; 5th Division, 41, 60, 80, 95–97, 237; and Hoengsong, 155; and Operation Roundup, 82, 85, 89–90; and Saemal, 135; and Wonju line, 174; 6th Division, 40–41, 45–48, 180, 242, 247; 8th Division, 38, 41, 60, 80, 89, 96–98, 125, 237; and Fourth Phase Offensive, 105; and Massacre Valley, 156; and Operation Roundup, 82, 89–90, 95–96; 10th Regiment, 90; 16th Regiment, 90; 21st Regiment, 88, 90; and Saemal, 133–34; 9th Division, 38, 55; forces of, 6–7; and Massacre Valley, 146, 150–51; and Operation Roundup, 82, 98; and Operation Thunderbolt, 65; organization of, 4; 10th Regiment, 57, 96–97, 105; 12th Regiment, 45; 16th Regiment, 96–97, 105, 114, 117, 125; 18th Regiment, 176, 179, 248; 21st Regiment, 89, 96, 98, 112–15, 137; 35th Regiment, 90–91; Ridgway and, 51–52; and Saemal, 124, 136, 140; and 2 battle of Wonju, 237; and Twin Tunnels, 67
Reyna, Andrew E., 218
Rhee, Syngman, 4, 12–13, 40; Ridgway and, 37, 51, 75
Richards, Lou, 233
Ridgway, Matthew Bunker, 1, 265–66; and First Phase Offensive, 21; and Third Phase Offensive, 46, 49–52; and Almond, 39, 140, 155, 158, 162, 240, 244; Chinese and, 50, 75, 77, 101, 260–61; and Chip'yong-ni, 180–81, 183; Collins and, 59–60; and commanders, 39–40, 58, 61–62, 209, 244–45; and Crombez, 224; and equipment losses, 157–59; and Freeman, 221; and "hold at all costs" orders, 175–76; and intelligence, 54–55, 63–64, 75, 101, 105; and Joint Chiefs, 59; and offensive spirit, 54–62; and Operation Killer, 243–44, 246–47; and Operation Ripper, 263; and Operation Roundup, 89–90, 96–97; and Operation Thunderbolt, 63–74, 78; plan for Operation Roundup, 79–84, 81f; taking command, 37–43, 263–65; and withdrawal from North Korea, 30–36, 41–43; and Wonju defense plan, 60–61
Roberts, Donald L., 249–52
Rochnowski, Arthur, 210, 214
Rogers, Jack, 131–32
ROK. See Republic of Korea Army
Route 1, 33–34
Route 2, 90, 114
Route 20, 67
Route 24, 68, 80, 179, 184
Route 29, 80, 88, 98–99, 112, 139, 176
Route 24-A, 184, 188, 210
Royal Ulster Rifles, 49
Ruffner, Clark L., 58, 73, 83, 132; and first battle of Chip'yong-ni, 190; and Hoengsong, 115–16; and Massacre Valley, 158, 160; and Wonju line, 173, 175
Saemal, 117, 145, 174; gauntlet at, 119–27; rescue from, 128–40
Sanchez, Carlos, 151
Scalzo, Frank, 151

Schmitt, Donald R., 212
SCR-300 radio, 129–30, 138, 203, 232
SCR-536 radio, 130
Second Phase Offensive, 27–29; plan for, 24–27
2d Infantry Division, 3, 30–31, 38, 41, 50, 55, 57–58, 60, 87, 247; and first battle of Wonju, 196–97; and second battle of Wonju, 227; and Fourth Phase Offensive, 105; and Third Phase Offensive, 52; Artillery, 115; and Chip'yong-ni, 182; at Kunu-ri, 27, 28f; and Massacre Valley, 156–57; and Operation Roundup, 82; Reconnaisance Company, 179–80, 191–92; and Saemal, 128; and Twin Tunnels, 67; and Wonju line, 171. See also 9th Regiment; 38th Regiment; 23d Regiment
segregated units, 120; and second battle of Chip'yong-ni, 215; Almond and, 90, 92–94
Seoul: liberation of, 10–13, 11f; withdrawal from, 49, 51
7th Infantry Division, 14, 38, 57; 2d Battalion, 95; and Chip'yong-ni, 180; 49th Field Artillery Battalion, 133; and Operation Killer, 247; and Operation Roundup, 82; 17th Regiment, 19, 42, 55, 61, 64, 133, 176, 237; 31st Regiment, 42, 119; 32d Regiment, 42, 101, 119, 237; 9th Regiment, 1st Battalion, 176; and Saemal, 135
70th Tank Battalion, 62, 210
75-mm main gun, 85
72d Tank Battalion, 139, 143–45, 150, 176, 191, 249
76-mm main gun, 96, 145
Shanahan, Jack B., 201–4, 241, 256
Sherman tanks (M-4A-3E-8; "Easy Eights"), 145, 210
Shoemaker, Harold W., 189
Sihn Sung Mo, 244–45
Sillim-ni, 248–50, 250f, 258
6th Tank Battalion, 210

60-mm mortar, 35, 118, 145, 149–50, 184, 215
Skeldon, James H., 177
SL-17 plan, 10
Smith, Charles B. "Brad," 7
Smith, Oliver P., 41–42, 246
Som River, 128, 179, 194–96
Soviet Union, 4, 6, 14, 261, 264
Spence, Sam, 204
Sperduto, Lewis, 254
Sprouse, Clarence B., 252
Spurr, Russell, 38, 83–84
Stanton, Shelby, 92
Stenson, Randal, 230, 232
Sterczek, Frank S., 99
Stewart, George Craig, 58, 227, 246, 266; and first battle of Chip'yong-ni, 190; and Massacre Valley, 160–61; and Operation Roundup, 82–83; and Twin Tunnels, 70–71, 73–74; and Wonju, 175–79, 195, 226
Stewart, Harry, 207
Stine, Harlan C., 191–93
Stratemeyer, George, 240
Strawn, lieutenant, 136
SU-76 self-propelled guns, 6
Sullivan, Robert E., 229
Sung Shih-lun, 18, 24–27, 29
Support Force 7: and Massacre Valley, 152–53, 155–56; and Saemal, 133–34
Support Force 21, 88–89, 98, 112, 114, 117, 124, 141; and Massacre Valley, 158; and Saemal, 126, 129, 132–36, 139
Support Force 32, 115
Support Team A, 89–90, 96, 114, 117
Support Team B, 89, 98–100, 114–15
Support Team E, 139–40, 143–44

T-34 tank, 6–7
Tack, captain, 153
Taebaek Mountains, 51–52
Tarkenton, James C., 18
Task Force Faith, 28
Task Force MacLean, 19, 21

Task Force Smith, 7–8

Taylor, Ira, 207

X Corps, 1, 16, 54–55; and second battle of Wonju, 227; and First Phase Offensive, 19, 21, 23–24; and Fourth Phase Offensive, 101; and Second Phase Offensive, 29; and Third Phase Offensive, 50; and beginning of war, 13–14; and Chip'yong-ni, 182; and Hoengsong, 141, 155; and intelligence, 64; intelligence, 102–3; and liberation of Seoul, 10–13; and Massacre Valley, 158–59; and Operation Killer, 243, 247, 249; and Operation Roundup, 79, 82, 85, 89–90, 96, 99; and Operation Thunderbolt, 78; Ridgway and, 42; and Saemal, 128, 132–33; and Twin Tunnels, 67; and withdrawal from North Korea, 34; and Wonju line, 171, 174

Terrain, 21, 90, 109, 205–6; of Wonju, 174–75

Thai Battalion, 41

Third Phase Offensive, 44–53, 47f, 84; plan for, 33, 39, 44, 52

3d Infantry Division, 21; and Third Phase Offensive, 50, 52; and Operation Thunderbolt, 65; 65th Regiment, 94

.30-caliber machine gun, 145

Thirty-Eighth Parallel, 12–13, 29, 40, 244, 263

38th Artillery Battalion: and Fourth Phase Offensive, 101; and Wonju line, 177

38th Infantry Regiment, 2d Division, 3, 27, 57, 87, 89, 98, 143–44; and first battle of Chip'yong-ni, 191–92; and first battle of Wonju, 197–98, 200, 202, 205–6; and second battle of Wonju, 234, 236, 241; 1st Battalion, 87, 119; 2d Battalion, 226; 3d Battalion, 114, 134; and Massacre Valley, 154, 156–57; and Saemal, 128, 133; Tank Company, 130, 148; and Wonju line, 176–79

32d Division, 19

37th Field Artillery Battalion, 68

Thompson submachine gun, 35

3.5-inch bazooka, 203

Travis, John E., 188

Treacy, Edgar J., Jr., 219–20

Truman, Harry S, 7, 12–14, 59, 94, 263

Turkish Brigade, 30, 40

25th Infantry Division, 30, 40, 48–49, 101; and Chip'yong-ni, 181; and Operation Thunderbolt, 65; 27th Regiment, 49, 54

21st Infantry Division, 1st Battalion, 7

24th Infantry Division, 7, 41, 45, 48; and Chip'yong-ni, 181; and Operation Thunderbolt, 65; 19th Regiment, 67; 21st Regiment, 100; 5th Regimental Combat Team, 242

23d Infantry Regiment, 2d Division, 57, 67, 87–88, 95, 100; and first battle of Chip'yong-ni, 184–93; and second battle of Chip'yong-ni, 209–25; 1st Battalion, 69–70; 2d Battalion, 69; 3d Battalion, 68–69, 71, 171, 173

23rd Regimental Combat Team: and second battle of Chip'yong-ni, 209; and Chip'yong-ni, 180, 182; and Operation Thunderbolt, 78–79; and Saemal, 128

Twin Tunnels, 67–74, 72f

2.36-inch rocket launchers, 7

Tyrrell, Stanley C., 68

United Nations forces, 13, 22f

United States Army: and first battle of Chip'yong-ni, 183–93; and second battle of Chip'yong-ni, 209–25; and first battle of Wonju, 194–208; and second battle of Wonju, 226–41; and Fourth Phase Offensive, 112–27; and Third Phase Offensive, 44–53; attitudes of, 18, 39, 54–62, 75–77, 122–23; and battle of Hoengsong, 141–54; and Operation Killer, 242–58;

organization of, 22*f;* planning, 75–84; readiness of, 9–10, 86; war aims of, 12–13, 29; and withdrawal from North Korea, 31, 32*f;* withdrawal from North Korea, 30–36, 32*f;* and Wonju line, 171–82
United States Marine Corps, 28–29; 1st Division, 41, 60, 181, 246; and Massacre Valley, 156–57; 1st Provisional Brigade, 10; readiness of, 10; 5th Regiment, 19; 7th Regiment, 16; Ridgway and, 41–42; and Twin Tunnels, 74
Unsan, 25
Uzzo, Francis, 130–32

Valent, Othon O. "Jumpy," 147, 235, 255
Van Fleet, James A., 264–65
Vandenberg, Hoyt S., 58–59

Wake Island meeting, 14
Walker, Forest, 94
Walker, Walton H., 7, 12, 14, 27, 57; and First Phase Offensive, 18–19; death of, 35–36; and withdrawal from North Korea, 30–36
Wall, corporal, 136–37
Waterhouse, Fred, 239

Weber, William E., 227, 229–33, 235
Webster, Wilbur, 121, 163–70
White, Barney D., 133–34, 152
White, David N., 207, 236
Whitson, William W., 24
Wilcynski, Thomas R., 232
Wilhm, Jack F., 99–100, 139, 143
Wilkes, Phillip, 146–47, 150
Williamson, Edward C., 181, 210
Willoughby, Charles A., 17–18
withdrawal: from North Korea, 30–36, 32*f;* Ridgway on, 41–43, 51; from Seoul, 49, 51
Wonju: first battle of, 194–208; second battle of, 226–41; analysis of, 236–37, 259–67; defense line for, 171–82, 172*f;* Peng on, 83–84; situation prior to, 1–4; terrain of, 174–75
Wonju Shoot, 194–96
Wonsan landing, 13
Wooley, Earl K., 234, 236, 255
World War II, 9, 24
Wright, Carl J., Jr., 268–69
Wright, Edwin K., 31

Ya Jai Hueng, 60, 80
Yangp'yong, 78, 83
Yenan Ban, 6
Yoju, 128, 209
Yoju-Wonju road, 69
Yu Jai Hueng, 96–97, 237, 245

About the Author

J. D. Coleman, a retired U.S. Army lieutenant colonel, served in Korea and Vietnam. In Korea, he was a staff sergeant with the 187th Airborne Regimental Combat Team. He made both combat parachute assaults with that unit and also participated in the Wonju campaign. In Vietnam, he commanded an airborne rifle company and received a Silver Star.

Following Army retirement, Coleman worked for the Georgia Department of Public Safety and, later, the Flathead National Forest in Kalispell, Montana, before leaving full-time employment and concentrating on writing. He is also the author of *Pleiku: The Dawn of Helicopter Warfare in Vietnam* and *Incursion: From America's Chokehold on the NVA Lifelines to the Sacking of the Cambodian Sanctuaries.* He lives in Kalispell.